MAKING A SPLASH

Dedicated to my mermaids and their mother

MAKING A SPLASH

Mermaids (and Mermen) in 20th and 21st Century Audiovisual Media

Philip Hayward

British Library Cataloguing in Publication Data

Making a Splash
Mermaids (and Mermen) in 20th and 21st Century Audiovisual Media

A catalogue entry for this book is available from the British Library

ISBN: 0 86196 724 7 (Paperback)

ISBN: 0 86196 925 8 (Electronic book)

Published by
John Libbey Publishing Ltd, 3 Leicester Road, New Barnet, Herts EN5 5EW,
United Kingdom   e-mail: john.libbey@orange.fr; web site: www.johnlibbey.com

Distributed Worldwide by
Indiana University Press, Herman B Wells Library—350, 1320 E. 10th St., Bloomington,
IN 47405, USA. www.iupress.indiana.edu

Printed and bound in the United States of America..

Contents

Acknowledgements

My interest in mermaids began through my association with Cornwall as a child. I visited the county with my parents, Ruth and Roy, on summer holidays during my school years. The mermaid has been widely present in the county's folklore, religious iconography and commercial signage for many decades and forms part of my earliest memories of the far west of England. It's fitting in this regard that Chapters 2 and 5 of this volume allowed me to excavate particular elements of Cornish folklore taken up by playwrights and novelists and subsequently represented in audiovisual media. Over the years, my parents have supported my interest in various ways, even acting as unpaid research assistants on various occasions. My late wife, Rebecca Coyle, also encouraged and supported my interests and indulged my fascination by allowing me to give our two daughters middle names derived from 20th Century mermaid media-lore (Miranda and Madison respectively).

My unexpected encounter with Avalon on Catalina Island, a town that had inscribed a block of mermaid associations from 20th Century media-lore into its vernacular signage, in 2012 prompted me to initiate another project that has proceeded in parallel with the writing of this volume – the curation of an exhibition of contemporary mermaid art at Macquarie University Gallery in Sydney (due to open in late 2017). My thanks to Rhonda Davis, Leonard Janiszewski and John Simons for agreeing to mount the exhibition and for collaborating with me on its preparation and organisation. The visual artworks involved, and my correspondence with the artists who produced them, has enriched my understanding of the nature of mermaid imagery in a range of contexts and has thereby fed into this volume, just as my work on the book has informed my curation and the production of accompanying materials for the exhibition.

A number of other individuals merit acknowledgement.

Special thanks to my frequent collaborator, Jon Fitzgerald, for co-authoring Chapter 3 with me and for giving me advice on the soundtracks of various audiovisual productions discussed elsewhere in the book. Also sincere thanks to those colleagues who acted as readers on drafts of various chapters: Nick Mansfield (Introduction and Chapter 7), Adam Grydehøj (Chapter 1), Pru Black (Chapter 2), Clarice Butkus and Alison Rahn (Chapter 4), Ronald M. James (Chapter 5), Marea Mitchell (Chapters 5 and 6) and Nancy Easterlin (Conclusion).

Also thanks to Karl Banse, Ib Bondebjerg, Alan Duncan, Mark Evans, Lauren Evans, Hannah Fraser, Waldo Garrido, Virginia Hankins, Kimmo Laine, Alex Mesker, Andrew Murphie, Rebekah Nazarian, Inga Tritt and Damon Trotta for various research assistances and to Hannah Murphy for her diligent proofing of the manuscript.

The patience and forbearance of my partner, Alison, has been much appreciated – she learnt more about mermaids than she ever wanted to know during my deep immersion in this project and she also contributed to the development of various aspects of the final volume through her diligent and insightful responses to the issues I raised with her. Her love and support was invaluable.

A final thanks to John Libbey for inviting me to write this volume and for his enthusiasm for its production.

Note on audiovisual material featured in this volume

This volume discusses a range of film, television and video material produced in North America, Europe and Australia in the period 1904[1]–2015 that represents mermaids and/or mermen in various ways. Discussion of this audiovisual corpus is clustered around particular themes and the extent of coverage of particular productions is related to the manner in which they relate to those themes.

Given the wide spread of genres and types of material I have included in my analyses and, in particular, my discussion of various non-commercial and/or amateur productions with limited distribution, it is likely that there will be some mermaid/merman-themed texts that have escaped my attention. I am nevertheless confident (with a few caveats) that I have identified and included discussion of all feature films and television programs that have included substantial representations of mermaids or mermen.

The caveats I refer to concern three main areas. The first concerns early films that are now deemed as lost in that copies are no longer available.[2] While I refer to a number of these in passing in Chapter 2, I have refrained from speculating on the representations they offer. The second concerns animated productions. While I discuss the film and television animation components of Disney's *The Little Mermaid* franchise at some length in Chapter 1, and also refer to aspects of Disney animation in Chapter 6, I have not attempted a systematic review of representations of mermaids in western audiovisual animation media. The third concerns music videos that feature mermaids. While I have discussed the small number of music videos that feature mermen in Chapter 7 I have made no attempt to survey, document and analyse the representation of mermaids in music videos beyond the note on this topic included in Chapter 7 and reference to a single video (TS Madison's *Feeling My Fish*) in Chapter 1. Research on the topic of the representation of mermaids in music videos is underway and will form the basis of a separate essay.[3] Also, for reasons of space and thematic focus, I have not extended discussion to audiovisual productions that reference mermaids as titular and/or thematic motifs without representing them in their narratives, such as *La sirène du Mississippi/Mississippi Mermaid* (Francois Truffaut, 1969), *Mermaids* (Richard Benjamin, 1990) and *Rusalka* (Anne Melikyan, 2009); or to films in which human females are represented in film titles *as* mermaids despite appearing in human form, such as *Tarzan and the Mermaids* (Robert Florey, 1948) or *Million Dollar Mermaid* (Mervyn Le Roy, 1952).

As I outline in the Introduction, mermaids have also been represented in a variety of animated and live action cinema and television programs produced in Asia. A preliminary examination of productions emerging from this region reveals a highly varied and complex set of representations that draw substantially on local mythology and folklore. I have not attempted the complex contextual analyses such productions merit and a comprehensive study of this field would fill a volume at least as long as this one.

---

1   The earliest mermaid-themed film that my research uncovered was *La Sirène* (Georges Méliès, 1904).

2   I have also not been able to access a copy of Charles Guggenheim's 1961 film *The Fisherman and his Soul* (based on Oscar Wilde's eponymous 1891 short story) and have not included it in analyses offered in the volume.

3   See: http://www.mermedia.com.au/mermaids-in-music-videos.html

3

The audiovisual material referred to in this volume is identified in the Filmographic Index at the rear of the volume. While noting the caveats given above, my research indicates that this represents the most comprehensive index of such material assembled to date.

Figure 1 – Decoration on the front gable of the Polytheama Cinema building, Manaus, Brazil (author's photo, June 2014)

Introduction

Tails, Tresses and Elusive Otherness

June 14ᵗʰ 2014 – Manaus, Brazil. Located 1500 kilometres up river from the Amazon's Atlantic estuary, Manaus is an unlikely location for mermaid imagery in that the folkloric figure is closely associated with oceans and their shores. But in a landscape dominated by the Amazon and its tributaries, and in a city established in 1694 by European migrants, its presence makes eminent sense. Its symbolism is inscribed on the front gable of one of the city's first cinemas, the Polytheama, built in 1912, which displays two long-tailed sereias[4] *(Figure 1). The imagery is subtle but functional. While bare-breasted and alluring, the* sereias *are also clearly marked as cultured; they*

---

4   *Sereia* is the Portuguese term for a siren and refers to both the classic fish-tailed mermaid and serpent-tailed variants.

grasp a lyre, which has traditionally symbolised their musical accomplishment, and a book and scroll, symbols of the literary and dramatic arts. In this manner they function as symbolic courtesans, luring patrons into the venue with the promise of sophisticated entertainment. Amazonia is also home to the Iara, a local syncretic form of mermaid, derived from the combination of indigenous mythology and settler traditions. Returning from a trip up to the 'Meeting of the Waters', where the clear, fast-moving upper-Amazon meets the murky, slow-moving Rio Negro, I was disappointed that I had not glimpsed the elusive Amazon river dolphin. As we docked in Manaus I looked back at the river as my fellow passengers disembarked. Then, in bright daylight, only metres from the stern, I saw a dolphin break the surface and twist lazily to its side, exposing a long pink flank that arched gracefully before dipping below the surface, leaving its tail erect as it descended. In this brief moment I gained a vivid insight into the sensual allure of such aquatic animals and of their ability to inspire and inform the myths of Iara and similar creatures that have circulated in many parts of the world.[5] Equally, in the signage of the Polytheama, I sensed a prefiguration of the role that cinema would play in establishing the mermaid as a prominent motif in 20th and 21st Century popular culture.[6] Given the global diffusion of mermaid symbolism and the global reach of modern audiovisual media, their interweaving in the material culture of a city in the heart of Amazonia was less surprising than it at first appeared.

Water-dwelling people with fully human, fish-tailed or other compound physiques feature in the mythologies and folklore of maritime, lacustrine and riverine societies across the planet. Recent developments in the field of Island Studies have opened up productive new perspectives on this phenomenon. One strand of research and theorisation has focused on the nature of what have been termed *aquapelagos*[7] (Hayward 2012a and Suwa 2012). This neologism refers to locations in which the aquatic spaces between and around areas of land have been fundamental to social groups' livelihoods and, consequently, to their senses of identity and of belonging. Maxwell (2012) made an important contribution to debates on this topic by emphasising the extent to which humans have "a radical continuity with our worlds" (ibid: 23). He has characterised this as a "primal intercorporeality"; that is, "rather than being set against the world we inhabit, we are given through and with it" (ibid). The concept of chorography is crucial to his discussion in that it "renders place in [its] chiasmatic idiosyncrasy, setting subjective and objective epistemologies into productive dialogue" (ibid). With regard to the characterisation that opened this paragraph, it is possible to view mythological and folkloric accounts of aquatic people as manifestations of an *aquapelagic imaginary*. In this imaginary, such figures reflect and transcend the limits of human existence and experience

---

5   There has been a continuing vein of speculation that misrecognition of manatees and/or similar marine mammals by seafarers may have inspired or reinforced belief in the existence of mermaids. While this is, at best, one filament in the mermaid's development as a cultural figure, it has a degree of credibility.

6   While there was a flourishing film production sector in Brazil in the first decade of the 20th Century, foreign films, and particularly ones from the United States (US), predominated after 1911 (see Rist [2005] for a discussion).

7   I was aware at the time of coining the neologism that the term 'archipelago' was derived from the Latin *archi* (meaning most prominent) and *pelagos* (meaning sea – a term that originally referred to the Aegean). While a pedantic etymology of my term might thereby characterise it as doubly referential to the sea (i.e. *aqua/pelagos*) it should be noted that my revision/subversion of the term 'archipelago' reflects its current usage (referring to a group of islands in a sea) rather than any archaic reference to a specific Mediterranean body of water.

in the aquatic realm. The identification and theorisation of aspects of cultural practice that evince aquapelagic sensibilities is in its infancy[8] and this book represents one attempt to advance this project in an extended manner. My engagement includes characterisations of particular forms of local practice that exemplify aquapelagic sensibilities and a broader investigation of the re-inscription of aquatic humanoid folklore in a range of 20th and 21st Century media practices. Fish-tailed aquatic humanoids have had particular prominence in contemporary culture[9] and subsequent sections of this Introduction (and the volume as a whole) address the manner in which their compound forms, derived from specific aquapelagic contexts, have been deployed to reflect various socio-cultural imaginations and representations of gender, difference and desire.

In one respect, mermaids are relatively straightforward. They are compound figures comprising the upper half of a female human and the lower half of a fish.[10] They are also amphibious, being able to live (and breathe) in water and on land (although their mobility is restricted in the latter context). But from here on, complexity abounds. One notable aspect of this concerns nomenclature. Etymologically, the English language term 'mermaid' is fairly straightforward (and easily deducible), comprising 'mer' (from the Middle English term 'mere'), referring to the sea, and 'maid' referring to a young/virgin female. Despite the lack of any linguistic element that specifies it, the term 'mermaid' has become so strongly associated with a compound figure comprising the upper half of a female human and the lower half of a fish that extensions of its usage to refer to fully human female forms are essentially allusive (in the sense of being metaphorical, symbolic or figurative). In contemporary anglophone culture the mermaid has a sister figure, the siren, which she substantially overlaps with. My stress on the *contemporary* context is deliberate. While the mermaid's form has been relatively constant since the medieval period, the figure of the siren has undergone significant transformations. As Holford-Strevens (2006) has discussed, the term has been applied to a variety of creatures, from the winged, harpy-like sirens of ancient Greece through to the more conventional fish-tailed mermaid figures evident in representations of themes from Homeric literature in 19th Century art (Kramer 2006). But whatever the historical usage, sirens are now confined within a narrow definitional 'bandwidth' as predatory creatures, while the term 'mermaid' has been applied to everything from innocent, child-like waifs through to seductive vamps with carnivorous proclivities. In this manner, the two terms interweave in English cultural usage, with the mermaid now dominant in the terminology used to describe popular cultural manifestations of the compound woman/fish form.

---

8   See Hayward (2015a) and Dick (2015) for discussions of the women's water splashing performance tradition of Banks Islanders in Vanuatu as an example of a cultural practice that embodies and expresses an aquapelagic sensibility.

9   One of the closest folkloric figures to the mermaid/merman is the selkie, which appears as a seal in the water but has an ability to shed its seal skin and take human form on land. Selkies have been the subject of representation in films such as *The Secret of Roan Inish* (John Sayles, 1994), *Selkie* (Donald Crumbie, 2000) and *Ondine* (Neil Jordan, 2010).

10 It should be noted that the Third Edition of *The Oxford English Dictionary* identifies the mermaid as having "the head and trunk of a woman and the tail of a fish or cetacean" (1973: 13111). While the latter element of the definition refers to occasions on which mermaids' tails are sometimes represented as more similar to dolphins' or porpoises' tails than to fish ones, mermaids are predominantly associated with piscine rather than cetaceous elements.

Scandinavian languages use terms that combine an initial reference to the sea and a following one that indicates gender. These refer to both fish-tailed females and to water-dwelling women more generally (Danish and Norwegian: *havfrue*, Faroese: *havfrúgv*, Icelandic: *hafmeyja*, Swedish: *sjöjungfru* and Finnish: *merenneito*). The Dutch language similarly uses the compound word *meermin*. Other languages offer complex clusters of names, meanings and associations. Contemporary German offers perhaps the greatest range of these. Two terms approximate the English term 'mermaid' – *meerjungfrau* and *seejungfrau* (compounds of *jungfrau*, meaning maiden, and *meer* [sea] or *see* [lake]) – neither of which specify piscine elements. German culture also offers an alternative in the form of the *nixe*, a water nymph/fairy that can be specified as a classic mermaid figure by the addition of the term *mit fischswanz* ('with fishtail') or can refer to a 'bathing belle' through the compound term *badenixe* (*bade* meaning 'bathing'). The term *sirene* is also used in German (derived from the Latin term *syreni*) to refer to both the Homeric half-human/half-bird figure and the more standard mermaid form. There are also specific regional forms such as the Lorelei, a recent folkloric invention (dating from the early 1800s[11]) who resides around a rocky outcrop on the banks of the Rhine and distracts passing boat crews. Further complicating matters, the melusine is present in both French and German folklore. The term refers to a fresh water sprite (or, in some versions, a woman who is periodically transformed into one) that occurs in a variety of forms: winged, eel-tailed, single fish-tailed or split-tailed.[12] Aside from the complexities of German usage, many contemporary Latin languages more uniformly use variants of the original Latin term *syreni* – *sirène* (French), *sirena* (Spanish and Italian) and *sereia* (Portuguese) – to refer to a variety of female aquatic entities. All the above also intersect with the figure of the undine (or ondine), an elemental water sprite that has been represented in both fully human female and fish-tailed form.

For reasons of convenience, and reflecting dominant patterns of English Language usage, the term 'mermaid' is used throughout this volume to describe the half-fish, half-female figures discussed in various chapters (except in those instances when variants of the term 'siren', or other folkloric terms, are specifically used in the nomenclature of texts, characters or tales).

The mermaid's beguilingly simple form has given it a particular durability in Western culture. The Arne-Thompson Motif-index of folk literature (1955–1958), a seminal resource in Western Folklore Studies, includes a lengthy list of international motifs concerning mermaids in folk tales (category B.81) and a further section identifying motifs of sirens "in mermaid form" in Irish/Breton folklore (B53.0.1 and B53.1–4). For at least a thousand years – despite changes in fashions of female beauty, or of social perceptions of the female, femininity and/or sexual difference – the mermaid has been present in Western visual, literary and, more latterly, audiovisual media. Somewhat surprisingly, Christianity

---

11   See Nickell (2014) for a brief summary of the origin of modern Lorelei folklore.

12   The split-tailed mermaid was an occasional variant of the single-tailed mermaid in medieval visual representations but largely disappeared from cultural representations in the 1800s until it was resurrected in the form of the initial Starbucks company logo, showing a bare-breasted mermaid holding her split tail apart. Concern over the suggestiveness of this image led it to be superseded by logos that 'zoomed in' on the centre of the image, de-emphasising the implied groin area of the initial logo, and obscuring her breasts with her hair (see Klara 2014).

has provided a significant context for its representation. Art historians such as Berger (1985) contend that mermaid imagery developed in Christian iconography in the 10th and 11th centuries as part of a shifting system of representations of female figures symbolising the divine and/or corporeal worlds. She identifies that the mermaid emerged as a clear "emblem of carnal temptation" by the 12th Century (ibid: 42) with the result that the figure "became very popular in the art of the Middle Ages" (ibid: 43). Indeed, the association of the mermaid with carnal temptation led the term to be applied to prostitutes in England in this period (and also extended to the naming of taverns to suggest their hospitality to male patrons). Pedersen (2015) also provides evidence of a wider diffusion of mermaid imagery in her examination of a number of late 16th to mid-17th Century theatrical and literary texts.

The prevalence of the mermaid as a figure in Western culture in the early modern era (c1600–1800), when a number of European powers began to explore, claim and colonise areas of Africa and North and South America – and to transport slaves from the former to the latter – appears to have facilitated the diffusion of the figure to other cultural contexts. In addition to the Western versions of the mermaid referred to above and discussed in detail elsewhere in this volume, there have also been interweavings and syncretic pairings with similar semi-human entities from non-Western cultures, most notably the figure of Mami Wata, which originated in coastal/estuarine areas in the south-east of present-day Nigeria and diffused through parts of Western, Central and South Africa (see Drewal et al. 2008). Similarly to the European siren and melusine legends, Mami Wata has various versions, including, most prominently, fish-tailed and serpent-tailed variants (ibid). In the United States (US), African-American reinterpretations of the legend have largely taken the form of 'black mermaids' (see Brown 2012).[13] Similarly, in Latin America versions of African Mami Wata and Western mermaid traditions have been syncretised with indigenous mythologies and folklore to produce mermaid figures with distinct local aspects. In Brazil these include forms such as the aforementioned Iara and the Jurema of the contemporary Umbanda religion (Hale 2009), while in Chile the mermaid has been interwoven with aspects of Mapuche folklore and has been recently activated as a symbol of local heritage values (Hayward 2011). Given the number and variety of types of mermaid in African-American and Latin American culture these have been markedly under-represented in 20th and early 21st Century screen media, in contrast to those showing European antecedence and skin tones.[14] Some representations of the pre-Christian Syrian goddess Atargatis, such as those at Ashkelon, show her in fish-tailed form and, based on this, she has been regarded by some as the earliest form of mermaid in Eurasian culture.[15] More recently, representations of mermaids in Middle Eastern culture, such as Mohammad

---

13   The only live-action film to include representations of African-American mermaids, to date, is Nijla Mu'min's short film *Deluge* (2013). The mermaids occur at the end of a narrative that reflects on the drowning of three young friends. See *Liberator Magazine* (2013) for discussion of the manner in which black mermaid heritage inspired the director (and her original ambition to provide a more ambitious representation of their undersea realm).

14   Indeed, performance historian Jennifer Kokai has contended that the predominantly Caucasian appearance of mermaids in public performance culture has reflected the manner in which such performance has been "a safe way for white women to express sexuality", with their upper bodies revealed and with their fish tails effacing their genitalia and providing them with a degree of innocence (Glenza 2015: online).

15   See Bilde (1990) for an account of the development of the goddess.

Ghorbankarimi's *The Desert Fish* (2014) and Shahad Ameen's short film *Eye and Mermaid* (2014), have shown syncretic blends of the ancient regional tradition and the more internationalised form of the figure.[16]

But whatever the inflection of the figure's uses, the durability of the mermaid myth has been premised on the *female* nature of the creature. This is underlined by the fate of the medieval mer*man*. While the merman is noted in several entries in category B82 of the Arne-Thompson Index, it has now fallen into such obscurity that the Third Edition of *The Shorter Oxford English Dictionary* extended it a rare, quasi-feminist definition as "the male of the mermaid" (1973: 1311). Some Scandinavian languages refer to mermen in similar terms to mermaids, modifying the second part of portmanteau terms to reflect the male gender (i.e. Danish: *havmanden*; Norwegian: *havmann*; Faroese: *havmaður*) whereas others use more generic terms for water spirits, such as the Finnish *näkki* and Swedish *vattenande*.[17] The German language refers to mermen as either *wassergeist* (water spirit) or *wasserman* (water man) and Dutch uses the term *meerman*. Like the mermaid, whose folklore and cultural representation interweaves and blends with the figure of the siren, the merman has a degree of overlap with another (albeit largely archaic) entity, the triton. In classical Greek mythology tritons (in the plural) were the offspring of Triton, the son of the sea gods Poseidon and Amphitrite. Unlike his parents, who were usually represented in human form, Triton commonly appears in mer-form. Like his father he was often shown brandishing a trident with magical powers and was also associated with a conch shell that he blew to control the sea. His offspring took mer-form and in the original mythological context were both male and female. By the medieval period, the term 'triton' came to refer to the male of the species, with the female form being absorbed within the figure of the mermaid. Latin languages defer to the mythological rather than folkloric traditions, identifying mermen as tritons (French: *triton*, Spanish: *tritón*, Portuguese: *tritão*, Italian: *tritone*).

The contemporary obscurity of the male figure of the merman/triton (in all but the instances discussed in Chapters 7 and 8 of this volume) is a significant pointer to the particular potency of the mer*maid* myth. The mermaid is paired with human males in almost all folkloric/mythic narratives. In the classic siren myths it is men who are lured to their watery doom. In the vast majority of mermaid-themed folklore and fiction it is men that she pursues, for either dalliance or longer-term relationships. In this regard, the potency of the mermaid can be identified as deriving, in substantial part, from aspects of masculine heterosexual desire, masculine perceptions of sexual difference and the manner in which women (and/or gay/bisexual men) have engaged with and/or interpreted these. The complexity of these aspects (with regard to the inhuman physiology of the lower half of the mermaid) is evident and there are various ways of seeking to understand and interpret the mermaid's continuing appeal. The work of Swiss psychologist Carl Jung offers one frame of reference. Jung sought patterns, themes and common tropes in diverse cultures and theorised the manner in which these could be characterised as primordial archetypes that populate the collective unconscious, manifesting in the dream-worlds of

16 Also see Mattson (2014) for reference to Ameen's inspiration.
17 Faroese and Icelandic also use the terms *marbendill* or *marmennill*.

mythology/folklore and in interior personal explorations of such archetypes. In Jungian theory, the female archetype is referred to as the *anima* and reflects the archetype of the female present in male consciousness that is represented by men in a range of cultural contexts. Its reverse is the male archetype of the *animus*. In his essay 'Archetypes of the Collective Unconscious' (1968), Jung identified the *nixie* as an "entrancing creature" who was a particularly "instinctive" version of the *anima*, alongside similar "sister" creatures such as sirens, mermaids and melusines (ibid: 25). Discussing this version of the *anima*, Jung speculated that:

> *Moralizing critics will say that these figures are projections of soulful emotional states and are nothing but worthless fantasies ... But is this the whole truth? Is the nixie really nothing but a product of moral laxity? Were there not such beings long ago, in an age when dawning human consciousness was still wholly bound to nature? Surely there were spirits of forest, field and stream long before the question of moral conscience ever existed. What is more, these beings were as much dreaded as adored, so that their rather peculiar erotic charms were only one of their characteristics.* (ibid)

This passage is so densely packed with contentions and qualified characterisations that it merits a more detailed analysis than this brief Introduction can provide. But for the purpose of this particular study it is notable that Jung clearly delineates between primitive/pre-modern states of consciousness (in a world in which "nature" [however defined] predominated and in which "moral conscience" had apparently not crystallised) and the modern condition, in which more complex "emotional states" prevail (ibid). This passage effectively contrasts historical folkloric forms of the *anima* with modern, more morally complicated manifestations in the human psyche. Jung continued to characterise that "an alluring nixie from the dim bygone" might today can be regarded as an "erotic fantasy" that "might complicate our 'psychic life'" (ibid) (with the "our" apparently referring to the male). Later on in the essay Jung identifies men's successful resistance to being overwhelmed by such disruptive allure as a morally strengthening exercise that suggests a particular function for the *anima* herself:

> *Behind all her cruel sporting with human fate there lies something like a hidden purpose ... It is just the most unexpected, the most terrifyingly chaotic things which reveal a deeper meaning. And the more this meaning is recognized, the more the anima loses her impetuous and compulsive character. Gradually breakwaters are built against the surging of chaos, and the meaningful divides itself from the meaningless.* (ibid: 31)

In accord with this vivid passage, Relke (2007) notes that (in contrast to the somewhat pallid male *animus*) the *anima* is:

> *a far more exalted projection, manifesting as goddesses, female demons, and powerful mythological women, such as Eve and Aphrodite, as well as the more prosaic projections onto wives and lovers. As well, she is an active protagonist in dreams and fantasies, not a passive pointer, like the animus.* (ibid)

Indeed, in a variety of folkloric and popular cultural manifestations the mermaid is more than just active, she is inherently inconsistent and unpredictable, offering a plethora of 'faces' and functions to male perception that are subsequently inscribed in culture and are available for interpretation in various ways. As Relke goes on to elaborate, drawing on her practice as a Jungian analyst:

> *in the dreams of men I have talked to, she can be cruelly provocative, taunting, seductive, and terrifying on the one hand, and gentle, solicitous, and wise on the other. Her mutable, untamable nature makes her a fascinating mythological creature, displaying opposing, compelling tendencies, often fatal to the other mythological beings she entices.* (ibid)

Relke also contends that female engagement with the mermaid (and similar manifestations of the *anima*) and women's representation of such figures in cultural practices also "complicate" matters and seem to imply different responses to them and/or lessons learned from engagement with them (ibid). In particular, she contends that women's spirited engagement with the *anima* (as a male reflection on female being) in preference to the *animus* reflects the weak nature of the latter and the corresponding strength and appeal of the former (to both men and women) (ibid). To render this more concisely, figures such as the mermaid appeal similarly (but differently) to both men and women (on a number of levels) and, as manifestations of the vibrant *anima*, have greater power and appeal than the more pallid *animus*.

As might be expected, there is also a plethora of Freudian interpretations of mermaid tales, many of which address the scenario of Hans Christian Andersen's 1837 short story 'Den lille Havfrue' ('The Little Mermaid') and its screen adaptation by Ron Clements and John Musker for Disney in 1989. As discussed in detail in Chapter 1, many of these read Andersen's story as an exploration of aspects of the Oedipus/Electra complex. As Soracco (1990) identifies, the female's pre-Oedipal/Electral developmental phase, which is dominated by identification with females, plays an important role in early sections of Andersen's story, before its protagonist fixates upon her earthly prince. Similarly, as also discussed in Chapter 1, the little mermaid's voluntary relinquishment of her voice as the price of access to the human realm can be seen as a symbolic castration and disempowerment that she struggles to overcome in order to try and attain the object of her desire.

In the mid–late 20th Century, Jacques Lacan's various engagements with and interpretations of Freudian theory prompted a number of theoretical perspectives of relevance to this volume. The strand of work in Film Studies in the 1970s and 1980s that focuses on the representation of the female in mainstream cinema is particularly noteworthy. While material culture, visual art, drama and/or literature may have been the prime media for the development and expression of the mermaid until the late 19th Century, cinema, television and video have been key agents in the 20th and 21st centuries. Indeed, to a substantial extent these can be seen to have set the agenda for the contemporary representation and perception of the mermaid more broadly. With regard to the aforementioned developments in film theory, the cinematic figure of the mermaid can be regarded as substantially determined by and expressive of processes that Mulvey identified in her influential essay 'Visual Pleasure and Narrative Cinema' (1975). The key aspects of her approach emphasised the Freudian perception that the crucial difference between the male and the female (as perceived within patriarchal culture) is the female's phallic *lack*, both physically and symbolically. As Mulvey argues, this produces two separate but inter-related (male) impulses: a fascination with the otherness of the female, which leads to the voyeuristic objectification of the passive female figure; and a parallel perception of the active female as threatening to the patriarchal order and therefore requiring control and/or punishment. As various film theorists have emphasised, these two aspects are particularly manifest in the complex erotic threat of the femme fatale represented in the narrative and visual aspects of classic films noir (such as *Gilda* [Charles Vidor, 1946] and *Out of the Past* [Jacques Tourner, 1947]).[18]

At this point, and recalling Jung's (1968) discussion of the mermaid as an "erotic fantasy", it is pertinent to note the most obviously intriguing element of the mermaid as a figure of erotic interest. Given her particular physique, conventional heterosexual coupling is 'off the menu' or is, at very least, tantalisingly opaque (mermaids must, after all, reproduce – and merchildren are represented in various texts[19] – but how do their parents manage it?[20]). The mermaid's sexual charge is therefore a complex one.

The visual pleasure scenario that Mulvey (1975) sought to explain provides a useful starting point to approach the representation of the mermaid in 20th and 21st Century audiovisual culture, as many aspects of her visual representation conform to classic tropes and styles of female representation. But, as will be evident, her tail marks her as different. The mermaid's tail may be understood in a number of ways within cinema's regime of visual pleasure. To begin with, it is rarely depicted as an object that shocks – let alone disgusts – humans who encounter it. Surprise is common, on first encounter, but rapidly subsides and is often replaced by fascination and affection. While no audiovisual productions the author has encountered include representations of characters who have overt sexual preoccupations with mermaid tails (let alone bodily gratification resulting from contact with them), the screen image tells another story, frequently lingering on the tail in a manner that suggests sexual partialism or fetishisation. The former term is one used to refer to an intense/exclusive fixation on one part of the body as an object of desire. In terms of male heterosexual desire, female breasts, buttocks or other areas (such as feet) are commonly recognised as subject to partialism. Fetishism refers more broadly to a non-genital or non-bodily sexual focus, with this aspect frequently addressed to objects such as shoes or to particular types of garment. The tail comes into play in this context since the mermaid possesses no visible genitalia[21] and no fixation with this element of her

---

18   See Kaplan (ed) (1978).

19   Merchildren are usually represented in fish-tailed form, although an episode of the TV series *Xena: The Warrior Princess* entitled 'Married with Fishsticks' (Paul Grinder, 2000) offers an alternative. The character Gabrielle (Renee O'Connor) appears in an extended dream sequence in which she takes on the role of Crustacea, the transformative mermaid mother of three offspring. Two of her children are aquatic humanoids and one resembles a small octopus.

20   See Joan Ashworth's short animated film *How Mermaids Breed* (2002) for one interpretation of the conundrum. The film shows mermaids dragging men into the water and 'milking' them for their sperm while they are unconscious. After going onshore onto a beach, a mermaid lays eggs from an orifice low on her tail and then squirts the collected sperm onto the eggs and covers them over with sand. The eggs subsequently hatch and the merbabies crawl like young turtles across the beach and into the sea.

21   It should be noted that there are a few exceptions to this characterisation, principally in the form of early medieval church carvings. The Roman House of Colonna also used the split-tailed figure as an emblem in the 15th and 16th centuries (representing Mixoparthenos, one of the sirens of antiquity) - with a (now unknown) artist making a striking bronze statue of the figure some time in the mid-late 1500s that is now housed in New York's Metropolitan Museum (see: https://commons.wikimedia.org/wiki/File:Mixoparthenos.jpg - accessed January 2nd 2015).

anatomy is therefore possible. In this sense, any human sexual interest in mermaids might be considered partialistic-fetishistic. The mermaid's lack of visible genitalia is compensated for by the presence of a large piscine tail that is often considerably longer than her upper torso and is usually portrayed as lithe and glittery – its design placing it at something of an unstable midpoint between (piscine) flesh and a garment when at rest, and as an element of a muscular body when utilised in swimming.

In this context it is also pertinent to consider the mermaid's frequent habit of gazing into a hand-held mirror. The representation of a woman staring at her reflection is usually understood to symbolise vanity. The mermaid might therefore be regarded as an incessantly and intractably vain creature. But the nature of the reflection seen in and the process of looking into a small hand-held mirror have particular aspects that merit comment. The spatial relationships apparent in such representations suggest that the image that the mermaid sees reflected back at her is her face or, at most, her face and upper torso. Consequently, what mermaids see in their mirrors is a representation that suggests them as human. There are affinities here with Lacan's notion of the 'mirror stage' (1977), in which the child recognises its reflection as something more integrated, coherent and complete than the body it conceives of through interior perception. The mermaid, as represented, is fascinated by a (fractured and partial) representation of her form that suggests it as other than it is in reality. It is possible, in this sense, to view the mermaid's mirror fascination as dysphoric. While disputed in its application (see Starcevic 2007), 'dysphoria' is a term used in psychiatry to refer to a condition whereby an individual primarily identifies with a biological gender other than the one they possess and wishes to be perceived as that gender in social and/or sexual interactions. An expanded notion of this might see the mermaid's proclivity to gaze into her hand-held mirror as evidence of her dysphoric identification as (fully) human, and – extending this a little – as a reflection of her primary sexual attraction to human males.

The presence of the tail and its unambiguous signification of difference go well beyond any characterisation of lack and, instead, suggest a range of possibilities for alternative engagement by spectators – particularly through the possibilities of various forms of 'Gay gaze' (Gokcem 2012), 'Queer gaze' (Wray 2003) and/or from transgender perspectives (Spencer 2014). It is notable in this regard that 1980s' feminist media arts practice offered a particularly striking engagement with the mermaid in the form of German video artist Ulrike Zimmerman's *Touristinnen: Über und unter Wasser* ('Tourists: over and under water') (1986).[22] In the video the performance artist Zora played a mermaid who comes to shore and transforms into a human. As Zimmerman has identified, "the image of the woman with her over-sized tail is also intended to be phallic ... in the sense of the phallic image of the screen goddess in popular films" (p.c. May 24th 1986). The latter point is significant. The mermaid's tail can be understood as a complex phallic object that evokes the male penis in several ways. Onshore her tail is often flaccid, as a sign and symptom of her powerlessness in the human domain (which can also be understood as that of patriarchy). If aroused – by various stimuli – the mermaid's tail is frequently shown

---

22   See Hayward (1989) for a more detailed contextual discussion.

jerking, uncurling or flexing. Once immersed, the tail allows the mermaid to move through her element with vigorous propulsive power.

Understood in this manner, human characters' attraction to the mermaid and her tail might best be understood to constitute a particular form of 'Queer' activity that merits analysis within such a context. Indeed, as a half-fish, half-human creature who has persisted in vernacular culture for many centuries the mermaid is both queer (in the everyday sense of the term) and those who are attracted towards her might be deemed Queer (in the more specific sense) for manifesting and indulging that attraction. Transgender Studies is also relevant here as an approach "concerned with anything that disrupts, denaturalizes, rearticulates, and makes visible the normative linkages we generally assume to exist" (Stryker 2006: 3). Approaching literary and audiovisual adaptations of Andersen's story from this perspective Spencer identifies the inherent polyvalence of the mermaid and her form as key to her complexity (2014: 125). As Mansfield argues, Queerness and transgender perspectives embody and emphasise the "both/and" logic of various practices and entities and, within these, "the fetish object both is and isn't the phallus and what the mermaid's body does is intensify all the contradictions of the woman as phallus: highly sexualised but completely unattainable, an object of desire that will always elude the practical manifestation of that desire" (p.c. May 25th 2015).

The partialist/fetishist representation of the mermaid in contemporary screen media and popular culture more broadly is compounded by another convention that results from continuing social taboos around female nudity. This involves the depiction of mermaids' unclothed breasts as covered by their hair, conveniently cupped by seashells and/or (in a post-World War Two era) covered by bikini tops. With regard to the former aspect, the mermaid's tresses provide more than just a means of covering (and, thereby drawing attention to) her breasts.[23] Hair is also a symbol and manifestation of the mermaid's allure in its own right (Milliken 2012: 123–133). This particular partialism is a well-recognised syndrome (known as *trichophilia*) that can be discerned in much of Hollywood's visual pleasure regime (perhaps most famously in Gilda's first entry into the frame in the eponymous 1946 film noir, where a surge of her luxuriant hair precedes the representation of her face and first vocal utterance). As Gitter asserts in her discussion of the role of female hair in the Victorian imagination, tresses of hair represented a woman's "transcendent vitality", "enchanting – and enchanted – her gleaming tresses both expressed her mythic power and were its source" (1984: 936). As she goes on to relate:

> the legends of alluring mermaids who sit on rocks singing and combing their beautiful hair, thus constitute a sexual exhibition. And the more abundant the hair, the more potent the sexual invitation implied by its display, for folk, literary and psychoanalytic traditions agree that the luxuriance of the hair is an index of vigorous sexuality, even of wantonness. (ibid: 938)

Pedersen provides a more direct interpretation of the allusive function of mermaids combing their hair:

> the Greek word for comb ketis and the Latin pectin can be used not only to

---

23   It is notable in this regard that the term 'mermaid hair' has entered English language as a description for long hair that is wavy and/or crimped. (See, for instance, Unattributed 2013: online.)

15

signify an item with which to smooth and fashion hair, but also female genitalia. Such a doubling arguably complicates a distinction between the biological and culturally constructed because it blurs the distinction between items assumed to create signs of gendered and sexed identity and the material body itself. (2015: 13)

With regard to contemporary visual representations of the immersed mermaid, the vitality Gitter refers to above extends to the movement of the mermaid's hair under water, floating and swirling as she swims, often surrounding her head with diffuse, animated haloes of fibres.

As Gitter (1984) identifies, the mermaid's hair and her seductive singing are often closely linked in visual and narrative representation. As Jon Fitzgerald and I detail in Chapter 3, mermaids are nothing if not elusive and plural. While their songs and manner of performing them may be alluring and erotic, the versatile mermaid also has access to more abstracted and reified vocal seductions and her melodies can appeal on various levels. As Austern identifies:

The mother's lullaby and the lover's exaltation share the essence of the siren's song. All are emotive and sometimes paralinguistic vocalizations of some primal place. The sirenic fantasy relies largely ... on conceptions of hearing as a passive, feminine sense, and on the link between woman, water and the insubstantial, affective flow of music. (2006: 58)

Zimmerman's aforementioned video takes a similar route by evoking those theorisations of the distinct *fluidity* of female discourse argued by theorists such as Irigaray (1996) in reaction to the work of Lacan (1977). Zimmerman has emphasised that her representations of the mermaid in *Touristinnen* were the result of "intuitively pursuing a mixture of myth and a desired image of bodily qualities which was related to the water ... a body which, through its closeness to the water becomes fluid, sensuous and mysterious" (Hayward, 1989: 17). In this regard, Zimmerman's text recalls Irigaray's (1996) reflections on the manner in which the mermaid's fundamental suspension between human identity and inhumanity echoes women's position within the patriarchal order, within which female subjectivity is itself problematic and evasive. Discussing Andersen's 'Den lille Havfrue' and literary accounts of the legend of the melusine from a female viewpoint, Irigaray identifies these stories as based on "something that attracts us, fascinates us" (i.e. women) "like a mystery, a key to our identity" (ibid: 474). In her perception, the compound monstrosity of the mermaid (and similar creatures) represents a stage (or "delay") in women's access to the divine or, rather, to the imagination and consequent embrace of a divine entity that embodies all that is female and that can allow women to establish their own subjectivity (ibid: 476). As will be apparent, this represents a very different reading of the mermaid's significance and symbolic power to that posed earlier by Jung (1968) with regard to the nixie/*anima*'s function to assist in the consolidation of male subjectivity and masculine order. These two readings are, of course, far from contradictory. Rather, they represent two markedly different gender interpretations of the mermaid's significance and suggest the tensions and negotiations between these that result in the mermaid's frequent recurrence in culture.

Media-Lore and Methodology

Cultural representations of the mermaid are premised on audiences' tacit acceptance of her unwieldy compound form. Her ubiquity allows her oddness to 'hide in plain sight' and she is more often regarded as a charming and graceful entity than as a bizarre and grotesque one. Her very ubiquity is seductive, lulling us into accepting her presence. In this regard, it is incumbent on the cultural essayist and critical reader alike to make her *strange* again in order to perceive the tensions and discrepancies central to her form and to the narratives she inhabits. Guinness (2013) provides a particularly useful perspective in this regard. Operating outside of the Freudian and Jungian psychoanalytic traditions sketched above, Guinness draws on Deleuze and Guattari to develop what she terms as a "virgulian" perspective. In their extensive critique of psychoanalysis (1972), Deleuze and Guattari identify the state of becoming as a thing-in-itself, as a constant, unresolved negotiation of aspects that variously attract and repulse each other, producing subjectivities that are locked in flux rather than cemented in place. Drawing on this, Guinness adopted the virgule (i.e. the slash symbol, "/") as a conceptual-analytical motif in her analysis of the work of German artist Rosemarie Trockel (2013). Characterising the virgule as a graphic character that "literally and figuratively cuts through two words or concepts", both dividing and combining them (2013: 24), she emphasises that to "place a virgule between two things is to say that they are similar enough to be linked ... but too different to be one" (ibid). Guinness uses this perspective to discuss a range of artworks produced by Trockel (including a grotesque mermaid sculpture featured in her mixed media work 'Pennsylvania Station' [1987]). As should be apparent, the virgule represents a singularly apposite way of conceiving the mid-section of the word 'mermaid' and the mid-section that conjoins the two parts of her body. The pertinence of this focus on the slash between forms, words and concepts is that, in Guinness's characterisation:

> The virgule is that space of combination without synthesis; it is all the intensities and cracks and connections that come from the rubbing of the two subjects. A virgule takes two separate entities and bridges them, creating a space in which binary constraints do not exist and there is a constant flux of becoming. (ibid: 24–25)

In line with Deleuze and Guattari, the state of becoming is never resolved. Indeed, in Guinness's framework "the virgule emphasizes separations; it shows the spaces in between ... not just the connectivity" (ibid: 30). In this aspect, the virgule embraces differentiation and "revels in the tensions between almost-connections that are ultimately impossible to synthesize" (ibid). This is particularly pertinent to this volume in that many of the mermaids represented in 20th and 21st Century audiovisual media embody in-betweenness in that they are able to transform from mer- to human form either via traumatic procedures (such as those enacted in *The Little Mermaid*) or through far easier and more easily reversible means (as in the case of those mermaids discussed in Chapter 4).

Throughout this volume I draw on elements of folklore/mythology and popular culture in a particular manner. Dundes (2002) characterises that folklorists perceive a triple schema of culture – high, mass/popular and folklore – in which the former two are distinct from the latter due to the fixity of their representations (in contrast to the fluid and variable nature of folklore and its multiple versions of tales and motifs). While this is tenable within the specific parameters he drafts, it is far less credible when applied to aggregates and/or series of texts that have various levels of intertextual relationships. In contemporary Western society, where few are more immersed in the traditional folkloric realm than in popular culture, it is possible to assert that interaction with popular cultural forms generates distinct contemporary social practices of interpretation, identification, engagement, development and/or serial representation. The case studies of thematically-linked and/or intertextually referential material presented in this volume are thereby posited as aspects of what might be regarded as forms of contemporary *media-lore*.

The concept of *media-lore* I invoke here is one that derives from the Russian Laboratory of Theoretical Folkloristics. The concept and its relationship to previous engagements with folklore were summarised in The Laboratory's orientation statement for their 2014 Conference 'Mechanisms of Cultural Memory: From Folk-lore to Media-lore'. Commencing with a characterisation of the classic oral culture of folklore, the statement goes on to characterise two subsequent phases of the maintenance and development of folklore as a form of "cultural knowledge":

> The emergence and spread of writing produced radically new mechanisms for storing and transmitting 'cultural knowledge'. The emergence of technical intermediaries made it possible to address a much wider circle of recipients decreasing the importance of interactive aspects of communication. The written text (reproducing an oral text or verbalizing a non-verbal text) ... often aims at substituting oral memory. A written version of some piece of 'cultural knowledge' (including the knowledge about the past) involves entirely different ways of interaction with tradition bearers.

> We live in the era of the third type of communication: 'screen based', chronologically following the written type but having more in common with the oral one with its immediacy and interactivity. Technical intermediaries which provide new opportunities for face-to-face communication become less prominent. A wide circle of recipients amalgamates into the image of the Other, who becomes the partner in the dialogue. This is a paradoxical similarity since the technology for information transmission and storing in the 'screen age' is radically different from those of the oral era. (Russian Laboratory of Theoretical Folkloristics 2014: online)

Framed by this schema, my methodology in this volume is as syncretic as the mermaid is herself. Within a broad (and relatively conventional) approach derived from Literary Studies, Media Studies and the over-arching framework of Cultural Studies (and, in some parts, employing aspects of Folklore, Art History and Musicology), I draw on strands of both Freudian/Lacanian/post-Lacanian and Jungian psychoanalysis (and allude, in passing, to aspects of Deleuze and Guattari's theories) in order to interpret aspects of texts and of intertextual aggregations.

The approaches I identify above are tendered as ways of negotiating and understanding cultural phenomena rather than as attempts to consolidate or critique aspects of various strands of psychoanalytical theory in themselves. As a result, areas of my analyses offer considerable room for interpretative play with regard to the mermaid's multiple incarnations in recent popular culture. The position I sketch is far from an unusual one for an author trying to explore facets of a topic diffused across a range of popular cultural niches. Reflecting on her study of the engagement and dialogue between the media and anthropology in 20th Century North America (1998) for instance, di Leonardo identifies the extent to which the "use of multiple appropriate methods" to address particular cultural questions can provide "varying optics on the same phenomenon [and] act as a check on and a test of the validity of particular interpretations" that helps to retain balance amidst various "equally valid epistemological frames" (2006: 205). In this regard, this volume operates within a well-established Cultural Studies tradition. Its motivation is essentially similar to di Leonardo's, with regard to her characterisation that she wrote her 1998 work of "blurred genres", "not as an escape from a troubled discipline, nor as a solipsistic technique for creating textual *jouissance*" but in the belief that "simultaneous engagement" with various disciplinary positions and methodologies can facilitate cogent arguments (1998: 23). The reader can, of course, evaluate whether such perceptions are correct with regard to the analyses I offer.

Following this Introduction, the book is divided into chapters that explore key elements of the mermaid's and merman's presence in 20th and 21st Century Western audiovisual culture. My decision to limit the scope of my study to North American, European and Australian material reflects the manner in which mermaid-themed media texts produced in non-Western contexts have drawn on aspects of national and regional folklore/mythology that lie outside my areas of expertise. East Asian cinema and television is particularly significant in this regard, with notable productions including the lost feature film *Ikan Doejoeng* (Lie Tek Swie, 1941), made in the Dutch East Indies, the contemporary Indonesian mermaid horror film *Arwah Kuntilanak Duyung* (Yoyo Dumpring, 2011) the Filipino *Dyesebel* series of films (1953–2015) and television programs (2008 and 2014), the idiosyncratic Japanese horror film *Manhoru no naka no ningyo* (Hidesho Hino, 1988) and the South Korean TV series *Ing-yeo gongju* (Baek Seung-ryong, 2014). Representations of mermaids are also plentiful in Japanese anime productions (and related manga material). While I am hopeful that the analyses of Western material I offer in my study might assist in future studies of this corpus of Asian productions there are also sets of significantly different cultural traditions that should be considered but that are outside of the scope of my investigations in this volume. I should also emphasise that my analysis of representations of mermaids in Western audiovisual media is far from exhaustive. While I have attempted to be as comprehensive as possible in my analyses of Western live-action media texts, I primarily engage with Western animated productions aimed at young audiences with reference to Disney productions relevant to the focus of Chapter 1. Similarly, while Chapter 7 includes discussion of representations of mermen in Western music videos my research into the more extensive representation of mermaids in this medium is still in progress and will be published in a separate context.[24]

Chapter 1 provides an extended contextual and analytical reading of the most prominent mermaid tale over the last two centuries, Hans Christian Andersen's 'Den lille Havfrue' (1837), its adaptation by Disney and related screen texts. Chapter 2 addresses various representations of mermaids in a group of dramatic and literary texts adapted for the screen in the 1920s and 1940s and the production of a group of films in the 1960s and 1970s that

---

24 See 'Mermaids in Music Videos' page (in progress) at: http://www.mermedia.com.au/ mermaids-in-music-videos.html – accessed February 9th 2015.

explored aspects of the sexual allure of mermaids. Chapter 3 provides an overview of the representation of mermaid song and vocality in screen soundtracks. Chapter 4 is addressed to the figure of the transformative mermaid established in Ron Howard's 1984 film *Splash* and present in a number of sexually explicit films produced in its wake. Chapter 5 then returns to the format of Chapter 1, analysing patterns of adaptation from folklore, through literature and on to the screen, with regard to Sue Monk Kidd's novel 'The Mermaid Chair' (2005). Chapter 6 discusses the nature of the representation of young mermaids for pre-teen and teen audiences, the aficionado culture that has developed around them and video drama productions that reflect this. Chapter 7 switches gender focus by considering the (relatively minor) strand of representations of mermen in 20th and 21st Century audiovisual culture. The latter topic is also addressed in Chapter 8, which considers the representation of mermaids and mermen in the two hoax television documentaries *Mermaids: The Body Found* (2012) and *Mermaids: The New Evidence* (2013). The Conclusion attempts to consolidate the various analytical strands developed in the volume and reflects upon aspects of the development of mermaid symbolism across a range of texts.

Chapter One

Becoming Ariel, Becoming Ursula

'D en lille Havfrue' ('The Little Mermaid') is Danish writer Hans Christian Andersen's best-known short story. Since its initial publication in 1837 it has been
translated into a variety of languages and has been the subject of numerous stage,
film and television adaptations. The first section of this chapter introduces the
folkloric context of the story, its original inflections and various psychoanalytic interpretations of its narrative and symbolism. Focus then shifts to the Disney company's
sustained engagement with the story before moving on to explore subsequent screen
interpretations of the scenarios and characters produced by Disney. The word "becoming"
in the chapter's title is used in two senses. The first refers to the duality of the little
mermaid's experiences. Not only does she have to negotiate the process of becoming a
young adult mermaid, she then has to cope with the implications of her decision to
transform into a young adult woman. Entwined with its exploration of these facets, the
chapter also characterises the manner in which the nameless principal protagonist of
Andersen's original work became 'Ariel' and the nameless sea witch became 'Ursula'
within a body of Disney texts and subsequent productions. The chapter thereby moves
from folklore through literary adaptation to media-lore, documenting the processes of
those transitions.

I. Danish Roots

It is impossible to understand The Little Mermaid *as Andersen intended without
first understanding the folkloric mermaid. Attempting to do so is the equivalent
of reading Beatrix Potter's* Peter Rabbit *without ever having heard of any rabbit
besides Bugs Bunny.* (Grydehøj 2006: 10)

There is a critical consensus that Andersen's short story 'Den lille Havfrue' was his own
invention rather than his interpretation of an existing folk tale. While this may be an
accurate characterisation it has resulted in limited address to prior representations of
aquatic people in the Danish cultural context from which Andersen emerged and their
potential linkage to and/or inspiration for aspects of his short story.

The modern nation state of Denmark comprises the Jutland peninsula together with over

400 islands (and many smaller islets), the majority located off the eastern coast of the peninsula. As a result of this geography, and its position at the mouth of the Baltic Sea where it meets the North Atlantic Ocean, the country has had a long association with the sea and with maritime livelihood activities. This orientation has, in turn, been reflected in various aspects of its folklore. Water-dwelling types of men and women, referred to as *havmænd* and *havfruer* (the plurals of *havmanden* and *havfrue*), have been recurrent and well documented motifs in its folklore. As discussed in the Introduction to this volume, while the Danish terms are now routinely translated as 'mermaids' and 'mermen' there is nothing in their linguistic basis that specifies piscine lower bodies and the terms refer to a wide range of water-dwelling folk. This stated, a substantial strand of *havmanden* and *havfrue* folklore does concern fish-tailed people. In 1833, for instance, Danish folklorist Andreas Faye provided the following account of aspects of *havmænd* and *havfruer*:

> *The males are of a dusky hue, have a long beard, and black hair, and above are like men but below like fishes; the females on the contrary are beautiful, and above are like the fairest women, but shaped like a fish below. Their children are called 'Marmaeler', sea talkers, and fishermen sometimes take them home to get from them a knowledge of the future. It is however a rare occurrence to hear the merwomen talk or sing. Seamen are very sorry to see these creatures because they portend a storm.* (translated in Prior 1860: 330–331).

A number of representations of fish-tailed *havfruer* also feature in Danish churches dating from the late medieval period.[25] Some are standard period images in which (as discussed in the Introduction and again in Chapter 5), the mermaid can be understood to symbolise the temptations of lust and/or vanity.[26] Other images are more ambiguous. In the case of the Fanefjord Church wall painting (Figure 2), the *havfrue's* voluptuous upper-bodily appearance would seem to indicate a figure symbolizing carnal desire, yet what is her purpose in the tableau of aquatic abundance? Who is she meant to be tempting? And what does the position of her arms signify? Is she raising them in alarm, or mimicking Jesus's gestures to the left of the image? Along with these individual examples, one of the most common uses of *havfrue* and *havmanden* images in Danish churches is their inclusion in representations of God's creation of living creatures (Mills-Kronborg Index 2004: online). This is somewhat curious on several counts. The most obvious is that the *havfrue* and *havmanden* are entirely absent from Christian creation myths and their presence in such images appears to have a more associative purpose. Yet that purpose is far from clear and scholars have not yet provided any convincing account of a singular allegorical function for the inclusion of the creatures in these scenarios. While acknowledging the latter uncertainly, it is still evident that late medieval Danish churches represented the *havfrue* and *havmanden* in a variety of symbolic contexts. *Havfruer* and *havmænd* were, thereby, figures 'in play' in the period in which they were painted and evidence of that play adorned Danish church walls through to Andersen's day, when various ballads derived from regional folklore were also in circulation.[27]

---

25   See Mills-Kronborg Index (2004: online).

26   Such as one depicted combing her hair at Raaby and a split-tailed *havfrue* at Vigertsted.

27   The presence of *havfrue* images in religious and folkloric iconography may also have influenced the Danish monarchy to acquire a collection of supposed *havfrue* body parts between the late 17th and early 19th centuries, before disposing of these by public auction in Copenhagen in 1826 (Bondeson 1999: 42).

Figure 2 – Detail from a mural at Fanefjord Church (c1480) showing a fish-tailed *havfrue* as a prominent motif, top right (photo: L. Pigott, Wikimedia Commons). (Note the similarity of the mermaid's positioning on a rock to Erik Eriksen's later bronze statue of Andersen's Little Mermaid erected adjacent to Langelinnie Promenade in Copenhagen in 1913.)

Andersen was born in Odense, on Funen Island, in 1805 and lived there until moving to Copenhagen in 1819. In the early 1800s Denmark had a strong marine orientation. The country relied on a network of small ships to move people and goods between various parts of its archipelago and to exploit its inshore and offshore fisheries. The country was also implicated into a broader pattern of Atlantic marine trade and transport through its colonial possessions, including the Faroe Islands, Iceland and Greenland in the North Atlantic, and the islands of Saint Thomas, Saint John and Saint Croix in the Caribbean. During Andersen's formative years Odense transformed into a port town, following its linkage to the sea by a canal that was constructed between 1799–1807. While the town was subject to major transformations, Easterlin has identified that folk traditions were still "vitally alive" in the early 1800s, noting that "although Andersen's father, a poor cobbler, was also a freethinker and man of some education, his mother was superstitious and nearly illiterate, as were her acquaintances" (2001: 262). One significant element of local folklore concerned a *nøk*. In 19th Century Danish usage, the term *nøk* referred to water spirits of various kinds, including human- and horse-formed ones.[28] One type of *nøk* reputed to live around Odense was believed to drown a man each year (Craigie 1896: 243–245). While functional explanations for elements of folklore tend to be reductive and conjectural, it is

---

28   Thanks to Adam Grydehøj for his information on this and his general discussions of Danish folklore.

23

nevertheless possible to view figures such as the *nøk* as serving a prohibitive function, deterring individuals from the perils of drowning at a time when canal networks and maritime activities were expanding in the area.[29]

The early 19th Century was a fertile period for research into Danish folklore and a series of contemporary publications presented material gained directly or indirectly from field research (see Tangherlini 1994). A number of writers also drew on folkloric motifs for their creative work. One notable example of the latter was Bernhard Severin Ingemann, a novelist, dramatist and poet with whom Andersen corresponded. Ingemann wrote several works that included *havfrue* motifs, including his poem 'Havfruen' (1812), which describes a young man's intoxicating nighttime encounter with a voluptuous aquatic female on a beach. The corpus of Danish folk ballads[30] in circulation in the early 1800s also included a number that concerned *havmænd*. Prior (1860), for instance, identified a group of tales about a young woman lured to live below the waves by a *havmanden* (e.g. n140: 265–268, n141: 269–271 and n153: 329–334), which included the legend of 'Agnete og Havmanden', discussed in detail below.

Andersen first used *havmanden* imagery in his prose work 'Fodreise fra Holmens Canal til Østpynten af Amager i Aarene 1828 og 1829' ('A walking tour from Holmen's Canal to the eastern point of Amager in the years 1828 and 1829') (1829). The text relates a short walk in Copenhagen made by its author-protagonist over the night of December 31st/January 1st. The disparity between the text's title and the actual duration of the 'tour' undertaken has been interpreted as an exploration of the creative space available to writers (see Kramer 2013). The imagery occurs when Andersen's author-protagonist reaches the far eastern end of Amager and contemplates moving on to the next island. At this point a bizarre *havmanden* appears, interrupting the author's perambulations to offer cautionary advice. The individual is essentially figurative and his function recalls the use of fabulous creatures at the margins of medieval maps, as in the aphoristic caution *hic sunt sireane* ('here be sirens') to designate uncharted areas of ocean. In the case of Andersen's story, the *havmanden's* allegorical function is manifest in a tail made from book covers and his caution is one concerned with the bounds of creativity. Rather like folklore concerning the Odense *nøk*, which may have deterred humans from entering into waterways, the *havmanden* succeeds in stopping the story's author-protagonist short at the water's edge by reminding him of the necessity of keeping his fiction within the bounds of his designated book title.

Andersen also addressed the *havmanden*, and related aspects of differences between the terrestrial and aquatic realms, in his subsequent poem 'Agnete og Havmanden' (1832). Andersen's poem takes its theme and title from a tale with German origins that circulated in Denmark in several variants in the early–mid 1800s (Prior 1860: 329). In the ballad a young woman is lured into the sea by a *havmanden* who wishes her to be his spouse. She

---

29 It is also significant in this regard that Andersen's mother erroneously anticipated that the prospect of crossing over from Odense to Copenhagen would have proved so intimidating to her son as to deter him from leaving his home island to explore his dreams of becoming an actor in the capital (Easterlin 2001: 262).

30 I use the term 'folk ballads' to refer to ballads with folkloric themes, acknowledging that there might be significant individual re-interpretation and/or embellishment to the folkloric sources by the writers of broadsheet or other published or sung versions of these.

agrees and lives with him beneath the surface, bearing him seven children in eight years. The scenario presented in Andersen's poem is one where the boundaries between the terrestrial and aquatic worlds are smoothly porous. Humans, such as Agnete, can easily relocate, without anatomical inconvenience and/or transformation. Similarly, the poem's *havmanden* can easily move onto land. The poem also conveys that the *havmanden* (and Agnete and the *havmanden*'s offspring) are human in form, having legs rather than tails. Many years after her relocation to the submarine world Agnete hears the sound of church bells underwater and asks her husband for permission to attend church on land. Her husband accedes to the request provided that she agrees to return to her children after her visit. She accepts the conditions and visits the church where she encounters her mother, who asks where she has been. The *havmanden* then enters to remind her of her family commitment but she rebuffs his entreaties and rejects her children, opting to remain on shore. Like its source, Andersen's poem represents its *havmanden* as fully human in form. It also maintains another aspect of its source in representing the *havmanden* as an ungodly creature who causes the materiality of the church to shrink from him as he enters it. This is a somewhat complex aspect with regard to the aforementioned inclusion of the *havmanden* and *havfrue* in a number of Danish religious creation images but it is related to a perception evident in a number of other folkloric accounts that *havmænd* and *havfruer* are soulless.[31] It is perhaps this aspect that weakens any moral claim the *havmanden* has over his wife and prevents him from exercising what might otherwise be perceived (in the early 1800s) as his standard patriarchal power. Andersen adapted the poem for the stage in 1842 and a production of it ran briefly in Copenhagen in April 1843 but received largely negative critical responses and was not subsequently staged elsewhere. Since then, both the poem and its dramatised version have had a low profile in his body of work. His short story 'Den lille Havfrue' was markedly more successful and has gone on to become his best known work (with its lead character immortalised in bronze by sculptor Edvard Eriksen in 1913 and installed on Copenhagen Harbour, where it has come to be prominent icon of the city).[32]

II. 'Den lille Havfrue'

In 1837 Andersen published 'Den lille Havfrue' ('The Little Mermaid'). There are distinct similarities between this story and his earlier poem in that both feature female protagonists who are unhappy in their submarine realms and who wish to relocate to land. There is also a sense of Andersen's story continuing some time after the earlier poem left off in that the (unnamed) protagonist and her sisters have been reared by their father – described as the *Havkongen* ("sea king") – without a mother. But while Agnete exerts agency and rejects male power in a straightforward and relatively unproblematic manner, the title figure of

---

31   See Grydehøj (2006: 18) for a discussion of the origins of this perception in Danish folklore.

32   In a significant (but often overlooked) deviation from Andersen's tale, the statue represents the mermaid as having legs that end in fins, rather than a full fish-tail. The persona embodied by the statue features in the short Danish documentary film *Alle mine skibe* ('All my ships') (Theodore Christensen, 1951) which includes images of the statue and a vocal performance of her character by actress Bodil Kjer, interacting with a welder as he works and reflects on his life in shipbuilding. (More controversially, the statue featured on the video cover and promotional poster for a porn film entitled *Love in Copenhagen* [Barny Nygaard, 2000] until the Eriksen family took legal action against unlicensed reproduction of the image, resulting in the withdrawal of the artwork and a fine against the producer [Lauritsen, 2001: online.)

Andersen's subsequent story is far more restricted by it. As elaborated below, the "little" and adolescent *havfrue* is constrained by patriarchy, in terms of the sea king's authority (as both her father and her king). Her resistance to that authority is articulated in terms of her desire to be loved by and marry a human male. In this regard, the story represents a classic example of what Jung termed the Electra complex (1913) and what Freud understood to be the female version of the Oedipus complex.[33] The complex refers to a developmental stage when women perceive that they are effectively born castrated, lacking the male phallus (in both its physical and symbolic aspects). As a result of this perception they first fixate on their father, in an attempt to gain access to the phallus (in an impulse that is thwarted by the incest taboo) and later turn to a male external to their family in order to gratify their desire. The substantial complicating element in Andersen's story is that (unlike the *havmanden* in his earlier poem) Andersen's little *havfrue* is represented as a fish-tailed entity (and, given this aspect, I subsequently refer to her as a mermaid). There is also a further complicating ambiguity. While the little mermaid and her sisters are described as having tails, which are key to the narrative and the story's symbolism, the sea king's bodily form is not specified. While subsequent illustrators and adaptors have often rendered him in fish-tailed form this is a subjective interpretation. Given that Andersen doesn't refer to him as anything other than the *Havkongen*, he may either be human-formed (like the protagonist of Andersen's earlier poem) or fish-tailed. Divergent interpretations of his daughters' physical forms follow from this ambiguity. If the whole family (and the other *havmænd* and *havfruer* referred to in the story) have fish-tailed bodies, they have a general physical aspect that restricts their sexual/reproductive capability with regard to interactions with humans. But if the sea king is human in form, his daughters' fish-tailed physiques are open to interpretation in other ways. With regard to the Electra complex, the sea king's daughters' lower halves might be regarded as biological chastity devices that keep them in thrall to the king by compromising their ability to secure human male partners.

Andersen's story describes the sea king's family as inhabiting a realm beneath the sea separate from humans. But the story also stresses the family's awareness of the human world of the surface and its ability to travel to it. The young mermaids' access to the human world is however strictly prescribed. They are forbidden to visit the surface until they are fifteen, with each visiting in succession on their birthdays and returning with colourful accounts of what they encounter. While all the sisters revel in observing the beauty of the surface world the youngest has a particularly intense yearning for it. She particularly cherishes "a beautiful marble statue … the representation of a handsome boy" that had sunk to the seafloor from a wrecked ship (1837: online).[34] What is striking here is that the mermaid longs for a fully-human male rather than a merman.

---

33   As Scott (2005: 1–24) identifies, the Electra complex is barely sketched in Jung's 1913 paper. Freud rejected the notion of there being a distinct Electra complex, perceiving it to be a female subset of the Oedipus complex (see Freud 2001a, 2001b and 2001c).

34   NB I have used Project Gutenberg's open-access English language translation of Andersen's story as my textual reference source throughout this volume: http://www.gutenberg.org/files/27200/27200-h/27200-h. htm#li_merma - accessed December 10th 2014. A pdf of the original Danish language version of the story is available online at: http://img.kb.dk/cgi-bin/AdlPgTif2pdf.pl?p_tiff_filepath=andersenhc/andersenhcev1/ tif/ahce1087.tif&dummy=iefake.pdf - accessed December 20th 2014.

The little mermaid's first visit to the surface is a dramatically impressive one, as she chances upon a ship upon which a group of men are partying, celebrating the birthday of a handsome prince:

> *The sailors were dancing on deck, but when the prince came out of the cabin, more than a hundred rockets rose in the air, making it as bright as day. The little mermaid was so startled that she dived under water; and when she again stretched out her head, it appeared as if all the stars of heaven were falling around her, she had never seen such fireworks before. Great suns spurted fire about, splendid fireflies flew into the blue air, and everything was reflected in the clear, calm sea beneath.* (ibid)

While she is thrilled by the spectacle and fixated on the prince, the little mermaid sees that a storm is closing in. Concerned to protect the young man who has captured her attention, she rescues him when the ship is driven onto rocks and wrecked. She pulls the unconscious prince to shore, where she kisses him and strokes his brow before hiding behind some rocks until he is found. As should be evident from the summary and quotations given above, there is much about this section of Andersen's story that is sexually suggestive. The mermaid longs for a (human) male, a living version of the statue she cherishes. When she sees a handsome prince, rockets go off, initially frightening but eventually delighting her. After she rescues her prince she holds him in her arms and kisses his unconscious face.

The little mermaid has problems with regard to her pursuit of the prince's affections. First, he appears to have a very limited memory of who rescued him from the wreck and, second, as a fish-tailed mermaid she has no means of pursuing her relationship with him on land. This frustration precipitates an existential crisis that reflects her grandmother's characterisation of the essential differences between humans and mer-folk:

> *We sometimes live to three hundred years, but when we cease to exist here we only become the foam on the surface of the water, and we have not even a grave down here of those we love. We have not immortal souls, we shall never live again; but, like the green sea-weed, when once it has been cut off, we can never flourish more. Human beings, on the contrary, have a soul which lives forever, lives after the body has been turned to dust. It rises up through the clear, pure air beyond the glittering stars.* (ibid)

This passage provides an original contribution to popular cultural perceptions and representations of mermaids[35] by embellishing the problematic soullessness of the *havmanden* in Andersen's earlier poem. It is also information that the little mermaid is profoundly unimpressed by. She presses her grandmother to tell her of any way she can escape the fate that has been prescribed for her and is informed that if she can win the deep and unqualified love of a mortal his soul will enter into her. But her grandmother informs her that her tail is a major impediment as it is ugly to humans and would prevent any man falling for her. Keen to circumvent this, she resolves to visit the sea witch's lair to seek a magical solution to her predicament. The sea witch is another of Andersen's

---

35 This is alluded to in a discussion of mortality between two of the mermaids in the TV film *Mermaids* (Ian Barry, 2003). When one discusses their issue of their soullessness with her sister, the latter scoffs that the characterisation is a folkloric rather than an actual one.

original creations, relocating and reconfiguring aspects of terrestrial witch folklore to an aquatic context. The little mermaid arrives to find that the witch is attended by suggestively phallic, "fat water-snakes" that she allows "to crawl all over her bosom" (ibid). The crude, unglamorous and corporeal sensuality of this intertwining of bodies is repellent to the little mermaid but she persists in her quest. The sea witch informs her that she can transform her tail into legs in order to help her to seek the prince's affections but is admirably frank about the trauma this will involve. Given that the mermaid's physique precludes her from possessing (anything like) human genitalia, the transition promises not just to deliver her legs but also a number of other useful anatomical features. The witch's description of the process of her tail cleaving as being "as if a sword were passing through you" (ibid) is suggestive of anxieties around a virgin's first experience of intercourse. Similarly, the witch goes on to stress that while the little mermaid will be beautiful and graceful in her new form, "every step" she takes "will feel as if you were treading upon sharp knives, and that the blood must flow" (ibid), a characterisation that can be regarded to allude to both initial coital bleeding and/or menstruation.

Along with her warnings about the pains of becoming a woman, the sea witch tells the little mermaid that the price she requires for the service is the mermaid's voice. When the young mermaid agrees – albeit with great trepidation – the witch makes a potion from her own breast blood and exchanges it for the little mermaid's tongue, which she cuts from her mouth, rendering her mute. This incident has considerable symbolic significance within a Freudian frame. Positioned within a patriarchal order that suppresses her agency, the little mermaid's singing voice is her most significant attribute and asset. As Bunker (1934) asserts, the male voice operates within the patriarchal order as the sonic embodiment of (masculine) power. Bunker and subsequent researchers[36] have identified that within patriarchal society men tend to talk and women tend to listen. Similarly, men tend to regard women's contributions to mixed-gender discussions as peripheral and regard women's talk in exclusively female groups as 'chatter'. This is, of course, a generalistic characterisation and Bunker's study also identifies exceptions to this tendency, such as women with particularly sonorous voices and/or those who possess singing skills that can attract male attention and approbation. Drawing on these exceptions Bunker contends that women with exceptional vocal charisma can be understood to exert a degree of phallic power. Removal of that power, in the manner represented in Andersen's story, can thereby be seen as tantamount to castration and it is notable that the castrating agent is a female who gains from her actions by increasing her (already evident) phallic power.

As Dahlerup (1990) contends, the witch's excision of the mermaid's tongue can also be compared to clitoridectomy, and the subsequent sensory and orgasmic disempowerment involved. While this comparison is a relatively direct one it has not been commonly acknowledged in psychoanalytic readings of Andersen's story. Nor has a significant corollary aspect been discussed. Within the spectrum of female vocal expression deemed as troubling by Bunker (1934) – and with not inconsiderable irony – the vocalization of pre-orgasmic tensions and of orgasmic release might be regarded as particularly phallic. Just as clitoridectomy serves to decrease female genital pleasure (and thereby diminish

---

36   Such as, most recently, Karpowitz and Mendelberg (2014).

the necessity of vocal expression of intense sexual responses), the removal of the voice also curtails the capacity to express these. There is a particular pertinence to this association, and to its invocation with regard to Andersen's short story, in that the (male-dominated) medical establishment of the early–mid 1800s showed a considerable concern over women's stimulation of their clitorises, the excited states that this activity generated and the (alleged) severe mental conditions that could result (such as hysteria, deterioration of mental capacities and eventual death). British surgeon Isaac Baker Brown went on to write an influential text on the topic (1866), to pioneer clitoridectomies and subsequently proclaim and publicise the supposed benefits of the operation on female patients (which he identified as including the more stable performance of spousal duties). While the vogue for such operations was short-lived,[37] the mindset that enabled such discourse represented a set of patriarchal attitudes about female physiology, sexual expression and mental and social stability that can also be traced in Andersen's story.

Leaving the undersea realm, the little mermaid goes to the shore, drinks the sea witch's potion, acquires legs, faints with pain and is found by the prince, who leads her to his castle. While the prince favours her (amongst a bevy of beautiful slave girls he has in his retinue), her muteness prevents her from gaining the love she desires and requires. This is doubly frustrating for her as the prince is fixated on a dim memory of the girl who saved him from the shipwreck (which is, of course, the little mermaid herself). Her predicament is further complicated by the fact that if the prince should fall deeply in love with another woman the little mermaid will die and will turn into sea-foam on the day of their wedding. When the prince falls for a neighbouring princess (whom he (mis-)recognises as the girl who saved him from the shipwreck) and resolves to marry her, the little mermaid fears all is lost. As Dundes and Dundes (2002: 56–57) identify, this scenario is a classic example of the European folkloric motif of the 'false bride' which, in Andersen's scenario, is a device used to thwart the little mermaid's attempts to escape the patriarchal prohibitions she has violated in seeking her prince. Recognising this situation her sisters try and intervene by selling their tresses to the sea witch in return for a magic knife that can restore their sister's mer-form, provided that she stabs the prince in the heart and soak her legs with his blood. But the mermaid cannot bring herself to kill him and instead throws the knife into the sea and dies. There is obvious symbolism here too – soaking her legs with blood can be seen to represent an intense version of the effects of the deflowerment she desires, just as the knife represents a phallic power that she is unwilling to appropriate and wield. In a coda to the story that softens the bleak ending she finds that instead of merely becoming sea-foam she becomes one of the ethereal "daughters of the air" and learns that if she accomplishes three hundred years of good deeds she can gain a soul.[38]

The short story moves far beyond the embellished folkloric form of Andersen's poem 'Agnete og Havmanden' and utilises the mermaid motif to address various aspects of desire, sexuality, transgression and redemption. The theme of the little mermaid's incapacity to express and consummate her desires with her object of affection (either in her

---

37   See Scull and Favreau (1986).

38   The ending has an even more saccharine coda. There is also a quicker option whereby mermaids can gain souls more rapidly if they enter the houses of families and find well-behaved children residing there (the flip side is that they have to wait even longer if the children are poorly behaved).

initial, vocally articulate mer-form or, later, in her mute human one) has led some critics to see the story as expressive and/or allegorical of Andersen's alleged sexual and experiential orientation as a celibate male seemingly attracted to both women and men (with a strain of recent scholarship arguing the latter to be his primary interest).[39] If such impulses are manifest in the text they are articulated through a vivid exposition of an Electral fantasy and related complexes that provided rich material for the screen media adaptations discussed below.

III. Enter Disney

Walt Disney began producing short animated films in 1922 with the *Laugh-O-Gram* series, which included adaptations of a number of European folk/fairy tale themes. While ostensibly addressed to a young audience, Zipes (2006: 200) contends that Disney's production team was aware of the need to include elements that might also (slyly) appeal to adults and, to that end, inserted a number of "erotic signs" in the company's early films (ibid), an aspect particularly apparent in the mermaid-themed productions discussed below. In the period 1929–1939 Disney produced a series of short animated films in the *Silly Symphony* series. The initial films were made in black and white and included *Frolicking Fish* (Burt Gillett, 1930), which features undersea creatures performing humorous balletic routines and an evil, dark octopus. The film is also notable for being the first Disney production to feature a mermaid, in the form of the figurehead of one with blonde curly hair playing a harp on the prow of a sunken ship. Swimming past it, a lobster, pauses, grins lasciviously and strums the strings of her harp. Shortly after a fish is shown bouncing behind the mermaid on a gangplank, smiling and slapping its tail suggestively before giving the mermaid's posterior a few swats. While the mermaid is a wooden statue rather than a live figure her function as an object of sexual titillation is clearly apparent.

In mid-1932 the *Silly Symphony* series shifted to colour. Its second colour film, *King Neptune* (Burt Gillett, 1932) appears to have been inspired by aspects of Andersen's 'Den lille Havfrue'. Opting to give its protagonist a fish-tailed form, it depicts King Neptune as the giant, grey-bearded king of an undersea kingdom who enjoys the playful attentions of a group of slim, young, bare-breasted mermaids who playfully swim around him and tug his beard, to his evident amusement. These actions are accompanied by a legato section of score in which high-set female voices, flowing wind arpeggios and orchestral string passages effectively complement the graceful swimming motions of the mermaids within their watery environment.[40] Their wordless soprano voices also combine in close three-part harmony, thereby providing an effective musical metaphor for the close underwater sisterhood portrayed in the sequence. The scene then changes to show the mermaids perched on a rocky islet singing, while one accompanies them on a harp. At this point, the film cuts to the image of a pirate ship on the horizon and then to a scene on deck where the crew are shown drinking and performing a raucous and rumbustious version of the shanty 'Blow The Man Down'. This is interrupted when a look-out in the crow's nest

---

39   Indeed, Easterlin contends that Andersen's adoption of the mermaid "as an emblem of outsider status coheres with a biographical perspective ... Indeed ... it would be difficult to imagine a set of circumstances more systematically apt to produce a constitutional outsider than those that governed Andersen's life" (2001: 265).

40   Thanks to Jon Fitzgerald for his observations on the score to this film.

espies the mermaids, prompting the crew to leave off their carousing and head to the islet. Sneaking up on the rocks, the pirates arrive and interrupt the mermaids' three-part harmonies, which shift to squeals as all but one manages to escape. In a disturbing scene, the captured mermaid is dragged on board and tormented by the crew, screaming in distress, while her sisters ring alarms that prompt an assembly of undersea creatures to come to her rescue. Locking the mermaid in a ship's chest for subsequent attention, the pirates then fight the creatures, holding their own until Neptune creates a maelstrom that capsizes the ship and drowns its crew. Sinking to the sea floor, the captured mermaid emerges from the sea chest draped in pearls and her eager sisters joyfully take other items of jewellery and join her in a final underwater ballet sequence.

The short film provides a representation of mermaids as flirtatious but essentially inno-cent adolescents (signified by their high, sweet harmonious singing) seized upon as objects of desire by drunken, lustful men who are only defeated by the intervention of an affronted elderly patriarch. The Disney production also hints at another aspect of mariners' sexu-ality and of the frustrations of heterosexuals spending prolonged periods afloat with a same-sex crew. During the sailors' raucous performance of 'Blow the Man Down', a single sailor's head pops out of a porthole and intones the line 'Yo ho, blow the man down' in a decidedly camp manner, as a result of which he is hit on the head with a jar and knocked unconscious, to general hilarity. While the use of the word "blow" in the original shanty does not appear to have had an overtly sexual connotation, the particular performance in the *Silly Symphony* production could be read as a sly double entendre in that a number of etymological accounts suggest that by the 1930s the term "blow" was associated with both homosexual oral sex and with sailors' experiences of being fellated by female prostitutes.[41] Even without confirmation of relevant members of the production team's knowledge (and knowing deployment) of the term's connotations, the particular nature of the vignette described above invites such a reading, particularly when followed by the sailors' frenzied dash to the mermaid islet and the subsequent scene that is suggestive of imminent gang rape of a creature lacking lower body orifices. Indeed, this aspect is so apparent that the official Disney online encyclopedia (disney.wikia.com) makes it the focus of its plot summary for the film:

> The King of the Sea becomes enraged when lustful pirates threaten violence and rape against his innocent mermaids. Creatures of the deep rise to do Neptune's bidding, and soon the pirate ship lies on the ocean floor. Peace and harmony are restored. (n.d.: online)

After leaving Disney for the Van Beuren company in 1934, Gillett revisited aspects of *King Neptune* in *Neptune Nonsense* (1936). In the short animated film Felix the Cat goes searching for a companion for his lonely goldfish. After being arrested by fish police for attempted kidnapping he is taken to an undersea castle where King Neptune is shown enjoying the attentions of a slim, blonde mermaid who is dancing a hula-style routine, swaying her hips and visible breasts and periodically arching to kiss him on the cheek. This 20-second-long dance is performed to an instrumental arrangement of the seminal

---

41 See entry on 'blow-job' in Urban Dictionary Online, for instance: http://www.urbandictionary.com/define.php?term=blowjob&deid=2741227&page=13 – accessed December 2013.

Hawaiian song 'Aloha Oe', which Neptune (seemingly) provides an accompaniment to by twanging on the points of his trident in synch with the song's melody line.[42]

Disney ceased production of the *Silly Symphonies* in 1939[43] and it wasn't until fifty years later that the company produced its feature-length adaptation of Andersen's original story.[44] Despite this, there is a significant text that sits between Andersen's original tale and the late 1980s' adaptation. This is the treatment developed by Disney in 1941 for a proposed short film. Given that the film was never made, and that its production notes and artists' sketches have never been published, it might seem, at best, an historical footnote to the study of mermaid films. But although obscure, aspects of it informed the development of Disney's 1989 film and merit discussion in that regard. As co-directors Ron Clements and John Musker made apparent in interview sequences in the 'making of' documentary *The Story Behind The Story* (2006),[45] they consciously appropriated elements of the scenario and designs drafted in 1941 and rejected and/or substantially reworked others for their 1989 film. The 1941 film treatment was developed by a team that included Walt Disney, Danish artist Kai Nielsen and director Sam Armstrong. Nielsen came to the project after establishing a reputation as a designer at the Royal Danish Theatre and through illustrating books such as an English language translation of Andersen's 'Fairy Tales' anthology in 1924 (which included 'Den lille Havfrue'). He relocated to Hollywood in 1939 and contributed to *Fantasia* (1940) before commencing work on an adaptation of 'Den lille Havfrue'. The adaptation reflected and attempted to reconcile contrasting impulses, namely Nielsen's desire to be faithful to the original and Walt Disney's contrasting direction for the team to "take a license" in adapting it for the screen (Elsa 1941: 2). One notable aspect of the treatment was its use of sonic and spatial-pictorial elements to introduce the narrative and its early establishment of mermaid song as a key element:

> *Open up on the open sea – the dolphins are playing and a flight of swans is going across the sky. Got the feeling of the sea – big and mysterious.*

> *Towards sunset, pick up a ship – an old galleon – coming towards us. Through*

---

42 This sequence bears a close resemblance to one that featured in an animation short produced by Warner Brothers in the preceding year. An episode of the 'Merrie Melodies' animation series entitled *Mr. and Mrs. is the Name* (Fritz Freleng, 1935) featured the child characters Buddy and Cookie venturing beneath the sea. The film opened with images of young mermaids frolicking around a shipwreck and then singing a Hawaiian-style ballad about ocean islands (referencing King Neptune and mermaids), accompanying another mermaid who manages to perform a hula while standing upright on her tail. Buddy arrives in the film as a merman chasing Cookie, as a mermaid, eventually catching up with her and pinching her tail. After exploring a wrecked ship Cookie finds a piano and plays a duet with a lobster. An octopus then arrives and carries her off before Buddy manages to rescue her.

43 A subsequent *Silly Symphony* production made after Gillett's exit from Disney explored aspects of the mer-form without the strong sexual subtexts of the aforementioned film. *Merbabies* (Rudolf Isling and Vernon Stallings, 1938) opens with the image of seafoam surging onto a rocky islet before revealing that it contains a host of mer-infants. These proceed to cavort underwater with various other sea-creatures until a whale's sneeze propels them back to the surface on air bubbles, which break at the surface with the mer-infants apparently vanishing into the air. This representation of the mer-babies as arising from and returning to seafoam has direct resonance with the end of Andersen's original short story as the only precedent for this association of mermaids, foam and 'unbeing'.

44 The only subsequent representation of mermaids in a Disney film production between the *Silly Symphony* shorts and the feature-length adaptation of Andersen's 'The Little Mermaid' in 1989 occurred in Clyde Geronimi, Wilfred Jackson and Hamilton Luske's 1953 animated feature adaptation of J.M Barrie's 'Peter Pan', which is discussed in the following chapter.

45 Available as a bonus DVD feature on the 2006 two-disc Special Edition DVD re-issue of the film.

the sound of the waves we hear the sound of singing voices growing into the sound of the mermaids.

As the ship comes close, we see the five mermaids on the waves singing to the ship. When the bowsprit is almost above them, they dive down. (ibid)

Nielsen's charcoal drawings for the mid-section of the above sequence represent the mermaids as possessing long dark tresses that hang far below their midriffs and also depict them as standing up on their tails in the water, with their upper bodies above the waves. While Clements and Musker did not retain these elements, a comparison of images from Nielsen's treatment (shown in the *Story Behind The Story* video) reveals that the storm sequence that sinks the ship in the 1989 film was closely modelled on Nielsen's original sketches. One aspect which Disney specifically directed his team to modify concerned the prince's coming-to on shore. In Andersen's original the little mermaid leaves the prince unconscious on the shore then waits, in hiding, to make sure that he is found. Disney introduced a new element in 1941 that Clements and Musker also utilised as a key aspect of their later narrative. Disney suggested that the little mermaid should linger on the shore and sing to the prince, only departing at the moment that he blurrily awoke to the song. The prince's memory of the girl he half glimpsed and heard singing, and his subsequent quest for her, became a key motif in the 1989 film.

While the Disney company has now acquired a reputation for sweetening and sanitising the material it adapts for the screen, not least in the case of its adaptation of Andersen's famous short story, the 1941 treatment had two elements that contradicted this tendency. The first involved a condensed narrative aspect. Instead of the little mermaid transforming into fully-human form and spending an extended time in the prince's court before he married another, the 1941 treatment had her arriving onshore ready to pursue her prince only to find the bells ringing to herald his wedding ceremony, leaving her a helpless and hopeless spectator, doomed to die due to her inability to secure his love. Harsh as this narrative condensation may have been, another aspect was even harsher. While the little mermaid in Andersen's version died and was transformed into an ethereal "daughter of the air", she was given the prospect of availing herself of an immortal soul in return for three hundred years of good deeds. The 1941 treatment offered no such escape clause, with its protagonist dying, forsaken and forlorn.

IV. 1960s'-1980s' Adaptations

While there was a substantial gap between the aborted 1941 Disney treatment and the company's 1989 feature film, there were a number of other screen adaptations in the intervening years. Two Eastern European feature films provided notable interpretations. Like Andersen's poem 'Agnete og Havmanden', *Malá Morská Víla* (Karel Kachnya, 1976), made in Czechoslovakia, represents its sea-people in human form, inhabiting a rocky, undersea cavern suffused with blue light. Given her human physique, the little mermaid's transformation at the hands of a sea witch in return for her voice is not so much physical as it is conceptual. Her fate is essentially the same as Andersen's original heroine though, in that she does not gain the love of the man she desires. In a poetic touch, the film's final images show the surface of the sea blooming with flowers after she dies. The Russian film,

Rusalochka (Vladimir Bychkov, 1976), takes different liberties with Andersen's original. The film commences with a young mermaid falling in love with a prince she sees on board a ship shortly before her sisters lure it onto a rocky islet where it is wrecked. The little mermaid rescues the prince and follows him onshore, hiding in waterways as he recovers. She is then befriended by a man who arranges for a (human) witch to transform her tail into legs in return for her hair. Despite this transformation (and her retaining her voice throughout) her love for the prince is impeded by his sense of indebtedness to the princess that he believes to have rescued him. On the day of the prince and princess's wedding he realises that the little mermaid was his real love all along but the realisation comes too late and the mermaid fades out of existence shortly after the marriage is concluded.

Along with these two features (which had limited circulation in the West), there were a number of shorter format adaptations that were more faithful to Andersen's original, including two animated films, Ivan Aksenchuk's *Rusalochka*, made in Russia in 1968, and Peter Sanders' contribution to the American *Readers Digest Presents* television series in 1974 (also titled 'The Little Mermaid'). Andersen's story was also featured in two American TV series that dramatised fairy tales in live-action form: *The Shirley Temple Show* (1961) and *Faerie Tale Theater* (1987). The former, directed by Robert Kay, had a number of aspects that merit comment in the context of this chapter. The episode featured Temple in the title role and represented the sea witch as a mature mermaid with a black tail. While the latter's appearance is less hideous than in Andersen's original story the witch was given a more monstrous 'familiar' (i.e. a spirit in animal form who serves a witch) in the form of a large, malignant black octopus with a female voice. However the most significant deviations from Andersen's original concerned the conditions of the little mermaid's transition into human form and her fate. In Temple's version the witch doesn't require the mermaid to lose her voice in order to have her legs transformed and she has also 100 tides on land to make the prince fall in love with her. Despite this, she doesn't manage to win the prince, who weds another woman instead. Keenly aware that she will soon be transformed into sea foam she calls to her relatives for help. Her grandmother trades fifty years of her life with the sea witch in exchange for a magic knife that the mermaid can use to stab the prince through the heart and save herself. In a twist on the original story that is unique in the corpus of screen adaptations discussed in this chapter, this action is promised to unite the couple by transforming the prince into a merman. Eschewing this radical option, the mermaid fails to act. But rather than let her die, her father shows mercy and intervenes to allow her to return to the ocean in mermaid form and reunite with her family. *The Shirley Temple Show* production thereby set a precedent for the softer ending for Andersen's tale that was delivered in Disney's subsequent feature-length adaptation.[46]

---

46   It is also notable that live-action treatments of the short story produced subsequently to the Disney film have also modified the ending. In the German television film *Die kleine Meerjungfrau* (Irina Popow, 2013), for instance, which is otherwise relatively faithful to Andersen's original, the heroine is rewarded when she is granted a soul for not killing Eric when she has the opportunity. A more novel approach to the ending of the story was provided in the 14-minute sequence included in Philip Saville's fictionalised television biopic – *Hans Christian Andersen: My Life as a Fairy Tale* (2003). The sequence ends on a 'cliff-hanger', terminating at the point when the little mermaid holds her dagger above Prince Eric as he sleeps. The anger that crosses her face suggests that she is going to carry through on her sisters' instructions for her to let his blood soak her legs and thereby save her life and restore her tail.

V. *The Little Mermaid* (1989)

Despite the circulation of the screen adaptations referred to above, none achieved anything like the success of Ron Clements' and John Musker's 1989 adaptation for Disney. While novel, the directors' take on Andersen's original was steeped in an awareness of Disney history. In addition to their engagement with the 1941 treatment discussed above, aspects of *King Neptune* were revisited by the 1980s' production team, with the titular character of the latter being the model for King Triton (the little mermaid's father) in their film. The choreographed ensemble actions of various sea creatures, including those represented as performing music in the film, are also similar to sequences in the Disney *Laugh-O-Gram* and *Silly Symphony* productions discussed above.

Disney's 1989 version of Andersen's story represents not so much a re-telling but, particularly in its latter parts, a comprehensive re-imagination of Andersen's earlier tale. While the central element of the little mermaid's sacrifice of her voice in return for legs and of her subsequent attempts to secure the prince's love on land remains, many other aspects are altered. In addition to adding musical numbers the Disney adaptation provides an individualisation of characters (such as all the mermaids having names), a re-imagining of the form and plot function of the sea witch and a significantly different narrative outcome.

The film opens with a pre-credit sequence that introduces the prince (named Eric in the film) on board a sailing ship. The jaunty, sea shanty-style chorus that accompanies this sequence has a double edge in that its lyrics refer, somewhat forebodingly, to mermaids and to King Triton waiting for the sailors below. After a title sequence the film shows a stream of mermaids and mermen arriving at the Sea King's impressively large palace for musical entertainment provided by the King's daughters, accompanied by an orchestra of sea creatures conducted by a crab named Sebastian. The concert's opening song, sung by the mermaids, is cut short when the final singer, King Triton's youngest daughter Ariel, fails to appear. The film reveals that she is off elsewhere, exploring a wreck. Upon her return she is admonished by her father and is strongly scolded when he finds out that she has been visiting the surface. The extent of her fascination with the human world is revealed when she is shown to have a collection of human artefacts secreted in a grotto. The narrative then closely follows Andersen's original, with Ariel rescuing Eric, visiting the sea witch to be transformed into a human and relocating to the land where she tries to charm the prince.

Andersen provides scant descriptions of the little mermaid in his story, only referring to her as "a strange child, quiet and thoughtful", and leaving it to the sea witch to make comments about her "beautiful form" and "expressive eyes" (1837 online). This gave Disney considerable latitude for interpretation. Ariel's appearance was designed by artist Glen Keane and features four main design elements: a green, scaled fish tail that ends at her waist with a small collar (which is unusual in mermaid folk- or media-lore[47]); long, thick auburn tresses (that swirl around in the sea and bob around in the air); a slim, naked upper body with breasts cupped in purple clam shells; and a pretty face distinguished by

---

47   While unique in 20th Century mermaid media-lore, it recalls medieval illustrations of mermaids' midpoints ornamented with frills or flipper like appendages.

large eyes and a gleaming smile. Keane's design used mature referents to create a representation of a mermaid on the cusp of adulthood. He reportedly used his wife Linda's face as the basis for Ariel's visage and used the (then 28-year-old) actress Sherri Stoner as a live-action body model,[48] exaggerating the narrowness of her waist and curve of her hips to match the curvaceous physiques of women represented in the paintings of French Rococo artist François Boucher (Connelly 2011: online).[49] Ariel's distinctive red hair colour was also derived from another art historical referent, John William Waterhouse's famous 1901 painting 'A Mermaid' (ibid).[50] Perhaps the most tellingly symbolic aspect of her design occurs at the vertex of the front of her tail. Here the tail splits open with a V shaped incision (as if unzipped), closing at a point where the pubic area would be if she had human form. This is something of an erotic tease. As Barthes famously asked, "Is not the most erotic portion of the body where the garment gapes?" (1975: 9) Answering his own question in the affirmative, he identifies that in "perversion" – which he identifies as "the realm of textual pleasure" – "intermittence" provides the erotic aspect, the "staging of an appearance as disappearance" (ibid).

Ariel's complex erotic package was recognised by a number of reviewers as a key element of the film's appeal.[51] As the *Los Angeles Time's* film reviewer colourfully summarised:

> *Ariel ... isn't much like Andersen's sad, noble sea-maid. She's a sexy little honey-bunch with a double-scallop-shell bra and a mane of red hair tossed in tumble-out-of-bed Southern California salon style. She has no gills, but, when she smiles, she shows an acre of Farrah Fawcett teeth.*[52] (Wilmington 1989: online)

As Cruz identifies, in an article addressed to *"The Little Mermaid's* 'Divisive Sexy Ariel'" (2014: online), similar perceptions of Ariel's attractiveness continue to be an enduring aspect of the film's appeal to males. Indeed, this aspect is the central element of *Merman* (Ryan Bosworth, 2015), a short film concerning a young man fixated on Ariel figurines who aspires to becoming a merman in order to be part of her world.[53]

One element of Andersen's story that was significantly expanded in the 1989 film was the role of the Sea King, who is a shadowy presence in Andersen's original. In the film he is named as King Triton, alluding to the figure from Greek mythology discussed in the Introduction to this volume. He is represented as a monumental, white-bearded patriar-

---

48   See reference footage online at: https://www.youtube.com/watch?v=f5BEKRtvKA0 – accessed December 31st 2015.

49   See Keane's preliminary production drawings of Ariel archived online at the Art of Glen Keane blog: http://theartofglenkeane.blogspot.com.au/2006/06/ariel.html – accessed December 26th 2015.

50   The Pre-Raphaelite painters often painted young female subjects with long, red hair (and/or used red-haired models) following a fashion that dated back to the late 1860s, when the character of Lydia Gwilt in Wilkie Collin's scandalous novel 'Armadale' was described as having luxuriant red hair, which symbolised her sexual worldliness (Ofek, 2006: 111). Waterhouse, who was heavily influenced by the Pre-Raphaelites, used red to signify similar aspects in several of his paintings, including 'A Mermaid' (1901).

51   Cruz has identified a common consensus among many adult male reviewers that Ariel was "above all hot" (2014: online). Research for this chapter also uncovered anecdotal evidence of male viewers of the film vocally expressing their perception of Ariel as sexually attractive during screenings of the film.

52   Fawcett was a tall, blonde actress and sex symbol who starred in the first season of TV series *Charlie's Angels* (1976–77) and was well known for a wide, toothy smile.

53   His attraction to the Disney heroine is explicitly acknowledged by his housemates when they return home and wonder where he is, with one saying, "He's probably in his room masturbating to Ariel."

chal figure who is more than double the size of his daughters. He bristles with patriarchal power and has a quick temper, both of which are expressed through his trident, which can shoot energy bolts and affect magical transformations. As discussed in Chapter 7, he is also, following the model of King Neptune in Disney's 1932 short film, fish-tailed in form.[54] Ariel's decisions to pursue her transformation and the man of her dreams are in direct contradiction to her father's command for her to abandon her association with the surface world, which he underlines by destroying the contents of her grotto.

Balancing King Triton's presence, the sea witch's role is also significantly expanded. Named Ursula in the film, her visage and upper half is based on the flamboyantly grotesque drag performer Divine (best known for starring in John Waters' film *Pink Flamingos* [1972], in which she was touted as the "filthiest person alive"[55]). Ursula's lower half transitions smoothly from her upper torso through a black bodice that morphs into six long, octopus-like tentacles. There's nothing subtle about her appearance. Described by one reviewer as "an obese lavender voluptuary ... squeezed into a cleavage-popping" gown (Wilmington 1989: online), she has also been characterised as a "gross and grotesque caricature of a femme fatale" (Dundes and Dundes 2002: 65). While the Disney's corporate Wiki site page on Ursula identifies her as a "villainous cecaelian sea witch" and charac- terises the cecaelia as "a legendary hybrid of human and octopus",[56] the figure of a monstrous tentacled female has little precedent in Western mythology or folklore. Rather than deriving from these sources, the cecaelia is a more modern figure that developed as a distinct entity within a dispersed node of fantasy aficionados and artists. The entity's name appears to derive from a single source text, a short pictorial story published in *Vampirella* magazine entitled 'Cilia' (Cuti and Mas 1972) that became the basis for the more general figure of the 'cecaelia' some time in the late 2000s.[57]

Cuti and Mas's story (ibid) concerns a mysterious and beautiful young woman whose lower body morphs into tentacles at the tops of her thighs.[58] After saving a ship's captain from a wreck she is seized, tortured and disfigured by villagers who initially mistook her for a mermaid when they saw her swimming out at sea. The villagers then head to sea to celebrate their brutality until a huge, monstrous kraken-like creature wrecks their boat and kills them.[59] While there is no evidence that Clements, Musker or Ruben Aquino (the

---

54 See Chapter 7 for further discussion of merman/triton figures.

55 As discussed in the 2003 'making of' video *Broadway comes to Burbank*, produced for the 2006 DVD release of *The Little Mermaid*.

56 http://disney.wikia.com/wiki/Ursula – accessed December 27th 2015.

57 This characterisation derives from my research into its earliest uses on the Internet and my inability to find specific references to it in printed material prior to this period.

58 The story identifies her as being a 'cilophyte'. This appears to be an invented term whose etymology is unclear.

59 Cuti and Mas's (1972) story is significant for subsequent mermaid media-lore for the manner in which it plays with readers' expectations by giving its female protagonist an identity that is not revealed until the mid-point of the narrative. It concerns two men, Zackery and Captain Spike, who survive a shipwreck in the Atlantic due to the intercession of a mysterious and beautiful young woman (who appears cloaked in the story's early frames). Captain Spike returns to an English coastal village with her and the graphics reveal her upper body to be that of a beautiful, slim young woman with long curly hair who needs to bathe in the sea frequently. Male villagers become suspicious and spy on her while she is out swimming. Misrecognising her as a mermaid and fearing that her presence onshore will bring ill fortune they abduct her. But rather than a mermaid they find that the upper female part of her body morphs into tentacles at the top of her thighs. Zackery and the captain then search for her and find her, hideously tortured and disfigured. The captain accedes to her pleas to put her out of her misery and kills her by plunging a harpoon into her heart.

film's supervising artist for Ursula) were aware of and/or drew on 'Cilia' in designing Ursula, both texts also include the appearance of a giant, menacing, octopus-like creature at the end of each narrative. Aside from these coincidences, Cilia is also identified within Cuti and Mas's story as being aligned to mermaids, both through the villagers' initial misapprehension of her and through elements of the narrative that recall Andersen's seminal mermaid story, such as her rescuing a young man from a wreck.[60] Despite the lack of evidence of the *Vampirella* story being a direct influence on the design of Disney's villainess, it is significant that since publication of the original story the term 'cecaelia' has become increasingly used to describe half-female, half-octopus entities such as Ursula, including on Disney's aforementioned Wiki page.

Whatever its relationship to Cuti and Mas's story (ibid), the filmic figure of Ursula represents a vivid innovation to both Andersen's source tale and mermaid-related lore in general. The symbolism of Cilia's and Ursula's composite bodies also merits comment. While Freud did not analyse tentacled female figures, Schnier (1956) contends that Mycenaean and Minoan octopus imagery could be read as symbolic representations of phallic females, with the single phallus of the male/patriarchy multiplied through what Silber characterises as the "polyphallic appearance" of the eight tentacled octopine form (1981: 162). Similarly, Trites characterises Ursula as a "perversion of femininity" with tentacles that "could be interpreted as eight phalluses" (1991: 50). Viewed from these perspectives, Cilia and Ursula are highly problematic to patriarchy, requiring them to be disfigured and/or killed in order to remove their disruptive presences.

Fittingly, in the above regards, Ursula is represented as the exiled and oppositional 'other' to King Triton. Ursula's theatrical, cackling villainy also functions as the opposite of Ariel's slim, doe-eyed, innocence – evoking earlier wicked witch roles in Western folklore and fiction. Ursula is cunning and totally heartless in the film, which represents her as granting Ariel's wish for legs as part of her feud against King Triton. Her most heartless act is of masquerading as the girl who rescued Eric early in the narrative, taking on a youthfully beautiful form (as 'Vanessa') and utilising the voice she has obtained from Ariel to trick Eric into marrying her. The marriage service commences on board a ship but is thwarted, at the moment of the final vows, by a sustained disruption by a group of sea creatures and birds. Although Ursula's trickery is revealed, it comes too late to save Ariel who has only been granted three days in human form to win Eric's love. At this point King Triton redeems himself by offering himself as a substitute for his daughter as a vassal to Ursula. Accepting the King's offer Ursula gains access to his trident, the symbol and embodiment of his phallic power, and grows huge and monstrous (like a giant kraken). Eric then comes to the rescue with his own phallic appendage, steering a ship into her torso and puncturing her with its bowsprit. With her death, order is restored, King Triton and Ariel are re-united and the King transforms her tail to legs with his trident in order that she can marry Eric and sail off into the future with him. Unlike the Electral nightmare of Andersen's original, where the mermaid disobeys and abandons her father only to fail

---

60   Cilia's appearance in the single narrative frame that reveals her full bodily form also has indirect echoes of representations of Andersen's story in that she is shown perched on a rock, with her separate legs morphing into triple tentacles, akin to the manner in which Eriksen's famous statue of the little mermaid in Copenhagen represents its mermaid with legs that morph into fins.

to win the heart of the man she desires, Disney delivers an Electral fantasy in which her father assists her departure with her object of desire.

Another notable aspect of the 1989 Disney film (shared with its sequels) is the manner in which it eschewed the various approaches to vocality and integration of melody and score in both *King Neptune* and those films discussed in Chapter 3 of this volume in favour of a more conventional musical theatre approach to score and vocal characterisation. The power and significance of Ariel's voice is central to the Disney feature but is rendered in a conventionally human manner. It first appears in a song entitled 'Part of Your World'. This is closely integrated into the narrative and functions as a classic Broadway-style 'I wish' number that outlines the aspirations of the central protagonist and lays the foundations for the development of the plot. As composer Alan Menken recalls, screenwriter Howard Ashman's contention was that:

> *every musical needs a point at which the central character sits down… and says 'this is what I dream of' and of course then the rest of the story's all based on creating obstacles that this character has to overcome to achieve their dream.* (2006 DVD audio commentary)

In the song Ariel declares her ambition to access the terrestrial world in a pure, clean soprano tone. Jodi Benson (who voiced Ariel) was coached by Ashman to interpret the song using an approach consistent with musical theatre.[61] Accordingly, Ariel's vocal delivery is theatrical in nature – with clear and precise diction, changes between singing and half-spoken articulation, and extensive use of rubato. In order to convey Ariel's youth Benson uses minimal vibrato and on occasions when vibrato *is* used, it is brief and rapid. The song structure is also suitably dramatic, beginning with a lengthy introduction before moving to a chorus that makes Ariel's wishes abundantly clear. After an introductory section the song moves to a pre-hook section that ends with a long high note (at the end of the phrase "I want more") – a typical musical theatre device that signals the pending arrival of the chorus. The chorus begins with mid-range vocals, and then rises again to reach a high-set climax, before the ultimate lyrical hook ("wish I could be/part of that world"). Ariel also sings a reprise of the chorus of 'Part of Your World' (with new lyrics) to Prince Eric as he lies unconscious on the beach after she has saved him from drowning. As he regains consciousness, he hears her song (as if in a dream) and becomes inspired to identify the singer. Musical ideas from 'Part of Your World' are also used at other prominent places in the film, further attesting to the importance of Ariel's voice within the narrative[62] and making its absence from the latter half of the film an even more poignant representation of Ariel's disempowerment on land.[63]

---

61   See *Treasures Untold: The Making of Disney's 'The Little Mermaid'*, documentary produced for the 2006 DVD release of *The Little Mermaid*.

62   Sonically-processed vocals based on the opening three-note rising melodic theme from 'Part of Your World' are also used prominently in a number of places. For example, when Ursula captures Ariel's voice, the rising vocal melody has echo effects added and is gradually shifted from the foreground to the background of the mix (while being simultaneously moved around within the stereo image), to signal its dislocation from her body. Similarly, when Prince Eric sees a hazy and distant vision of Ariel on the beach, the rising vocal motif is presented with a large amount of reverb effect added – giving it a complementary ghostly, distant quality. In the scene in which Ariel regains her voice, the processing techniques used when she lost it are reversed, with reverb and echo effects gradually removed. The vocal motif is moved from background to foreground and the 'natural' order is restored.

39

VI. Sequels and Prequels

The massive commercial success of *The Little Mermaid*, which grossed US$222 million in cinemas upon initial release and accumulated a further $289 million in DVD and Blu-ray sales,[64] prompted Disney to explore spin-off productions for television. In 1990 puppeteer/director Jim Henson proposed a TV series entitled *Little Mermaid's Island* to Disney, intended to feature an actress playing Ariel together with puppets playing the key animal roles from the film. Two 25-minute pilot episodes of the show were made in 1990, featuring adult actress Marietta DePrima as Ariel, but the series' proposal was abandoned following Henson's death shortly after completion of the pilots.[65] Instead, Disney invested in an animated television series set before Ariel's transformation into human form, also entitled *The Little Mermaid*. Thirty-one episodes of the series were produced and were broadcast on CBS in 1992–1995. Many of the characters from the original film were present in the series, which also featured musical sequences inspired by and often similar in style to the original film. Set prior to Ariel's transition into human form, the TV series lacked the film's key transformative motif and rich set of symbolic associations. Episode-based, the series mainly concerned Ariel's undersea adventures as a young mermaid and her efforts to foil occasional disruptive characters. One particular episode, entitled 'Wish upon a Starfish' (1993), is notable for revisiting aspects of the original film. The episode involves Ariel encountering and striking up a relationship with a mute mermaid named Gabriella. When Ariel finds a ballerina figure musical box she aspires to acquire legs and the ability to dance. Gabriella also craves a voice so that she can sing. Together they set out to find a magical starfish that can make their dreams come true. After crossing hostile aquatic terrain they find the fabled starfish only to be disappointed when it does not have the power to transform them. Reflecting on their experiences they realise that they are happy with the abilities that they have. The narrative and thematics of this episode are obviously strikingly different from the original film – transformations are not attempted and the mermaids accept their physical forms and do not seek to disrupt the symbolic order of the undersea kingdom.

A feature-length prequel was also produced in 2008, directed by Peggy Holmes and entitled *The Little Mermaid: Ariel's Beginning*. While the film represented a fresh take on Ariel's early life, rather than adapting elements from the TV series, it covered similar themes to the 'Starfish' episode described above, particularly with regard to the device of a music box with dancing figures triggering memories and desires. *Ariel's Beginning* only features humans briefly, albeit in a pivotal sequence, and does not include any transformations of mer-form. The narrative commences with the undersea kingdom (now specified as 'Atlantica') in an idyllic state, ruled by King Triton and his Queen, Athena. The film's narration specifies that it "was a magical time, the pure joy of songs filled life". In order to celebrate his love for Athena, an accomplished singer, the King gives her a music box

63 My thanks to Jon Fitzgerald for his insights into 'Part of Your World'.
64 Source: http://www.the-numbers.com/movie/Little-Mermaid-The#tab=more – accessed June 11th 2015. (I have not been able to ascertain videocassette sales figures.)
65 The initial pilot episode, entitled *Sebastian's Birthday*, is currently online at: https://www.youtube.com/watch?v=3MpN7PHjw7Y – accessed October 5th 2015.

with two dancers, representing the couple. An idyllic sequence of young mermaids and mermen frolicking, singing and playing instruments in a lagoon is interrupted by the arrival of a pirate ship. The merfolk scatter but Athena delays in order to retrieve her music box and is crushed by the ship and dies. The film's main narrative occurs ten years later, when Ariel is in her early teens, living in an underwater society where music has been banished, since it reminds the King of the love he has lost. Rather than a sea witch, the evil female role established in the first film, is assigned to an older and slightly grotesque mermaid governess named Marina Del Ray. Ariel, who loves music and song as much as her mother, resents the ban on music and stumbles across a clandestine music club run by Sebastian the crab. Marina also discovers the club and informs the King, who arrives, arrests everyone and demolishes the venue by blasting it with his trident. Ariel resists patriarchal authority and escapes the palace and frees the imprisoned sea creatures. She then finds and retrieves Athena's long-lost music box and attempts to present it to the King to remind him of joy. Knocked unconscious by Marina as she is about to do this, she is revived by her anxious father who sings her a snatch of her mother's theme song to comfort her. Upon her awakening, social and musical harmony is restored to the kingdom with the King's blessing. The film thereby combines a representation of an arrested grieving process with a rejection of (overly harsh) patriarchal power. Ariel desires to escape her father's regime in order to return to the (literal and metaphorical) harmony she associates with her experience of an earlier developmental stage when she primarily identified and interacted with her mother and her sisters.

In addition to the prequel TV series and feature film, Disney also produced a feature-length sequel entitled *The Little Mermaid II: Return to the Sea* (Jim Kammerud and Brian Smith, 2000), which centred on Melody, the daughter of Ariel and Eric. The narrative commences with a sequence that shows Ariel, now a human, returning to the sea to introduce her baby (human-form) daughter to King Triton. He welcomes her and gives his granddaughter a locket that contains images and sounds from Atlantica. At this point a new character, Morgana, the sister of Ursula from the original film, arrives. Like her sister, she is tentacled, albeit slimmer, less grotesque and green skinned. Morgana tries to steal Melody in order to ransom her for the Sea King's trident but is driven off. Ariel then resolves to keep her daughter away from the sea until Morgana is found. The narrative then jumps forward a decade to show a teenage Melody, who does not know of her mer-roots, yearning for the sea. She then finds the locket (which she has no memory of) and is drawn to the sea where she is persuaded by a fish to visit Morgana in icy, polar waters. Morgana delights her by turning her into a mermaid for a short duration and offers to make that condition permanent if she steals the King's trident for her. Melody does this, with the aid of friendly sea-creatures, and takes it to Morgana. In the meantime the King has transformed Ariel back into mer-form in order to search for her daughter. Ariel arrives at Morgana's lair, where Melody realises that her mother is a mermaid. Feeling deceived by this discovery Melody gives the trident to Morgana, who assumes gigantic proportions (like her sister in the first film). Morgana then imprisons Melody in an ice cave and traps Ariel in her tentacles. After Eric, the Sea King and a group of mermen fail to defeat Morgana, Melody returns to the surface, having being freed by sea creatures. She grabs the trident and throws it to the King, who then uses it to seal Morgana in a block of ice and exile her to the seafloor.

As the above description suggests, *Return to the Sea* lacks the considerable symbolic charge of its predecessor and the transformation from human to mermaid that both Melody and Ariel undergo in the narrative is not represented as in any way traumatic (nor does it require them to lose any other attributes). The trident plays a strong role again, as a symbolic phallus that a monstrous female covets, but has a different symbolic aspect in that Melody (in mer-form with her phallic tail) is able to steal it from the King and then appropriate it again at the end of the narrative. The final scene shows King Triton and his retinue accompanying Eric, Ariel and Melody back to land. When the King gives Melody the offer of either living on land, as a human, or in Atlantica, as a mermaid, Melody chooses a third course. She takes the King's trident from him and uses it to blast down the wall that separates Prince Eric's kingdom from the sea in order to allow the two realms and their populations to interact more freely. Melody's propensity for accessing the phallus, even after her initial appropriation causes calamitous events in the main part of the narrative, marks her out as a more empowered individual than Ariel in the first film and moderates the King's patriarchal power in that regard. Unlike Ariel (and the disempowerment caused by her reverse transformational process), Melody's acquisition of mer-form empowers her and gives her substantial agency in the narrative and in the undersea realm.

The various sequels and prequels discussed above can be regarded as reinterpretations of the core situation and scenario of Disney's 1989 adaptation of Andersen's story. By fixing the timeframe before and after the story of Ariel's vexed and traumatic transformation, the subsequent Disney versions provide ample opportunities to reinterpret the Electra complex central to the original in ways that either 'wind back' to Ariel at earlier stages in her youth, or else represent her as successfully realigned to another male, as in the film's sequel, where she has her own daughter. *Return to the Sea* is also notable in that Melody provides one of the most assertive incarnations of youthful (human and mer-) womanhood in any of the Disney productions discussed above, through her determination and capacity for autonomous decision-making and action. Actively making a reverse transition to that undertaken by Ariel and seeking a tail (and the phallic power and agency it represents), she embodies the power and autonomy of 'becoming mermaid' that is also manifest in the audiovisual material discussed in Chapter 6.

VII. Pornographic Interpretations

The success of *The Little Mermaid* (and of a subsequent musical theatre adaptation[66]) spawned a plethora of related texts. In addition to the Disney productions referred to above, there were a number of unauthorised appropriations of Ariel's, Eric's and Ursula's characters in several short, sexually-explicit (and often untitled) animation sequences that have been circulated online (primarily via YouTube) *The Little Mermaid* was not the first Disney production to receive such treatment. In 1973 British porn film producer David Grant and animator Marcus Parker-Rhodes produced a re-imagination of scenes from *Snow White and the Seven Dwarfs* (David Hand, 1937) entitled *Snow White and the Seven*

---

66   See Coyle and Fitzgerald (2010) for discussion.

Perverts. The film shows a variety of the film's characters engaging in graphic sexual activities with each other. These can be considered 'porn parodies' in that they present hyper-sexualised interpretations of an identifiable referent text. The form, which has notable antecedents,[67] variously teases out and/or amplifies potential sexual elements of referent texts.[68] As Booth (2014) outlines, while porn parodies principally provide distorted imitations of prior texts intended to amuse and arouse audiences, aspects of their representation can stimulate recognition of deeper cultural tropes and patterns within the source texts in manners that may be illuminating. Framing any specific critique or reinterpretation of individual texts that a porn parody may offer, the overall genre suggests a repression of sexual content in cinema and of sexuality in society more generally that it can loosen (creating a classic 'return of the repressed' in a carnivalesque context in which norms of sexual propriety and prudence are inverted). With regard to the specific representations discussed in this volume, the form of the transformative mermaid can be seen to facilitate such a process in itself, and her insertion into porn parody contexts can be seen to let her 'off the hook' of her anatomical restriction and allow her to explore human/genital sexuality.

The Little Mermaid porn parodies most notably respond to the 'hot' aspect of Ariel's character noted by several contemporary film reviewers and to the unresolved sexual tensions suggested in the Disney original. Perhaps intent to avoid any paedophilic connotations of involving Ariel's somewhat prepubescent form in X-rated activity, most of the porn parodies feature a slightly older, physically more developed version of her. One of the more widely circulated of the animated videos presents an alternative version of what may have occurred after Ariel dragged the unconscious Eric ashore after his shipwreck. Rather than departing the scene she looks lustfully at the prince and then takes his penis from his trousers and expresses vocal delight as she masturbates him to orgasm, with a look of surprise and delight as he ejaculates on her face. Another take on Ariel's beachside visit in mermaid form occurs in a scene in which Ariel returns to shore, removes her bikini top and peels off her tail before manually arousing herself in anticipation of Eric's arrival. Evidently pleased to encounter her in naked and aroused form, Eric quickly undresses and is fellated by Ariel before he penetrates her in various positions, eliciting standard porn-style vocal exhortations from her (despite her supposed muteness), before he withdraws and, again, ejaculates over her face.[69] Similarly, a number of animations represent explicit sexual activity between Eric and Ariel subsequent to her metamorphosis into fully-human form.[70]

The live-action porn film *The Little Spermaid* (Jordan Septo, 2014) represents its titular

---

67   The porn parody film is a contemporary genre that has notable precursors, including Henry Fielding's novel *Shamela* (1741), a novel that parodied Samuel Richardson's novel *Pamela* (1740) by representing its protagonist as sexually complicit (unlike the protagonist of the original).

68   Both porn parodies and sexually explicit mainstream films have been regarded as a symptom/by-product of a more general pornographication of cinema, whereby graphic sexuality has been implanted in genres that previously either eschewed it or treated it more discretely (see Nikunen, Paasonen and Saarenmaa [eds] 2008 for discussion).

69   The animation is collated, together with other sexually explicit animations, in a Cartoon.valley.com compendium online at: http://www.xxx-18.xxx/xxx-18-videos/84288.html – accessed 8th December 2013.

70   Online at: http://www.xvideos.com/video539285/little_mermaid – accessed December 9th 2013.

character in sexual activity in both mer- and human form and transfers elements of *The Little Mermaid* to modern day America, with characters loosely based on those from Disney's film – Riley Reid stars as Princess Areola and Ryan Driller as Eric Prince. As with many porn features, the film is based around a number of extended sex scenes linked by a skeletal narrative. The film commences with Eric about to get married but haunted by vague memories of a mermaid whom he believes once rescued him from drowning at the beach. He is then shown walking along a cliff path, falling off into the sea and being rescued again by a mermaid (dressed in an approximation of Ariel's garb in the Disney film). She awakens him, introduces herself and initiates fellatio (while managing to balance upright on her tail). A voice-over then introduces the Ursula character (named Curse-Ola) as Areola's rival for Eric's affections. Curse-Ola then turns up in human form and has extended sex with Eric's housemate before vanishing from the narrative. Following a third sex scene between two extraneous characters, the mermaid-theme recommences when Eric explains to his fiancé that he can't marry her because of his attraction to Areola. Their interaction is interrupted by the arrival of an older man in a crown and blue cloak who introduces himself as King Two Ton. Asking Eric whether he truly loves his daughter, Areola, the King then instructs him to go off in search of her while he attends to his (now former) fiancé's needs by having sex with her.[71] The final scene shows Eric meeting Areola by a swimming pool at night and professing his love for her. Taking her from the pool into his house she spontaneously transitions to human form, setting herself up for a final sex scene between the characters that concludes the narrative. As this summary suggests, there is little that is particularly insightful about the film's contemporary re-imagination of its Disney referent.

Taking another tack, the incestuous (taboo) aspect of the Electra complex is vividly transgressed in another short animation (credited to Cartoon Gonzo, 2011), which features six scenes in which Ariel and King Triton interact with each other in fully-human form. Significantly, in terms of her propensity to flout patriarchal authority, the first scene features Ariel being spanked by the Sea King (whilst self-stimulating). The following four show her being penetrated anally and vaginally while the final one draws attention to her transgression in seeking and gaining human lower-body form by showing the King achieving a climax between her feet. Aside from this, one of the more novel porn parody animations produced to date, entitled *Wild Little Mermaid* (2012), eschews the heterosexual angle altogether by providing a sequence in which Ursula and Ariel (whose fishtail is represented as commencing just below her pubic area) perform oral sex on each other underwater (accompanied by an orchestral arrangement of the original film's main theme). Ursula then moves behind her, wraps her in her tentacles and penetrates her with one (in the style of Japanese *shokushu goukan* pornography[72]). This scene provides a graphic realisation of the implicitly phallic nature of Ursula and her array of tentacles noted in the previous section and foreshadows further reconfigurations of Ursula's form and role, such as those discussed in Section VIII.

71 He explains to her that his name was given to him by his mermaids in reference to the ample size of his "royal jewels" (i.e. his genitals).

72 *Shokushu goukan* is a Japanese erotic convention involving the vaginal and/or oral penetration of women by the tentacles of an octopus or squid.

The productions referred to above might be best understood as attempts to both realise aspects of the sexual dynamics variously evident and latent in the original film and also to subsume the complicated aspects of mermaids' sexuality arising from their tails, absent genitalia and powerful melodic vocality within representations that derive from a heterosexual pornographic imagination. The majority of *The Little Mermaid's* porn parodies are premised on the clichéd repertoire of porn dramas,[73] effectively rendering Ariel as a sexual stereotype. In this way, and perhaps even more profoundly, the little mermaid is significantly more of a loser in these porn texts than she is in Andersen's original short story, where her ending, although poignant, is imbued with dignity as she becomes liberated from human form and transformed into a daughter of the air.

VIII. Ariel and Ursula Redux

In addition to their appearances in the animated prequels, sequels and unauthorised pornographic reinterpretations discussed above, Ariel and Ursula also feature as characters in the third and fourth seasons of the US TV series *Once Upon A Time* (2011–) (henceforth referred to as *OUAT*). The series has a complicated narrative structure involving characters drawn from fairy tales who interact in a New England town called Storybrooke and in parallel fantasy locations. Ariel arrives in the narrative in adult form, played by Joanna Swisher,[74] in Series 3 Episode 6 (Ciaran Donnelly, 2013). After rescuing Snow White (Ginnifer Goodwin) from the sea she explains that she is visiting land to pursue the affections of Prince Eric, who she rescued from a shipwreck a year before without his being aware of her identity. These aspects represent a fairly straightforward adaptation of Disney's Ariel character to a live-action television context but a far greater degree of creative license was taken with the representation of Ursula, who appears in the same episode.

Ariel reveals to Snow White that she can attend the ball in human form since Ursula, an entity who has not been seen for a thousand years, created magic that allows mermaids to assume human form for 12 hours once a year. Ariel then goes on to attend the ball, wins Prince Eric's affections and secures an invitation to accompany him on an extended voyage. Troubled by how to reveal her real form to him, she returns to the seashore and forlornly calls on Ursula to advise her. Much to her surprise the mythological figure arises from the water in front of her. Like the sea witch in the original Disney film, Ursula is tentacled but, unlike the 1989 version, the upper half of her body is slender and youthful (more akin to Celia, in Cuti and Mas's 1972 visual narrative). Ursula responds to Ariel's plight by giving her a magical bracelet that allows her to switch to human form at any time. Shortly after, Ariel realises that what she had perceived to be Ursula was in fact Regina, the Evil Queen (Lana Parrilla), trying to use her to trap Snow White. Having presented Regina as impersonating Ursula for her own ends the episode provides a further

---

73 It is notable in this regard that a short film entitled *The Little MerMILF* (2013) parodies the production of a (live-action) porn parody of *The Little Mermaid*. The film uses elements of the original's score, including a lyrical parody of 'Under the Sea' that satirises working in the porn industry – online at: https://mail.google.com/mail/u/0/?hl=en&shva=1#sent/142f7b2e456ada44?projector=1 – accessed December 15th 2013.

74 See *The Tale of Ariel*, a short 'making of' documentary included in the Series 3 DVD set.

twist when the real (i.e. mythological) Ursula appears in her mirror as a gleaming, bronze-coloured apparition that warns Regina never to impersonate her again.

As the above description suggests, depictions of Ursula in *OUAT* are complex. The inclusion of Ursula as a powerful, ancient sea goddess is a novel conceit that is not suggested in the Disney film. The entity that appears to the Evil Queen in her mirror is very different to the grotesque figure of Disney's film and both are markedly different to the form that Regina assumes to impersonate the entity. A third Ursula also appears in Series IV (2014–2015), debuting in an episode entitled 'Poor Unfortunate Souls' (Steve Pearlman, 2015). She is different again, being a mermaid who chose to take on tentacled form in her youth (providing an implicit back-story to Ursula's appearance in the original Disney film). A further innovation is provided by the casting of two African-American actresses in the role, Merrin Dungey, playing Ursula as an adult, and Tiffany Boone, as a teenager. This casting is notable in a series that is otherwise largely populated by Caucasian actors portraying a range of fairytale characters derived from European traditions. The casting appears to derive from Ursula's black bodice/tentacle composite in the original Disney film, an aspect that appears to have been based on the traditional European association of blackness with evil, rather than any attempt to represent Ursula as African-American in appearance. Unlike the plump and late middle-aged rendition of Ursula in the original film, Dungey and Boone play younger, slimmer and more conventionally attractive versions of the character. They are also notably less malicious.

'Poor Unfortunate Souls' initially introduces Ursula as a sonic presence. A flashback sequence shows Captain Hook's pirate ship being drawn towards an unseen mermaid (singing the melody from 'Part of Your World', Ariel's signature song from *The Little Mermaid*). The ship narrowly escapes being wrecked on a rocky islet when the song ceases abruptly. The episode then reveals that the singer is the youthful Ursula, the daughter of Poseidon, God of the Sea (who is represented as fully-human and is also of African-American appearance). Poseidon berates his daughter for sparing the ship and the dialogue reveals that his hatred of humans is motivated by his wife's death at the hands of a pirate. Ursula's refusal to follow his orders and lure the ship onto the rocks derives from the value she places on her accomplished singing voice as representing the last trace of her beloved mother's presence. After her disagreement with her father, she steals a magical bracelet from his treasure trove that allows her to transform into human form and leaves for the terrestrial realm. She next appears in a tavern, where she sings for the patrons.[75] Captain Hook recognises her voice as that of the mermaid he had encountered earlier but befriends her rather than revealing her true identity. At this point Poseidon re-enters the narrative and persuades Hook to use a magic shell to trap Ursula's voice in order to convince her of the perfidy of humans. Traumatised by her father's and Hook's treatment of her, she dives into the sea and swims away. A subsequent scene shows her back on the rocky islet that she previously sang on. Denouncing her father for his role in depriving her of her singing voice, she snatches his trident and uses it to transform her fishtail into tentacles, in conscious imitation of the mythical sea goddess Ursula. Compensating for the loss of her

---

75 Singing a version of 'Fathoms Below' (the song sung by the crew of Prince Eric's ship in the opening scene of *The Little Mermaid*).

singing voice with the multiple phallic power of her lower body she then warns her father to beware her new powers and departs.

Ursula subsequently appears in the Storeybrook strand of the narrative as one of the three evil female characters from Disney history that Rumpelstiltskin entices to accompany him in order to seek the happy endings that their original fictional roles denied them.[76] In this context Ursula is represented as a human woman who has the ability to extrude lengthy tentacles at will. After various adventures with the trio she exits the narrative when Captain Hook returns her singing voice to her in return for her co-operation in revealing Rumpelstiltskin's plans. Unlike Ariel, Ursula shows no interest in acquiring a human mate but her happy ending is still constrained by patriarchy as it involves her being reconciled with her father and returning to the sea with him. In this regard, despite her agency and transgressions on land, she is neatly re-affiliated with her father in the developmental phase in which she was first (unhappily) represented.

Following on from *OUAT's* precedential representation of a powerful African-American mermaid/Ursula figure, an independent video entitled *Feeling My Fish* (Mitchell Hardage, 2015) opened up further readings and reinterpretations of the characters' forms. The production was a music video-style[77] visualisation of an original song sung by TS Madison Hinton that incorporated substantial elements of the lyrics and vocal melody of 'Part of your world' (Ariel's signature song from *The Little Mermaid*). Hinton, usually referred to as TS Madison, is an African-American, transgender performer and producer[78] who is known for appearing in online videos asserting transgender rights.[79] *Feeling My Fish* commences with the singer in role as Ariel and then combines this with her doubling as Ursula (see Figure 3). Opening with images of the surface of the sea and accompanying wave noises, a simple synthesised rhythm part commences the song, over which TS Madison whispers, "Ursula has very great powers", as those words appear on screen. The image then introduces TS Madison's glamorously made-up face, wearing a red Ariel-style wig as she states "A sea witch? I couldn't possibly ..." before starting the first sung line "Look at this stuff", with the image showing her ample bosom (clad in shell-like decorations) and a long, pearl-coloured glittery tail. Emphasising lines like "wouldn't you think I'm the girl ... who has everything" by stroking her breasts, and reiterating "everything, everything that a girl could want, everything, just everything" in spoken asides, the video contrasts the singer's ample curvaceousness and sexual confidence with the fragile uncertainty of Ariel's performance of the song in the original film. Around the midpoint of the video a caption states "Make all your dreams come true" followed by a vocal aside "where am I gonna go?" These prefigure the singer also assuming the role of Ursula, wearing a swept-up white wig as she cackles and invites Ariel into her lair. While Ariel initially looks shocked by the sea witch's appearance and invitation to trade her voice in return for the

---

76   In addition to Ursula, the trio comprises Cruella de Ville, from Disney's *101 Dalmatians* originally released as an animated film (Clyde Geronimi, Hamilton Luske and Wolfgang Reitherman, 1961) and re-made as a live-action film (Stephen Herek, 1996) and Maleficent from the eponymous film (Robert Stromberg, 2014).

77   I specify 'music video-style' since the video does not appear to be a promotional vehicle for a music release.

78   TS Madison established Raw Dawg Entertainment in 2009 to produce porn videos featuring African-American trans women.

79   See her online discussion of her identification and gender position at: https://www.youtube.com/watch?v=K-eO8nD9bpM – accessed December 12th 2015.

Figure 3 – TS Hinton as Ariel losing her voice in *Feeling My Fish* (Mitchell Hardage, 2015).

transformation, she eventually agrees. She then sings her signature melody in order to allow Ursula to capture her voice – represented by rays of green light leaving her throat (Figure 3) and travelling into a sea shell around Ursula's neck. Empowered by her possession of Ariel's singing voice, Ursula declares, "I am now the new supreme", as Ariel sadly declares, "I've given up my fish". The video then cleverly superimposes Ursula's image over frames from the original film that show Ariel's sisters recoiling in horror as chorus vocals state "all hail the new goddess" and "bow down". Ariel responds to the latter instructions with the screen showing a multiplied image of her bending from the waist in submission as Ursula declares that "Now I have the power of all the oceans" (Figure 4). The video ends with the words "the new supreme" spoken on the soundtrack and superimposed over images of ocean waves.

The song and its visual representation offer a number of original inflections and revisions to images, associations and characters from the original Disney film. TS Madison's performance of Ariel as a mature and voluptuous African-American mermaid gives its version of Ariel's predicament in the video (and presented in the lyrics of the original 'Part of your World') a very different inflection. Rather than adolescent innocence, TS Madison's enactment of the role exudes a confident and sassy sexuality. There is also a stream of knowing double entendres to the song lyrics made most apparent in the references to her being a girl who has "everything". As a male-to-female transsexual who has retained her penis, she has both an actual phallus (underneath her tail) and a tail that (in her case somewhat redundantly) compensates for its apparent absence. TS Madison's enactment of Ursula is also notable for involving a trans African-American enacting a role substantially based on that of a Caucasian male drag performer. There is also a complex aspect to the song's repeated reference to the singer "feeling my fish". While the "fish" in question seems most obviously to refer to Ariel's tail, the term also has another subcultural meaning that is pertinent to its use in the video. In recent years some transsexuals and gay men

Figure 4 – TS Hinton as Ursula and multiplied Ariels in *Feeling My Fish* (Mitchell Hardage, 2015).

have used the term 'fish' to refer to cisgender (i.e. biologically 'real') women and, similarly, the term 'serving fish' has come to refer to "an ultra-feminine" version of drag performance (Clay 2013: online[80]). While debates about the derivation of the term and/or its pejorative aspects remain unresolved,[81] Ariel's and Ursula's references to variously feeling, losing or gaining "fish" involve complex double entendres. When Ariel allows Ursula to take her voice she sadly states, "I've given up my fish". This could be interpreted as an association of the mermaid's vocality and tail (and to the loss of both) but this is complicated since Ariel retains her tail for the remainder of the video. The "fish" that she has lost thereby appears to be phallic vocality. In her vocally disempowered state she is shown as passively subservient to Ursula. Ursula in the meantime declares that she is now "feeling her fish", indicating that the acquisition of vocality has given her an essential aspect of femininity (despite her retaining her tentacled form). The video's final scenes also offer a very different interpretation of the closing scenes of the original Disney film by virtue of showing Ursula victorious, lording over Ariel as she abases herself and closing on the slogan "worship her" without the necessity (or even suggestion) of male power coming to Ariel's rescue. The music video's scenarios are strikingly complex with regard to sexual identity. TS Madison's enactments of Ariel's and Ursula's roles from the Disney film shift their symbolic associations and further refract, parody and problematise the complex gender identities that they represent.

---

80 The term is also explained by transsexual performer Shangela in the lyrics and visual track of her music video 'Uptown Fish' (Brad Hammer, 2015), which includes the spoken introduction: "When a diva is so fabulous that she must have been sent by the mermaid goddesses of the ocean we call that... 'Fish'" – online at: https://www.youtube.com/watch?v=nAocUKwRxf4 - accessed December 25th 2015.

81 See Clay (2013) and the various responses to her Blog post on the use of the term 'fish' by transsexuals.

Conclusion

In the original and various adaptations of Andersen's story, mermaids may visit land temporarily but can only stay if they become humanised in form. The price of the little mermaid's access to her dreams (i.e. of becoming the prince's wife and living on shore) is the renunciation of her essence, of her very *mer-ness*. In the Andersen-Disney texts, mermaids' existence in the patriarchal/terrestrial order is tenuous. However alluring, the price of their entry into the arena of human sexuality is either death (as in Andersen's original 'Den lille Havfrue') or domestication via monogamy (as in the Disney film adaptation). In the contexts of Andersen's original story and the initial Disney film, the little mermaid is marked by her lack; as a female she lacks the phallus and aspires to its power, but as a mermaid she lacks a vagina and desires human anatomy in order to appeal to and interact with men. Once converted to human form she also lacks her voice and aspires to having this (and the phallic power of her accomplished vocality) returned to her. And then there is her tail. Casting this aside, she loses the power that resides in it. Ursula cuts across this tangle. In the first Disney film she is 'other' to both mermaids and humans. Her transformation to human form comes without pain or trauma and it is rather her unmasking that provokes her monstrous wrath. Her phallic power, as represented by her multiple tentacles, *almost* overwhelms the patriarchal order – until she is run through, deflated and dispatched to oblivion. Ursula in *OUAT* interconnects with these positions in a complex manner. She appears in multiple forms, as a deity, as an impersonation of that deity and as a mermaid who has transformed herself into an approximation of that deity in order to enact vengeance upon the patriarchal order. In one sense, Ursula is presented as an alternate version of Ariel. Whereas Ariel seeks (the adult) Ursula's assistance in changing her fishtail into human legs, the youthful Ursula represented in *OUAT* takes the initiative of using her father's trident to transform her tail into tentacles. Unlike Ariel she acquires the power to combine human and octopus form on land. TS Madison's *Feeling the Fish* video offers an alternative scenario whereby its Ursula inhabits a trans-world in which the fixed gender and racial positions of Disney's original are dissolved and refigured. But aside from TS Madison's subversions of gender roles, in all of Disney's *The Little Mermaid* texts, the safest and most free realms of experience for female characters are those pre-pubescent ones represented in the original film's prequels. In these, the young mermaids escape definition in terms of lack and are not preoccupied with transforming their anatomies in order to achieve coupling with human males.

Author's note: I have not been able to secure permissions to reproduce images from *The Little Mermaid* and related Disney productions in this chapter. These can, however, be easily accessed via online search engines.

Chapter Two

Flauntation and Fascination: The Alluring Mermaid and her Charms

While Andersen's short story 'Den lille Havfrue' and Disney's film adaptation are the best known examples of 19th and 20th Century mermaid themed fiction they are, perversely, somewhat aberrant within the wider pattern of modern mermaid media-lore. While the central theme of their story concerns a mermaid striving to relinquish her fish-tail in order to become fully human (on a permanent basis), the majority of mermaids represented in 20th and 21st Century screen media are either stable (and apparently happy with their mer-physique) or else can transition easily between mer- and human form. This chapter focusses on the nature and appeal of what might be termed 'fixed-form' mermaids (with Chapter 4 addressing mermaids with transformative abilities). Rather than seeking to renounce and replace their tails, the mermaids discussed in the opening sections of this chapter are more confident in their anatomies and, indeed, often flaunt these in order to attract the attention of human males. While well established in folkloric and cultural traditions, male fascination with mermaids' unique anatomies functions outside the usual realm of male heterosexual proclivity. In particular, there is a notable slide between the male's attraction to the familiar upper, humanly bodies of mermaids and their inhuman tails; one in which the mermaid's overall symbolic/erotic figure is greater than the sum of her disparate parts.

In this manner the fixed-form mermaids discussed in Sections I and II embody *virguility*, a constant – and, paradoxically stable – "flux of becoming" (Guinness 2013: 25) which coalesces the complexities of women within the symbolic order into a single, iconic anima.

I. The Stage and the Early Screen

Two significant representations of mermaids appeared in Western Europe in 1904. The first took the form of her cinematic debut, in Georges Méliès's three minute 'trick film' *La Sirène* (1904). Its skeletal narrative involves a conjuror and a fish tank that magically reveals a reclining mermaid, playing with her tresses and blowing kisses to the audience. The mermaid then transforms into a diaphanously clad human maiden (with the conjuror subsequently transforming into Neptune). The second occurred on the London stage in the form of J.M. Barrie's 1904 play 'Peter Pan' or 'The Boy Who Wouldn't Grow Up'. The drama, its subsequent novelisation (as 'Peter and Wendy' [1911]) and a series of stage and screen adaptations have provided an enduring filament to 20th and 21st Century media-lore.[82] Unlike Andersen's diminutive mermaid, who sought to replace her tail in her quest for human love, the mermaids who occur as incidental characters in Barrie's narrative are far more comfortable with their piscine lower halves and are, indeed, happy to display them. The mermaids feature in Act III of the play, set around a lagoon that Peter and his companions, the 'Lost Boys', also frequent. Barrie's introduction to the act sets the following scene:

> There are many mermaids here, going plop-plop, and one might attempt to count the tails did they not flash and disappear so quickly. At times a lovely girl leaps in the air seeking to get rid of her excess of scales, which fall in a silver shower as she shakes them off. From the coral grottoes beneath the lagoon, where are the mermaids' bedchambers, comes fitful music.
>
> One of the most bewitching of these blue-eyed creatures is lying lazily on Marooners' Rock, combing her long tresses and noting effects in a transparent shell. Peter and his band are in the water unseen behind the rock, whither they have tracked her as if she were a trout, and at a signal ten pairs of arms come whack upon the mermaid to enclose her. Alas, this is only what was meant to happen, for she hears the signal (which is the crow of a cock) and slips through their arms into the water. It has been such a near thing that there are scales on some of their hands. They climb on to the rock crestfallen. (1904: online version)

This description emphasises the mermaids' allure. They attract attention by leaping into the air, shedding excess scales which fall "in a silver shower" around them and the most "bewitching" of them is a "lovely" individual who reclines languorously, combing her hair

---

82   Disney produced an animated feature version in 1953, directed by Clyde Geronimi, Wilfred Jackson and Hamilton Luske. The film included sensuous renditions of the mermaids in a lagoon sequence that features (apparently adolescent) mermaids with elaborate tresses in a variety of colours and with starfishes or shells covering their breasts. They are shown performing standard mermaid activities such as playing lyres, considering their reflections in hand-held mirrors, arranging their hair and – in something of an innovation – showering under a cascade. A number of further screen adaptations followed, including P.J. Hogan's 2003 live-action film, which featured a very different rendition of the mermaids, as malicious, blue-skinned and facially unappealing creatures. Two related live-action films also featured representations of mermaids, Stephen Spielberg's 1991 *Hook* (a live-action sequel to *Peter Pan*, featuring the adventures of an adult Peter, played by Robin Williams), which is discussed in Chapter Four, and *Pan* (Joe Wright, 2015), a prequel to Barrie's original play, which features three identical mermaids with luminous tails (played by Cara Delevingne) who rescue a youthful Peter from the clutches of a giant crocodile.

while observing herself in a mirror. As the Introduction to the Act goes on to describe, Peter is quite taken with the mermaids' charms and frequently plays and swims with them. The mermaids are, in turn, quite fond of him. Indeed this aspect is underlined by their reaction to Peter bringing his new human companion, Wendy, into their lair. Their jealousy prompts one to try and drag her into the water and drown her. While relatively incidental to the main narrative of the play, the mermaids' representation on stage in the original 1904–1905 theatrical run in London was given an added dimension in a modified version of the drama staged in the city in 1905–1906. This featured an additional musical number in which the mermaids celebrated their tails in a humorous lyrical interplay with Peter Pan and the Lost Boys (Hanson 2010: 76).[83] A single mermaid commences the exchange, flicking her tail to emphasise her final points:

> When waters of the never-land are naked to the moon
> Then wakes the fair mermaid-en from her sleep in the Lagoon
> And I raise my coral mirror my drooping locks to tend
> But the part of me I'm proudest of is at the other end
> The mermaid's tail
> The mermaid's tail
> It fans us when we're hot
> We whisk it thus!
> If we are pleas'd
> And so! If we are not

A chorus of mermaids then chimes in, emphasising:

> And when we take to flirting
> It fascinates the male.
> No lady would dress in skirts
> If she could show a tail

The mermaids' flauntation[84] of their attributes in this manner is striking. The tail is openly acknowledged as both a captivating asset and one that gives them a competitive edge over human females.

Following a series of popular productions in the United States (US), 'Peter Pan' was first adapted for the screen in 1924 (as *J.M Barrie's Peter Pan*) in a version directed by Herbert Brenon. While the film was widely applauded for its use of special effects to animate the fairy figure of Tinker Bell, the Mermaid Lagoon scene was less vividly rendered. The film nevertheless provided the spectacle of a substantial group of mermaids reclining on rocks and swimming out to sea en masse (Figure 5). The presence of mermaids in Brenon's film was far from unusual in the final stages of the 'Silent Film' era,[85] but analysis and discussion of a number of mermaid-themed films from this period is problematic since the majority are now lost (i.e. there are no longer complete copies available to view).[86]

---

83 Lyrics by Barrie and music by John Crook.

84 A modern slang term referring to the shameless flaunting of assets. See: http://www.urbandictionary.com/define.php?term=flauntation – accessed November 12th 2015.

85 A period that is more accurately described as the pre-synchronised sound film era given the use of live musical accompaniment to film screenings.

86 Estimates vary but the German national Kinemathek has suggested that between 80–90% of all early films are now unavailable (2008: online).

Figure 5 – Promotional still from *J.M. Barrie's Peter Pan* (1924).

While the first mermaid-themed film appears to have been produced in the US in 1910,[87] the subject experienced a significant vogue from the mid–late 1910s to the early 1920s. Its popularity can be seen to have arisen from the cross-association of the folk-loric/mythological theme with the assertive manifestation of female physicality pioneered by specialist swimmer turned film actress Annette Kellerman. After commencing her career in Australia, Kellerman relocated to the US in the early 1900s and performed in water ballets enacted in large glass tanks in New York, such as 'The Big Show' of 1916 at the Hippodrome, which included a sequence in which two hundred mermaids clustered around an artificial waterfall (Slide 2012: 287). Kellerman also caused public scandals by appearing in tight, one-piece bathing suits on stage and on public beaches[88] and by appearing nude in Herbert Brenon's film *A Daughter of the Gods* (1916). Drawing on detailed research into Kellerman's career development, Woollacott contends that the "central motif of Kellerman's performances was a blend of the mermaid, the water nymph and the South Sea Islander, a modernist pastiche of the primitive and the exotic" (2011: online). The latter aspect is significant, in that Kellerman used folkloric motifs to assert a distinctly modern female persona and identity. She utilised aspects of the mermaid both allusively, with regard to her aquatic prowess, and literally in a number of films in which she donned a fabric fish tail to play mermaid roles.

In 1911 Kellerman appeared in two short underwater themes films, *Siren of the Sea* (director unknown) and *The Mermaid* (director unknown) and followed this with *Neptune's Daughter* (Herbert Brenon, 1914), *A Daughter of the Gods* (Hubert Brenon, 1916) and *Queen of the Sea* (John Adolfi, 1918). Similarly themed lost films from the period include Henry Otto's *Undine* (1916), starring Ida Schnall. Otto's film was promoted by a poster showing its star amidst a group of mermaids reclining on a sandy beach, accompanied by the tagline "The most Beautifully formed Woman in the World and Thirty-five Diving Nymphs". The poster also immodestly claimed the film to be "Much more wonderful than 'Neptune's

---

87 In the form of the Thanhouser Company's lost comedy short *The Mermaid* (1910), which is documented as representing a young woman who impersonates a mermaid so as to attract custom to her family's hotel. This plot is similar to that of *Fish Tale*, short British film made over a century later. Set in a Welsh seaside town, the film (directed by Steve Lewis in 2015) involves a woman (Sarah Morris) in mermaid fancy dress being mistaken for an actual mermaid. A news item featuring shots of her taken by a pier shop proprietor are shown on television resulting in tourists flocking to the area and to his pier shop.

88 Leading on one occasion, in 1907, to her arrest on indecency charges in Massachusetts.

Daughter'". Two further lost films by
Captain Leslie T. Peacock (*Surf Maidens* [1913] and *Neptune's Bride* [1920])
also had similar themes. A promotional leaflet for the screening of the
latter at the Philharmonic auditorium
in Los Angeles announced that the
film featured 'Pluvia' "the most perfectly formed girl in the world" and
that the screening was "augmented by
a Gorgeous Prologue Dance of Mermaids and Wood Nymphs".[89]

While the majority of early mermaid-
themed films are lost, fragments of
these and/or production stills produced for promotional purposes (such
as those reproduced in Figures 5 and 6
above) indicate that mermaids' tails
comprised tight fabric sheets that followed the actresses' contours before
flaring out into tail-like extensions –
resulting in a distinct mermaid silhouette.[90] Surviving images suggest that
the figure-hugging garments provided

Figure 6 – Publicity still of Kellerman (left), young
mermaid and fairy in *Queen of the Sea* (1918).

a somewhat risqué representation of the female form that was a significant element of the
films' appeal. *Neptune's Daughter* and *Queen of the Sea* also featured Kellerman as a mermaid
able to transform into human form,[91] anticipating the types of transformative mermaids
discussed in Chapter 4. While none of Kellerman's US mermaid-themed feature films
remain extant, one subsequent production survives. *Venus of the South Seas* (James
Sullivan, 1924), shot in New Zealand after she left the US, following a decline in her
popularity. While the film lacks the spectacular sequences and sexual risquéness that
reviewers noted of its US-produced predecessors, it provides evidence of Kellerman's lithe
physicality and of her prowess as an aquatic performer, particularly in an underwater
fantasy sequence where she has fish-tailed form. But despite the cycle of mermaid-themed

89 See material reproduced online at: http://ladailymirror.com/2013/02/12/witzel-photo-found-on-ebay/ –
    accessed August 14th 2015.

90 It is notable, in the latter regard, that a style of figure-hugging, full-length gown that flares out below the knee
    into a fan shape is commonly been referred to as a 'mermaid dress'. The dress style was first popularised in
    the 1910s and became prominent again in the 1940s–1950s. The design has been subsequently reworked in
    various ways, including as a fancy dress garment that directly imitates aspects of the representation of mermaids
    in screen media. For a notable recent example of the latter, see media celebrity Kim Kardashian's
    Splash-influenced mermaid dress as worn at a Halloween party organized by Midori in New York in 2012
    (visually documented at: http://www.justjared.com/photo-gallery/2746528/kim-kardashian-kanye-west-
    mermaid-sailor-for-halloween-25/fullsize/ – accessed December 12th 2015).

91 See the surviving six-minute fragment available online at: https://www.youtube.com/watch?v=ds7v4jdFZ3s
    – accessed December 25th 2015.

productions that enjoyed a vogue in the 1910s and early 1920s, mermaids disappeared from live-action cinema by the mid-decade and remained absent until the late 1940s, when they appeared on screen in films adapted from literary and theatrical sources.

II. The 1940s and 1950s

Just as the vogue for mermaid-themed films in the mid-1910s was preceded by a rise in the popularity of live aquatic shows featuring skilled and charismatic female performers, the return of mermaids to the screen in the late 1940s was preceded by a revival of such shows. The revival gained prominence in the late 1930s, most prominently in the form of the Aquacade Theatre, a performance space centred around a large pool featuring various performers and water effects. This attraction premiered at the New York World's Fair in 1939, where it showcased the abilities of celebrity swimmers such as Gertrude Ederle and swimmer and actor Jonny Weissmuller (best known for playing the role of Tarzan in a series of films made between 1932–1948).[92] A similar performance space was then constructed on an artificial site named Treasure Island in San Francisco Harbour in 1940 as part of the Golden Gate International Exposition. Young and (then) unknown swimmer Esther Williams joined the ensemble for its San Francisco residency and her performing talents and photogeneity secured her a contract with MGM Studios. Williams went on to appear in a number of films that showcased her aquatic abilities (such as *Bathing Beauty* [George Sidney, 1945] and *Neptune's Daughter* [Edward Buzzell, 1949]) together with more conventional dramas.[93] The popularity of the Aquacade and of Williams's aquatic-themed films prompted Hollywood underwater stuntman Newt Perry to establish a permanent aquatic theatre site at Weeki Wachee Springs in Florida in 1947.[94] The attraction (which continues to operate) rapidly established a reputation for accomplished underwater choreography performed by young, lithe (and exclusively Caucasian) young women in tight bathing suits (see Kokai 2011). In its early phase the attraction referred to its female performers as 'aquabelles'[95] but the term 'mermaids' was increasingly adopted following the use of the Springs' large swimming tank for the underwater sequences in the feature film *Mr Peabody and the Mermaid* (Irving Pichel, 1948). Various stages of the film's production were publicised by Universal-International Films, and coverage included frequent references to and representations of the Springs.[96]

---

92   The last installment of the series was entitled *Tarzan and the Mermaids* (Robert Florey, 1948). Despite the film's title, it does not represent fish-tailed females but rather concerns an African coastal community whose women are closely involved with the sea.

93   In 1955 she starred in her best-known film role, in Mervyn LeRoy's fictionalised biography of Annette Kellerman, *Million Dollar Mermaid*, complete with ornate water ballet sequences designed by Busby Berkeley. While Williams did not appear as a conventional fish-tailed mermaid in live or in on-screen roles, her popularity (and the title of the Kellerman biopic she appeared in) fostered the association.

94   There are various publications on the attraction's history, Vickers and Dionne (2007) and Vickers and Georgiadis (2012) being the most extensive and most copiously illustrated.

95   Also rendered as 'Aqua Belles' in some publicity material.

96   The film's regional premiere at nearby Tampa also served to promote the Springs as a tourist attraction. Perry accompanied the film's initial screening at the Park Theater with a number of related events that also secured publicity for Weeki Wachee Springs. These included installing a performer with a fishtail in a glass tank outside the city's courthouse and organising a beauty contest for the title of Florida's 'Mermaid Queen'. The competition was contested by young women in conventional beauty pageant attire and was won by a regular Springs' performer, Mary Dwight Rose. At the awards ceremony Rose was dressed in one of the fishtails used in the film, placed on a throne and then crowned by the city's mayor.

Mr Peabody and the Mermaid was based on 'Peabody's Mermaid', a novel by Guy and Constance Jones that was originally published in *Cosmopolitan* magazine in two parts in October–November 1945. A book version followed in 1946, with illustrated chapter title pages and a frontispiece that combined a highly stylised representation of a mermaid with a quotation from English Metaphysical poet John Donne, "Teach me to hear mermaids singing". The quotation is taken from his poem 'Song: Go and catch a falling star' – in which he conjures a number of improbable phenomena (such as catching a falling star and hearing mermaids) in the course of lamenting the impossibility of finding a true and devoted woman. Together with the book's title, which stresses the ambiguously generative/possessive relationship of its protagonist to the mermaid in question, the quotation offers a significant insight into the book's theme, which revolves around its male protagonist's quest for a woman who can satisfy his various desires.[97]

The novel is set in the Saint Hilary's Islands, a fictional British colony in the Caribbean. Arthur Peabody (principally referred to by his surname throughout the volume) travels to the main island, Saint Hilda's, on the eve of his 50th birthday to recuperate from ill health and what is described as "spiritual exhaustion" (Jones and Jones 1946: 1). The book goes on to describe how this represents (what later came to be known as) a male mid-life crisis.[98] Arriving with his wife Polly, he initially becomes attracted to Cathy, a glamorous American singer and stage performer on vacation, and then to a young mermaid he encounters while sailing offshore. The novel represents Cathy and the mermaid through similar associations (both are beautiful, alluring and accomplished singers and swimmers) and signals this through individual chapter titles: Chapter 8, introducing Cathy, is entitled 'Land Sirens', while Chapter 10, concerning the mermaid, is entitled 'Sea Sirens'.[99] The novel centres on Peabody's attempts to keep the mermaid concealed in a large, ornate swimming pool at his rented house, causing various misunderstandings with his wife and local people. As his somewhat unflattering name suggests, Peabody is represented as an ineffectual male whose lack of romantic and sexual inclinations exasperate his confident and self-sufficient wife. While there is no direct allusion in the text, the novel shares a number of affinities with T.S Eliot's poem 'The Love Song of J. Alfred Prufrock' (1915), with particular regard to its middle-aged male protagonist's ennui and its references to mermaids as existing on a romantic plane outside of mundane everyday existence. As the poem famously states, "I have heard the mermaids singing, each to each/I do not think that they will sing to me". The novel provides a twist to this by delivering Peabody a mermaid who not only sings to him but also welcomes his attentions.

Cathy and the mermaid represent two distinct types of 'other women' that destabilise his marriage. Cathy is beautiful, worldly-wise, vocally articulate, flirtatious and something of a bon vivant. The mermaid, by contrast, is mute, other-worldly, unaffected and reclusive. The mermaid's distinct physical charms are vividly rendered in the book's description of

---

97 NB discussion of aspects of mermaid song in the novel and its film adaptation are included in separate analyses in Chapter 4.

98 A term attributed to Jacques (1965).

99 The novel includes a sequence where the mermaid finds Cathy's dress and wears it as she sits by the pool singing, confusing Peabody as to her identity.

the moment when he catches her while out fishing. This passage exemplifies the tendency whereby men find both halves of the mermaid's form attractive and alluring:

> *Peabody saw a beautiful sinuous tail, iridescent in the bright rays of the sun with blue and green fires ... The cobalt blue and emerald green scales of the tail appeared to meet a silver-white back, and the marine creature had floating golden tentacles.* (ibid: 64)

This description of the vivid blue/green hues of the tail, of its iridescence, its sinuosity and of the floating golden tentacles emphasise its beauty, rather than any repellent piscine otherness. Startled to find that the upper half of his catch is female, the passage continues to describe how

> *She lay on the bottom of the boat with her eyes shut and her long pale hair clinging to her white shoulders. She was smaller than most women, the size of a child, but there was nothing adolescent about her. Her little breasts were pointed and rosy tipped. On a minuscular scale she was maturely voluptuous.* (ibid: 65)

This is a colourful passage that represents her as both adult, in terms of her voluptuousness, and child-like, in terms of her diminutive size. Her "delicate white" face appears to Peabody as "cold and serene as the moon" and suggestive of "all innocence and all knowledge" (ibid). Yoking elements of the two descriptive passages referred to above, the paragraph ends with the characterisation that:

> *Indubitably she was a woman; rather, half a woman. At the slim waist, her white body curved into magnificent shimmering blue-and-green fish scales.* (ibid)

The detailed descriptions of the colour and sheen of the mermaid's tail are striking. Indeed, the vividness of the description is close to fetishistic, recalling the particular attraction that shiny and/or sequined materials can hold for wearers and/or voyeurs. The repetition of the term "white" in the above, along with reference to her pale hair, establishes her as a mermaid imagined in Northern European terms. Her diminutive physique also invites comparison to the "little" mermaid of Andersen's celebrated short story and, appropriately, Peabody names her 'Min', after an 11-year-old girl of German ancestry he knew as a child.[100] The mermaid is thus firmly rooted in the cultural imaginary of Peabody's European antecedence rather than representing any aspect of Caribbean folklore (such as the Aycayia[101] or the Haitian La Sirene).[102] Yet, for all this, she is also intractably 'other'. Peabody's appreciation of her appearance occurs on Cay Oro islet, a 'contact zone' (Pratt 1991) between marine and terrestrial realms. Like the enacted aquapelagic spaces referred to in this book's introduction, Spyer describes such contact zones as "fissured, performative spaces" (1998: 2). She also identifies that fetishism occurs in these spaces as one expression of "forms of difference" that it "both marks and negotiates in the process of producing or alluding to novel, creative hybridities" (ibid).[103] It is also

---

100 Who he recalls as having eyes "sea-blue like the Caribbean; skin white as foam on a wave; and straight hair hanging down her back as palely yellow as the morning sun" (ibid: 31).

101 Whose name evokes the cay on which Peabody's mermaid resides.

102 Indeed, Peabody himself surmises this, asking himself whether "this specimen" of mermaid was "peculiar to the Caribbean Sea" before responding that he "thought not ... he had the feeling that she had wandered a long way from her native habitat" (ibid: 68–69).

pertinent that Spyer's observations make particular reference to situations that arise from European colonialism (such as that enacted in the fictional Saint Hilary's Islands) and allude to fetishism's "capacity to fix and unsettle borders and essentialisms that hold these in place" (ibid).

While the mermaid's upper body appeals to Peabody in a conventional manner, the mermaid's defining aspect is her otherness. She is neither implicated within nor bound by specific codes of human social behaviour. This is made apparent in the book in a scene not included in the film. Concerned and somewhat embarrassed by the nakedness of her upper form, Peabody purchases the upper portion of a two-piece bathing suit for her. But the mermaid rejects the garment and his attempts to wrestle her into it and signals her displeasure at his actions by biting his thumb and drawing blood. It is possible to interpret this as the mermaid's resistance to having her human physique interpreted as sexual and concealed on that account. In this perspective, her attack on Peabody's thumb can be analogised as a rejection of the phallus, of phallic sexuality and of his attempt to utilise male power to restrict female choices as to their presentation in public. But despite her violent response to his actions, the incident proves little more than a 'lovers' tiff', with the mermaid remaining both highly enamoured of him and anxious as to whether his commitment to her is sincere. This is crystallised in a scene when he approaches her near a swimming pool at night, where she "seemed as nebulous and translucent as the cloud over the moon" (ibid: 129). Responding warmly to his reassurance that he won't abandon her, she transports him to a primal place of serenity:

> She put her arms about him, drew him to her and kissed him. As her lips touched his, Peabody knew that he had lived fifty years for that kiss. (ibid: 129)

With regard to Peabody, 'his' mermaid crosses the dualisms of childhood and adulthood and appears as both pre-pubescent/pre-sexual *and* maternal. She is impossibly ideal and wholeheartedly devoted to him. She is the embodiment of an innocent (yet attractive) female child and an ideal mother who can calm, protect and envelop him. She makes no sexual demands of him and, instead, offers him a line of flight from the constriction of his roles as husband, businessman/provider and father. The mermaid's crystallisation outside of this nexus proves intoxicating to him and his distracted demeanour convinces his wife Polly that he is having a (far more conventional) affair with Cathy, the actress. Fearing that his concealment of the mermaid in his house pool has been discovered, Peabody takes her back to her isolated cay and tries vainly to live with her before he is discovered by British police and taken off by them. While he initially seeks to take his mermaid with him, concealed in a beach robe, he changes his mind and dives off the boat with her, allowing her to escape. Realising that his adventure is at an end he leaves the island and returns to the US.

The mermaid is so closely associated with Peabody that she suggests herself as a figure of his imagination, reflective of a childhood memory of an ideal, pre-sexual girl that has been refigured as a Jungian anima sent to test him at a mid-life crisis point. But while she primarily appears to and for him, she is also perceived by and interacts with others. The

---

103 It should be emphasised that Spyer's characterisations refer to broad types of fetishism, predominantly in colonial and post-colonial contexts, rather than to sexual fetishism in particular.

most dramatic interaction with another human occurs when Cathy dives into the villa pool to see what kind of fish Peabody has hidden there. The mermaid responds to Cathy's intrusion into her realm (and, implicitly, her relationship with Peabody) by biting Cathy on a part of her body that a mermaid doesn't possess (and a part that Peabody had enjoyed looking at when he first encountered Cathy on the beach). As the novel specifies, "Blood was streaming down one slim leg from a double row of neat punctures" (ibid: 111). As this scene suggests, the mermaid has agency in the narrative and is represented as an entity with desires and the capacity to act on them (although the reasons for her attraction to Peabody and the gratification she seeks from him remain obscure).

The book ends on a brief interaction between Cathy and Fitzgerald, a colonial press agent, in which they discuss whether Peabody's claims to have caught a mermaid during his visit to the island were evidence of his madness. Fitzgerald contends that, even if deluded, Peabody had attained something considerable in believing that he had encountered a mermaid. Fitzgerald then quotes Matthew Arnold's poem 'The Forsaken Merman' (which represents the scenario of the folk tale of 'Agnete and the Merman', discussed in Chapter 1) referring to a "heart sorrow-laden, a long, long sigh for the cold strange eyes of a little mermaiden, and the gleam of her golden hair" (ibid: 182–184) before concluding, in an echo of the John Donne poem that prefaced the novel, "at least ... it's something to have heard a mermaid singing" (ibid: 184).

The Jones's novel was adapted for the screen by screenwriter Nunnally Johnson and made into a feature film in 1948, directed by Irving Pichel. The film's re-titling as *Mr Peabody and the Mermaid* dispensed with the possessive/generative associations of the novel's title and rather suggested the two characters as more equally posed. The film retained key narrative elements of the novel but also included some significant modifications. Fifty-five year old actor William Powell played Peabody and petite (5-foot-tall) 19-year-old actress Ann Blyth played the voluptuous, child-sized mermaid. In one deviation from the novel, Blyth's hair appears as dark on screen rather than blonde. In another, the mermaid is named Lenore, after Edgar Allen Poe's eponymous 1834 poem (which celebrated a beautiful woman who died at a young age and is ever after remembered as being in her youth). While the novel described Peabody as appreciating the appearance of the mermaid's bare and "rosy tipped" breasts, the film (in accordance with prevalent standards of modesty in US cinema in the period) conceals these either through the use of particular camera angles, in the early scenes, and then later via her willingness to don the bikini top that Peabody brings for her. The latter aspect represents a significant deviation from the scene in the book where her rejection of the garment signals her resistance to being included within a particular symbolic order and its related mores. But this appears largely functional with regard to the filmic decorum of the period, particularly as Blyth's tresses are not of sufficient length to conceal her breasts.

As Figure 7 reveals, the (black and white) film did not attempt to approximate the subtle descriptions of blue/green iridescence offered in the novel and instead opted for a bright, pale sheen and scale patterned fabric that ends, via an abrupt virgule, above the actress's navel. Unlike the mermaids who appeared in earlier films, her midriff is bare and a patterned bikini top covers her breasts. Her tail also appears firmer and more functional than the more flimsy versions presented in early cinema and is worn in underwater

Figure 7 – Ann Blyth as Lenore in a publicity photo from *Mr Peabody and the Mermaid*

swimming sequences, where it appears to assist her through movement through the water. As discussed in Chapter 4, Lenore's singing abilities are vividly described in the novel and are also inscribed in the film score, providing her with key aspects of her allure.

In both the novel and film, Peabody's Caribbean sojourn and his interaction with a mermaid comprise brief interludes in his staid, mainland existence and no sense of either the mermaid's motivations to bond with him nor of her life subsequent to her departure are explored or even suggested. In contrast, a British mermaid film that was also released in 1948 specifically addressed these aspects in its scenario.

Miranda was directed by Ken Annakin and adapted for the screen by dramatist Peter Blackmore from his eponymous three-act light comedy, which was first staged at the Embassy Theatre in London in 1948. The entire play was set in the lounge of a London apartment belonging to Sir Paul Marten, a doctor identified as being around forty years old, and his wife, Clare, who is in her thirties. Paul arrives back from a fishing holiday in Cornwall with Miranda, a female patient with an unspecified condition who is unable to walk and who requires a nurse. As is revealed to the audience by dialogue in Act I, Miranda is a mermaid. Aside from Paul, the only other character who is in on the knowledge (until the end of the final Act) is the nurse he hires to look after her. Over the course of the three Acts, Paul, his servant, Charles, and Nigel, a close friend, are shown to be infatuated with Miranda, each believing that she is favouring their attentions. Clare's suspicions about her guest are increasingly aroused until she forces Miranda to reveal her true identity. Shortly after Miranda has been 'outed' she manages to slip away from the flat in her wheelchair and exit the narrative.

While Miranda does not appear in mermaid form in the drama in front of any other cast members, with her lower body always covered by shawls or blankets, brief dialogue in Act I and sustained discussion during the narrative's denouement establish her credentials as a mermaid. Dialogue also reveals that she was found around Pendower Cove in Cornwall and that her surname is Trewella (two clear associations with Cornish folklore concerning the Zennor mermaid).[104] Miranda's tail is only made visible to the audience in a brief solo scene at the end of Act II that is described by the dramatist in a highly sensuous manner:

> (*Exit* NURSE CARY *flat door. Mysterious watery music "fades in" on the radio.* MIRANDA *manipulates her chair over to the French window, where she is bathed in soft grey light.*)
>
> (*Outside rain starts to fall*)
>
> (*The light turns faintly green.* MIRANDA *loosens her hair, so that it cascades down over her shoulders. The chair is now at the open window. Suddenly she removes her négligé, and reveals her silver fish's tail.*)
>
> (*There is a long shimmering flash of lightning, which sets her tail all sparkling, as she slowly raises it through the open window into the rain. She sings with the wireless music, and draws a comb through her hair.*) (ibid: 52)

This scene offers a highly condensed representation of the sensuality of the mermaid. She is shown activating the erotic signifier of her hair, loosening it so that it "cascades down over her shoulders" allowing her to comb it. The sudden revelation of her "sparkling" "silver" tail, as she dispenses with her négligé, is accentuated and illuminated by a "long shimmering flash of lightning" that might be regarded as attempting to convey an erotic shock. In an echo of male phallic erection, she slowly raises her tail and pushes it through the open window's aperture into the moist space beyond. The scene vividly delivers on an element of dialogue earlier in the play when Paul and Miranda are recalling their initial encounter:

---

104   As discussed in detail in Chapter 4, the tale concerns one Mathey Trewella, who was seduced away to live in the sea by a local mermaid. The story of his disappearance only became known when a ship moored in Pendower Cove was asked to move by a mermaid who was living in an underwater cave with Trewella and their children. The tale has it that the mermaid was initially attracted to the man by his accomplished singing voice.

MIRANDA (laughing) *I shall never forget your face when you first saw my tail.*

PAUL. You looked so cool and alluring sitting there in the seaweed. (ibid: 21)

Her mer-allure is also revisited in the final scene when Miranda refers to her tail in front of Clare:

MIRANDA. It's quite pretty when it's wet. Isn't it Paul?

PAUL (rather embarrassed). *Charming ... perfectly charming.* (ibid: 65)

Aside from discussions of the charms of Miranda's tail, and of Paul's attraction to it, the drama manages to deliver another surprising twist to the play's representation of Paul's devoted interaction with Miranda. Disapproving of Miranda's flirtations with Paul, Nigel and Charles, Clare asks Miranda whether there are mermen she could consort with:

MIRANDA. Oh yes ... a few. But they have little eyes and flat noses, and they're awfully cissie. (She smiles at *CLARE* rather ruefully). *That's why we're practically extinct.* (ibid: 65)

This statement indicates that Miranda desires strong, virile masculinity (rather than its antithesis). Shortly after her unfavourable characterisation of mermen's charms and their unmanly/effeminate nature, Miranda slips into the conversation that her sisters have gone to Majorca, where she also wants to be in May. This comment is left hanging until the final lines of the script:

CLARE. Majorca, yes. I wonder why she said she wanted to be somewhere very lovely in May. (She thinks for a moment, and then suddenly starts counting on her fingers) *September, October, November, December, January, February, March, April, May.* (With darkening suspicion) *Paul!* (ibid: 67)

Clare's mental arithmetic indicates that Miranda has planned to be in Majorca nine months after her dalliance with Paul in a cave "deep in Pendower cove" (ibid: 66). Eliding the complex issue of the location and nature of the mermaid's genitalia, the implications are clear: that Miranda has been impregnated, and that Clare regards Paul as the culprit. While this ending may appear light-hearted in the contemporary context, it was significant in that British Theatre was tightly regulated in the 1940s by the Lord Chamberlain's Office, which routinely censored play scripts and removed a wide variety of material that it deemed sexually suggestive (see Nicholson 2011: 301–354). In this regard, the scene in which Miranda's *négligé* is removed to reveal her tail can be also considered as particularly risqué.

In Blackmore's play Miranda is represented as a powerful and disruptive *anima* who possesses a knowing (and even conniving) mature sexuality that is unlike Min/Lenore's childlike erotic aspect in the Peabody novel and film. Indeed, Miranda is more like the Cathy character from the Jones's story in mermaid form than she is the pliant mermaid from Cay Oro. While Min/Lenore threatens the stability of Peabody's marriage (mainly by confusing his wife, who thinks that he is having an affair with a human), Miranda threatens the stability of a trio of relationships with her extreme flirtatiousness and disregard for social restraint. Her tail is a symbol and manifestation of her phallic power and of her disregard for patriarchal rules and stereotypes. In this manner, she resembles both a number of femme fatales from US films noir and a number of the bold, adventurous women present in British cinema in the late 1940s (typified by Margaret Lockwood's starring roles in films such as *The Wicked Lady* [Leslie Arliss, 1945] and *Jassy* [Bernard Knowles, 1947]), which have been regarded as filmic reflections of the changed nature of women's social and sexual roles following the disruptions of World War Two.

Miranda's sexual agency and the erotic charge of her tail were made even more apparent in Annakin's screen adaptation. The film starred actress and singer Glynis Johns in the title role and was a major hit in a post-War Britain still suffering from the impact of wartime privations and seeking escapist diversion in theatre and cinema. In addition to the use of score (discussed in the following chapter), the film also made good use of Johns' distinctively husky vocal timbre in spoken dialogue. Miranda is as diametrically opposite to Lenore in that she is vocally articulate, speaking and understanding English with ease, rather than being mute. Her vocal huskiness, combined with her clear diction and an unhurried, lilting sense of vocal phrasing, gave her an appealing and seductive quality perfectly in-tune with the flirtatious nature of much of her scripted dialogue. Indeed, one of the pleasures of the film is the manner in which Johns' spoken vocal performance, using a range of affectations, combines with her languorous poses, as she is variously carried or wheeled around onshore by men or else reclines in baths, beds or on couches, suggesting her own sexual interest and availability. While the film retained the primary setting of the London apartment it provided a preface and final shot that visualised aspects of the external narrative, together with two additional scenes that complemented the play's themes.

The film opens with Paul's encounter with Miranda while fishing and shows the mermaid's underwater cave, revealing Miranda's nature and her elegant tail early in the narrative (and thereby obviating the need for the revelation scene at the end of Act II of the play). Her tail is long, smooth and sheath-like with a high sheen (Figure 8) and without the fish scale patterning of Lenore's in *Mr Peabody and the Mermaid,* and her long, fair tresses are elegantly curled, falling down over her breasts. As in the play, Miranda behaves flirtatiously throughout the film but the extent and nature of her interaction with males onshore is only made explicit in the film's visual postscript. Unlike the play, which ends on Clare's calculation and unspoken question to her husband about what he might have done with Miranda, the film answers her question about why Miranda wanted to be in Majorca by showing the mermaid six months later, sitting on a rock in the sea cradling a merbaby.

Six years after *Miranda's* release, a sequel entitled *Mad About Men* was produced. Written by Peter Blackmore and directed by Ralph Thomas, the film was shot in colour (in contrast to its black and white predecessor). Johns reprised her role as Miranda and also doubled as her (fully-human) lookalike relative Caroline Trewella in a narrative largely set in Cornwall. The plot involves Miranda first meeting and then switching roles with Caroline in order to enjoy the pleasures of life on land for a brief duration. Miranda-as-Caroline's sudden inability to walk is explained as the result of an accident, requiring her to be moved around in a wheelchair or carried by various male characters. The basic plot again revolves around Miranda-as-Caroline's interactions with men who are entranced by her vivacity and flirtatiousness. This is complicated by the unexpected arrival of Caroline's dull and pedantic fiancé from London, who cannot understand why she has become so disinterested in him. In contrast to the initial film, Miranda's (silvery blue) tail is not revealed to any of the men who court her attentions. The narrative also features a female character, Barbara, who resents her husband's fascination with Miranda-as-Caroline and discovers her secret identity. Barbara then invites Miranda to sing at a gala concert where she plans to reveal her true identity. Miranda becomes aware of this and gets the real Caroline to substitute for her on the night in question. When Barbara acts to reveal that Miranda is a mermaid the action exposes Caroline's legs rather than a fishtail. Emphasising her conventional human physique, Caroline then gets up from her wheelchair and dances around the stage.

Figure 8 – Miranda and merbaby in publicity photo For *Miranda* (1984).

One significant difference between the films was the introduction of an additional mermaid companion for Miranda named Berengaria (Dora Bryan). Berengaria is a unique character in live-action cinema as a result of her *not* embodying the graceful, mellifluous and seductive traits typical of mermaids and, instead, being distinguished by her clumsiness, her vocal inadequacies (as detailed in Chapter 3) and her propensity to dress in odd combinations of found human clothes (and wearing what looks like a lampshade on her head at one stage)[105]. Berengaria's comic take on mer-form and character highlights Miranda's glamorous appearance as a mermaid at the same time as it shows the essential absurdity of the mermaid form and legend. *Mad about Men* concludes with a scene where Miranda sees Caroline in a boat kissing the human suitor who she has been most impressed by during her time on shore impersonating her. As befitting her tastes in her previous film, the individual is a strong, rugged man-of-action and her expression shows disappointment that it is Caroline who is enjoying his attentions, rather than her. In this manner the film

105   See Chapter 3, Figure 12.

does not offer its (lead) mermaid the gratification that the preceding film gave her as a result of her time on shore. Rather, it suggests that Caroline's problem with regard to her (now) ex-fiancé was her inability to engage the feminine wiles that appear to come naturally to her mermaid cousin.

A mermaid also graced the screen in a further European comedy, *Pekka Ja Pätkä Sammakkomiehinä* ('Pekka and Pätkä: Diving Agents'[106]), a Finnish film directed by Armand Lohirski in 1957. The film was part of a series that ran between 1953 and 1960 starring the male comedians Esa Parkarinen (as Pekka) and Masa Niemi (as Pätkä). The duo has been compared to US comedians Stan Laurel and Oliver Hardy and their comedies centred on their characters' interplay and the various mishaps they get into. *Sammakkomiehinä* was their ninth film and included a plot line that involved them training as divers off the coast of southern Finland. During their training they encounter a young, beautiful and affable mermaid with a glittery, scaly tail named Helmi ('Pearl' in Finnish), played by Sirkka-Liisa Wilén. Bringing her onshore (which they perceive as safer than the sea), they keep her in a bath before she is found by a janitor and taken to Helsinki's Linnanmäki amusement park, where she becomes a performer in a sideshow attraction. While the mermaid only features in a small section of the film her visual representation is notably less modest than those featured in the previously discussed 1940s' and 1950s' films. Although she has long and wavy hair, her breasts are shown uncovered, with her nipples obscured by starfish-like pasties,[107] in a manner that anticipates the types of representations discussed in the following section.

III. Transitional Representations: De-Tailing the Mermaid

Despite the popularity of *Mr Peabody and the Mermaid*, further mermaid-themed live-action films were not produced in the US until the 1960s. When they did reoccur they took a variety of forms.[108] Whereas the 1940s' and 1950s' films discussed above represented their mermaids as fantastic creatures in whimsical comedies, the genre contexts for the representation of mermaids in 1960s' live-action cinema were significantly different. The first of these, *Night Tide* (Curtis Harrington, 1961), was an atmospheric thriller set around California's Santa Monica Pier. The film featured a young sailor named Johnny (Denis Hopper) who becomes fascinated by Mora (Linda Lawson), a mysterious young woman who works as a mermaid in an arcade attraction on the pier (Figure 9). Mora appears in a mermaid costume in the arcade and, briefly, as a fish-tailed figure in one of Johnny's dreams but otherwise retains human form and identity throughout. This ambiguity tantalises Johnny and Harrington's direction creates an oblique, mysterious narrative that draws on his earlier work in avant-garde cinema to show its male protagonist caught up in a dark, erotic web. The film is ultimately ambiguous as to whether Mora actually is a

---

106   *Sammakkomiehinä* literally translates as 'frog agents', with the former term being used in the sense of 'frogmen' (i.e. as divers).

107   Pasties are adhesive patches that cover the area around the nipples and aureolae.

108   A mermaid also appeared in *Diver Dan*, a TV series featuring live actors and marionettes that initially screened in the US in 1961. The series featured a mermaid named Miss Minerva (played by Suzanne Turner) who mainly attempted to evade the intrusion of the Diver Dan character onto her marine kingdom and sided with the fish marionette characters.

Figure 9 – Mermaid pier show signage from *Night Tide* (1961).

murderous siren in human form (in addition to her performance of a mermaid on the pier) or else has been persuaded to accept that fiction; and her death at the end of the film leaves this aspect unresolved.

The second mermaid-themed feature film of the decade capitalised on a vogue for underwater adventure films that was derived from and closely associated with the introduction of the aqua-lung underwater breathing system. Developed in France during World War Two, the aqua-lung gave divers greater freedom of mobility than previous systems. The device was closely associated with its co-designer Jacques Cousteau and the opportunities it presented for divers were publicised by Cousteau and Frédéric Dumas in their 1953 book 'The Silent World', the contents of which were summarised in the book's subtitle, 'A story of undersea discovery and adventure, by the first men to swim at record depths with the freedom of fish'. A number of American film-makers were quick to realise the potential of using aqua-lung equipment to shoot underwater sequences, including producer/industrialist Howard Hughes, who commissioned and oversaw the production of a diving adventure for RKO entitled *Underwater* (John Sturges, 1954). The film starred Jane Russell and was publicised with poster images of her swimming underwater in a skimpy red bikini. The production was given a novelty premiere in January 1955 at Silver Springs in Florida. Reviewers were given the option of either wearing aqua-lungs to view it while swimming underwater or else watching it through the portholes of mini submarines brought in for the event (AFI 2015: online). Despite this unusual launch, the film had limited box-office success. The cinematic possibilities of using aqua-lungs to shoot documentary and action sequences were explored more successfully in Cousteau's collaboration with director Louis Malle on the 1956 feature-length documentary film *Le Monde du Silence* (released in anglophone markets as *The Silent World*). The film's technical accomplishments and vivid representation of the marine environment (including sequences of shark attacks and undersea explosions) secured it an Academy Award for 'best documentary feature' in 1957. In the following year the TV series *Sea Hunt* (1958–1961) debuted on American television. This centred on the exploits of Mike Nelson (Lloyd Bridges), a freelance aqua-lung diver involved in various underwater adventures. While most episodes concerned relatively predictable scenarios, one episode in series 1 ('Legend of the Mermaid', directed by Leon Benson) departed from these by exploring accounts of a mermaid seen off the Florida coast, which Nelson prove to be mistaken.[109]

---

109 The episode involved Nelson being drawn to an underwater location by mysterious bell-like sounds. Returning to the surface, he is informed by a local fisherman that the location is known as the Cave of the Mermaid on account of a "thing that looks like a woman" that "lives in the cave beneath us" and "kills divers". He then meets an older diver who also claims to have heard the music and a flashback sequence shows an indistinct mermaid face in the cave. A subsequent dive by Nelson reveals this to be a figurehead from the prow of an old wreck and the bell-like sounds as being (somewhat implausibly) produced by an old anchor chain.

Drawing on elements of the abovementioned productions, film-maker John Lamb developed a feature film entitled *Mermaids of Tiburon* that was released in three versions (in 1962, 1964 [released as *Aqua Sex*] and 1985), each upping the ante in terms of explicit representations of the female form. Lamb worked as a diver, cameraman and occasional actor on a number of films in the 1950s and developed his abilities in underwater production by working on *Sea Hunt* before writing and directing his low-budget, black and white feature. The film was shot on location around La Paz Bay on the south west coast of the Baja California peninsula and in the Marineland of the Pacific Oceanarium, south of Los Angeles. The film has a simple plot line that concerns Dr Samuel Jamison (George Rowe), an American marine biologist who travels to Tiburón Island to search for giant pearls. Upon arrival he finds the waters around it populated by a shoal of (stereotypically young, attractive and predominantly Caucasian) mermaids who befriend and fascinate him. Drama is generated by the activities of an unscrupulous, near-psychotic rival, Milo Sangster (Timothy Carey), who attacks Jamison and tries to get the pearls for himself before dying when his oxygen tank runs out of air. Despite this narrative thread, much of the film's screen time is taken up with extended sequences of mermaids cavorting for the camera in scenic marine locations.

The film starred actress, dancer and model Dianne Webber as the lead mermaid and her appearance, with a conventional fish-tail and breasts adorned with undersea flowers, provided the film with its principal marketing image (Figure 10). Webber had a diverse career in the 1950s–1960s. She first became acquainted with Lamb while working alongside him as a stunt swimmer on *Ghost Diver* (Richard Einfield and Merrill White, 1957) but was best known as an erotic model who first attracted attention as a *Playboy* magazine 'Playmate of the Month' in May 1955. She appeared in the magazine again in February 1956, when she featured in underwater shots taken by photographer (and later erotic film-maker) Russ Meyer.[110] Webber went on to become a high profile proponent of nudism and was also associated with the atmospheric musical styles commonly referred to as lounge music and/or exotica[111] by appearing as a featured model on the covers of albums such as Nelson Riddle's *Sea of Dreams* (1958) and Martin Denny's subsequent 'response' album *Jewels of the Sea* (1961). While the mermaids featured in the film were not represented as being able to speak, the film opened with a female voiceover, implicitly that of a mermaid, directly addressing the audience. Evoking J.M. Barrie's 'Peter Pan', and the fairy Tinker Bell's conviction that if children believe in fairies she will be able to survive misfortune,[112] Webber's voice opens the film by stating "Won't you believe in me? If you

---

110   Meyer's first feature film, *The Immoral Mr Teas* (1959), was the first commercially-released American synch-sound film to include depictions of female nudity outside of representations of the Naturist movement and was a major commercial success for the director, launching his career as an exploitation cinema director. Meyer also featured Webber in a short film entitled *This is my Body* in 1960, which involved the star posing by the surf and taking a lengthy nude swim before discussing the sensual nature of the experience.

111   Exotica drew on various elements including jazz, Latin American music and the work of modernist composers such as Debussy and Stravinsky and featured elements such as chromaticism and pentatonicism, the use of a wide variety of instruments (to increase timbral range) and the use of devices such as arpeggios (often on harps) to provide colourful flourishes.

112   At the end of Act IV of Barrie's play Tinker Bell swallows poison intended for Peter Pan. Close to death she whispers a message to Peter who relates it to the audience "she says she thinks she could get well again if children believed in fairies! ... Do you believe in fairies? Say quick that you believe".

do, there will always be mermaids" as the screen shows water bubbles floating up through the sea.[113] Accompanied by a score by Richard la Salle that draws on Debussy-esque modernism and exotica (and thereby invites comparison to albums such as Riddle's *Sea of Dreams*), the film shows Jamison observing the mermaids and providing a narration that relates his scientific speculation as to their status as an evolutionary digression. His familiarisation with the local mermaid pod is facilitated by the rapport he develops with Webber's mermaid as he courts her with

Figure 10 – Promotional poster for the original version of *The Mermaids of Tiburon* (1962) featuring Dianne Webber.

sea-flowers and follows her on dives around the island. The final scenes of the film show him resigned to leaving the mermaid who has captured his affections after she withdraws from him following Sangster's death. As his narration declares, "perhaps she had come to realise that I was a different species from another world and she was born to live forever under the sea". As he departs he echoes the film's opening female voiceover by speculating that, "if our world had been less cynical and disbelieving through the ages, we would have never lost our belief in such wonderful beings".

Emphasising the somewhat risqué nature of its representations of skimpily clad female torsos (for the period), *Mermaids of Tiburon* was initially distributed to US military bases rather than to mainstream cinemas. As the decade progressed, representations of female nudity began to gain traction in fringe cinema circuits as a result of the popularity of productions made by directors such as Meyer. Attempting to capitalise on this, Lamb re-edited his film in 1964, sacrificing narrative logic and continuity by inserting a number of sequences of naked women (without fish-tails) and re-released the film under the title of *Aqua Sex*. The latter tendency was made complete in a third version in 1985 (which returned to its original title), in which the mermaids' appellation is as much allusive as descriptive. None of the mermaid/women's interactions with humans in any of these versions involve any sexual contact and they principally functioned as objects of pleasure for the gaze. This sexual aspect was made clear in the promotional tagline on posters for *Aqua Sex* that proclaimed "Dazzling, Untamed – these shimmering Sea Nymphs love and frolic in an undersea Shangri-La".[114]

---

113   Aside from this introductory voiceover, mermaid vocality is only indicated around the midpoint of the film, when Jamison follows Webber's mermaid into a cave and first encounters her pod. The presence of the pod is foreshadowed by the disembodied sound of female laughter and subsequently by a squeal when one of its mermaids sees Jamison entering their cave.

114   See the reproduction of the poster online at: http://www.allposters.com/-sp/The-Aqua-Sex-Posters _i7675605_.htm – accessed July 15th 2015.

69

Webber reprised her role in *Mermaids of Tiburon* in an episode of the TV series *Voyage to the Bottom of the Sea* (1964–1968), which concerned a high-tech US submarine exploring the undersea world. The episode, entitled 'The Mermaid' (Jerry Hooper, 1967), not only featured her in similar attire to her earlier film, wearing a green, leaf-like bikini top adorned with flowers, but also re-used some of her swimming sequences from Lamb's original film. In the episode she catches the attention of the submarine's captain (David Henison) as she swims past the bridge of his vessel. Intrigued, he searches for her underwater, captures and tranquilises her and brings her on board. While she cannot speak, she bewitches him via a psychic connection, exercises telekinetic powers and finally secures her release by agreeing to help the captain locate an undersea nuclear device that is about to explode. The episode concludes with the captain and his admiral (Richard Basehart) agreeing to quietly forget their encounter and concurring that mermaids are better left as myths.[115]

While mermaids occasionally featured in the mid–late 1960s as incidental characters (as in William Asher's *Beach Blanket Bingo* [1965][116]), in the form of women impersonating mermaids for comic effect (as in Frank Tashlin's *The Glass Bottom Boat* [1966]), as mermaid performers initially mistaken for actual mermaids (as in an episode of the TV series *Rip Tide* [1969][117]), or in title sequences for films that did *not* include representations of them in the main narrative (as in Lee Sholem's *Catalina Caper* [1967][118]), their next reoccurrence as major characters in screen drama occurred in very different contexts and in very different physical forms.

The tendency towards loosening censorship noted above with regard to the US in the early 1960s accelerated as the decade progressed and resulted in explicit representations of sexual acts becoming commonplace in adult-restricted films.[119] Hardcore pornographic films, representing actual (rather than feigned) sexual activity began to achieve significant commercial success in the US in this period, typified by Gerard Damiano's fellatio-themed *Deep Throat* (1972), starring Linda Lovelace. As Williams (1989) has discussed, the early phase of US porn film production was marked by experimentation in theme, narrative and visual style and a range of topics and sexual tastes were explored. During this period two films were produced that represented mermaids (or, at least, young women designated as mermaids by the narrative and publicity) involved in sexual activity. Both of these films were produced in 1976 and both alluded to Damiano's film and to another, albeit more mainstream, cinema hit of the period, Stephen Spielberg's *Jaws* (1975). The first of these,

115 Also see the discussion of the appearance of a merman (of sorts) in Chapter 6.
116 One of a number of youth exploitation 'Beach Party' films set on California's coast that featured teen idols such as Frankie Avalon and Annette Funicello, frequent shots of photogenic young people in skimpy beach attire and pop music (usually supplied by composer Les Baxter). *Beach Blanket Bingo's* innovation was the inclusion of a mermaid named Lorelei (Marta Kristen) as a minor character who rescues and befriends a character named 'Bonehead'. Given her fleeting presence in the film, it is perhaps the other characters' relative lack of surprise at her association with them that is the film's most curious feature.
117 In an episode entitled 'Catch of the Day' (Michael Lange, 1969).
118 This feature, the last of the 'Beach Party' series of films, commenced with an animated title sequence that depicted a curvaceous, red-haired mermaid attracting the attention of a scuba diver (despite this element not featuring else where in the production).
119 Such as those given an X rating (initially restricted to persons over 16 but later raised to over 17) in the US. This was the most restricted category of the Motion Picture Association of America's voluntary rating system, which was introduced in 1966 to replace the previous Motion Picture Production Code.

Gums (Robert J. Kaplan) is recognised as one of the earliest examples of the cinematic porn parody genre, whereby an (identifiable) mainstream production is loosely reworked into a porn film, using elements of the plot, thematics and/or iconography of the referent film.[120] *Gums* is a relatively complex porn parody text with regard to its referentiality. While the majority of porn parody films (such as those discussed in Chapter 4) have a single referent text, *Gums* parodied aspects of both *Deep Throat* and *Jaws*. Its parody was also relatively unusual in that porn parody films conventionally sexualise aspects of films in which sexuality is latent, suggested and/or discretely represented. This is clearly not the case with regard to *Gums* (which is *less* sexually graphic than *Deep Throat*, see Figure 11).

Gums' plot involved a local sheriff and scientist tracking down a marine predator that was terrorising local beaches and killing male swimmers. An early scene identifies the killer's modus operandus. It – or, rather, she, as it transpires – approaches men underwater, fellates them and then kills them by biting off their genitals. A number of sequences show these attacks, in which the men are at first startled, then delighted and then die as a result of the attentions accorded to them. The culprit is revealed to be a young, slim female (played by actress Teri Hall) clad only in a tiara and a thin shell belt, with elaborate eye make-up and painted shimmery legs. She is identified as a mermaid by a scientist named Dr Smegma, who is described (in a notice shown briefly on screen) as a "world renowned fellatiologist". In one of the longer and more complex spoken passages in the film (all things being relative), the scientist identifies that attacks such as those that have occurred in the area have been made by "lovelorn mermaids". Responding to the local sheriff's query as to whether the culprit can be a mermaid since she has been reported as having legs, Dr Smegma states that:

> It is said that a mermaid is a semi-human being who can dwell in the sea and also live on land and enter into social relations with human beings ... The typical mermaid has the head and body of a beautiful woman [and] below the waist has a fish tail with scales and fins. However the ideal of a fishtail is unimportant, for the true Teutonic mermaid has no fish tail at all. The idea of a fish tail is a psychological one, you see, the mermaid is a mother figure.

This passage is significantly different from any other in the film in that it is discursive rather than comic or incidental and appears as to be less directed to the sheriff than the audience, which might be wondering why the mermaid referred to by the characters is in fact fully human in form (presumably since it was easier for the producers in that the actress concerned did not need to be fitted with a prosthetic tail). Although much of the film's dialogue appears to have been semi-improvised, with various glitches left in,[121] the passage is notable for stressing a strand of mermaid folklore that concerns their ability to visit land and to interact with humans socially (and, implicitly, sexually).[122] It also refers

---

120 Also see Chapter 1 Section III for a discussion of porn parody versions of sequences from Disney's *The Little Mermaid* (Ron Clements and John Musker, 1989).

121 Earlier in this sequence Dr Smega also says "Mermaids have been known through history as sirens, tritons, dragons" (the latter characterisation clearly being an error).

122 While mermaid singing is absent in the film, the film has an inventive score, composed by Brad Fiedel, that parodies well-known pieces of music such as the *Jaws* theme (composed by John Williams) and Brecht and Weill's 1928 song 'Mac the Knife'.

Figure 11 – Promotional poster for *Gums* (1976)
(Note the representation of a conventional
fish-tailed mermaid [which does not feature in the
film]).

to the mermaid's symbolism as a mother figure, which is a slender and ambiguous element of mermaid folklore, and introduces a novel concept, that of the "true Teutonic mermaid" (such as, perhaps, Wagnerian Rhinemaidens?) that are fully human in form.[123] Amidst its somewhat confusing narrative, the film also includes an innovation in the cinematic representation of mermaids in the form of a sex scene between the mermaid and the sheriff's female secretary. This takes place on the sea shore, where the mermaid engages in ardent oral sex with her human partner before, apparently, killing her (or rendering her unconscious by sexual satiation – it's unclear which) before dancing triumphantly around her. Given the mermaid's apparent inability to speak and the lack of contextual material presented in the film we are led to assume that her status as a "lovelorn" mermaid identified by Dr Smegma explains her serial violence towards men. In this manner, she manifests as a pornographic femme fatale, revenging herself on men due to her unrequited passions.

Somewhat confusingly, another mermaid-themed comedy porn film released in the same year, *Deep Jaws* (directed by Perry Dell), was a satire on a small, declining Hollywood studio that decided to diversify into porn production as a way of turning its finances around. After a discussion of the runaway commercial success of *Deep Throat*, a female member of the management team proposes a film featuring "nympho mermaids", which the studio head enthusiastically accepts. The film is made on a shoestring budget, using money creamed off of another project being shot simultaneously. Much of the film's humour concerns its complex pre-production, with different actresses vying for the leading role and with regard to the logistics of trying to shoot two dissimilar films in the same location. Aside from some scenes with near-naked women interacting with men underwater while wearing loose fishnet wraps around their legs (which may or may not be part of the planned mermaid film, it's difficult to tell), the only shots featuring an actress in a conventional mermaid tail occur right at the end of the film, as the star performer waits around to be filmed. As Chapter 4 relates, the types of film that *Deep Jaws* satirised were made in the following decade and marked a significantly new inflection of mermaid media-lore.

---

123   The latter reference ties into a bizarre element of the film, namely the presence of an ageing Nazi, dressed in uniform, who has been employed by the town to hunt and kill the mermaid (with the narrative giving no explanation for his presence in 1970s' America).

Conclusion

The mermaid-themed material produced between the early-1910s and mid-1980s can be seen to have tracked changes in standards of screen censorship and related film industry practices. During the 1910s and 1920s, when feature films were developing as a form, a number of Hollywood productions included representations of barely clothed or naked female bodies and/or sexually suggestive interactions between characters in period piece and/or fantasy films.[124] In this regard, Annette Kellerman's performances were typical of a broader cycle of production that waned in the early 1930s as the Motion Picture Association of America accepted a self-censorship regime under the so-called Hays Code. The return of the mermaid to the screen in the 1940s occurred at a time when restrictions on nudity and/or representations of sexual (or, even, sexually suggestive) situations or scenarios were tightly maintained. In these contexts, the mermaid conveniently occurred outside of conventions regarding the representation of human females, with her fish-tailed lower half distancing her from concerns over genital sexuality at the same time as her demeanour and behaviour clearly implicated her in sexual interactions. In this context, the ending of *Miranda* (which indicated that the film's mermaid protagonist has [some-how] achieved copulation with a male character) is all the more surprising for its diver-gence from conventional cinematic morality. The loosening of censorship regulations during the late 1950s and early 1960s removed the mermaid's niche appeal in this regard (in a manner that is manifest in the serial reworking of Lamb's *Tiburon/Aqua Sex* films to transition from representing mermaids to naked women).[125] Similarly, the representation of mermaids in anatomically human form in *Gums* in 1976 can be seen as an attempt to carry the mystique and allure of mermaids generated within folk- and media-loric contexts into the representation of fully-human females in exploitation cinema. In all but the latter films, the mermaid's tail is a key element of her allure, camouflaging genital sexuality in a fetishistic manner and sublimating conventional heterosexual desire. As the following chapter details, this aspect has also been explored on screen in tandem with the repre-sentation of mermaids' seductive vocality.

124 Such as *Hypocrites* (Lois Weber, 1915), starring Margaret Edwards, and *Queen of Sheba*, (J. Gordon Edwards, 1921), starring Betty Blyth.

125 In addition to the films produced between 1948 and 1976 discussed in this chapter, a later film entitled *Mermaid: A Flippant Tale* (Adele Smith and Charlie Simonds, 1992) represented something of a throwback to the period. Produced by Parafotos Films, a British company that makes naturist films similar in style to 1960s' nudist-themed films (in that they neither represent nor allude to sexual activities), the film weaves a mermaid motif into the shooting of a film promoting the virtues of Fuerteventura Island as a naturist destination. A silver-tailed mermaid (played by co-director Smith) appears briefly in several sequences but neither speaks to nor interacts with human characters.

Chapter Three

Sonic Seduction: Mermaid Vocality and its Expression in Screen Soundtracks

Jon Fitzgerald[*] and Philip Hayward

Whereas Chapter 1 analysed the manner in which the protagonists of Andersen's short story and Disney's film sacrificed their voices in order to gain human form, this chapter analyses the nature of mermaid vocality in a series of films in which the protagonists retain both their voices and tails. More specifically, we explore the manner in which the musical scores and sound design of a series of live-action films made between the late-1940s and mid-2010s have facilitated diverse explorations of the mermaid's voice. Both the classic mythology of the sirens and a substantial strand of European mermaid folklore represent the creatures' voices and sung melodies as accomplished, appealing and often seductive. While some mermaids have been represented as being able to sing songs in human languages, they are more commonly represented as singing pure melodic lines that make a deep impression on their (over-whelmingly male) listeners. Naroditskaya and Austern argue that:

> More than any other quality, it is the siren's music that positions her in the flowing spaces between the human, animal, and spirit worlds, between past and present, danger and delight ... The song of the siren belongs to the threshold between time and eternity, the plane of reference for the metaphors of myth. (2006: 3)

* Jon Fitzgerald is an adjunct associate professor in the School of Arts and Social Sciences at Southern Cross University, Lismore, Australia.

Similarly, Austern asserts that the siren's song is essentially similar to "the mother's lullaby and the lover's exaltation" in that these are all "emotive and sometimes paralinguistic vocalisations of some primal place" wherein "woman, water and the insubstantial, affective flow of music" intermingle (2006: 58). Film sound designer Walter Murch offers a complementary characterisation of the womb as sound's primal place and describes it as offering the foetus a "continuous and luxuriant bath of sounds" supplied by the mother's biomechanical processes and the sound of her own speech, heard internally (1994: vii). Chion's essay on uses of sound and music in Mizoguchi Kenji's film *Sanshō Dayū* (1954) takes a similar course, arguing that the siren's song and its diffusion across water evokes the baby's perceptions of sound and space in utero, characterising that:

> Sirens are creatures of the borderline *between land – a solid body, circumscribed – and the sea, which is uncircumscribed, formless. Sirens inhabit the in-between that they invite us to negate, since they invite confusion of land with sea, speech with voice.* (emphasis in original, 1999: 114)

Chion's interest in the role of the siren's voice in Kenji's film derives from what he perceives as the unusual manner in which a female voice is used *acousmatically* in the film; that is, without a readily identifiable source. As Silverman (1998) asserts, in the course of a psychoanalytic consideration of the role of the voice in cinema, acousmatic voices (such as those supplying voice-overs) are habitually male and on the rare occasions they are not are often used in a disturbing manner rather than to provide meaning and stability (ibid: 181).

This "borderline" referred to by Chion (1999) is complex in that both the womb and the maternal body more generally have a dualistic aspect. In one sense, both offer a fluid realm of peace and comfort. In another, they offer a claustrophobic enfolding that constrains the future individual in a pre-natal state. Both of these polarities are evident in the contextual and affective representations of singing mermaids discussed in subsequent sections of this chapter. This duality about the "primal place" that mermaid songs appear to emanate from and promise access to gives them an unsettling and uncanny aspect that is, if anything, amplified by the mermaid's pleasure in singing her songs (to herself, to those who overhear her and/or to those who she might direct her songs to). She vocalises outside of the terrestrial/patriarchal order precisely because she *is* outside of it. Her frequently depicted fascination with men and/or material goods is premised on their exteriority to her world. Even when she is represented as singing song *words* – rather than pure vowel sounds – her melodiousness commonly stresses the affective dimensions of melody and timbre over language. In this manner, the mermaid and her songs touch deep aspects of the psyche and draw their symbolic/affective power from them.

The discussions of aspects of mermaid vocality, score and sound design we advance in the following sections are informed by their particular historical and cultural contexts, providing senses of the potential plurality and shifting nature of representations of the vocal mermaid. Cinematic mermaids' songs occur in different contexts (generic, historical and/or geographical) but share aspects that consolidate vocality as a key motif in 20th and 21st Century mermaid media-lore that is specifically enabled by the conventions of diegetic vocal tracks, extra-diegetic scores and elements of sound design that incorporate these.

I. 1940s' and 1950s' Mermaid features

As discussed in Chapter 2, cinematic mermaids re-emerged after World War Two in two films released in 1948: the US production *Mr Peabody and the Mermaid* (Irving Pichel) and the British film *Miranda* (Ken Annakin). Both films featured mermaids with alluring voices and both integrated these elements into their scores. The following discussions complement the broader analyses of the films offered in the preceding chapter by analysing their sonic aspects.

'Peabody's Mermaid' (1946), the novel by Guy and Constance Jones that was the basis for Pichel's film, contains a number of vivid descriptions of the seductive power of the mermaid's song and is prefaced by a quotation from English poet John Donne, "Teach me to hear mermaids singing". As previously discussed (in Chapter 2), it concerns a middle-aged American businessman encountering and becoming besotted by a mermaid while on holiday in the Caribbean. His first encounter is a sonic one. Soon after arriving at his holiday villa Peabody finds himself inexplicably drawn to an offshore islet known as Cay Oro, where he becomes beguiled by a mysterious voice:

> *Above the sound of the wind and water came strains of clear sweet music. It seemed like the voice of a woman, but unlike any song that he had ever heard. It moved him profoundly and he shivered ... It came again, swelling louder till it seemed all about him, dying away to a thrilling vibration in the air. It filled him with longing and a deep self-pity, then stirred him to exaltation and a feeling of high power.* (ibid: 20)

Keen to discover the identity of the singer, he at first suspects Cathy, a glamorous American stage performer also on vacation on the island, and persuades her to sing for him one afternoon. But in contrast to the ethereal voice he heard on the Cay, Cathy has a "rich, throaty" voice that reveals itself in her impromptu rendition of Saen-Saën's mezzo-soprano aria 'Mon coeur s'ouvre à ta voix' ('My heart opens at the sound of your voice'). The authors' choice of this particular song is clearly far from incidental, as its lyrics represent the affective power of a lover's voice to inspire intense emotion, but it is the mermaid rather than Cathy who enraptures Peabody. This is made explicit later in the novel as she sings to him one night and transports him to a place of serenity:

> *The stars paled. The mermaid lifted her head to the sinking moon and sang. There was no one but Peabody to hear her. The strange music sank voluptuously low, rose triumphantly and ecstatically clear, died away to a lullaby of incomparable peace. Peabody slept in her arms.* (ibid: 129)

These elements of the novel are richly realised in the film's soundtrack. As in the novel, the mermaid (played by singer and actress Anne Blyth) cannot speak but is possessed of a fine and highly seductive singing voice. The film's score, written by Robert Emmett Dolan, highlights the mermaid's role in the narrative by providing her with a distinct leitmotif. This is first heard during the film's opening titles when a sweet, pure soprano voice sings a rising sequence of descending fourth intervals in the upper vocal range. Although Peabody thinks he hears a distant female voice soon after his arrival at the beach house, the first clearly audible use of Lenore's leitmotif within the film occurs when Peabody sails towards her home on a rocky islet. As he climbs out of his boat onto the shore Lenore's voice becomes louder (although she is still unseen) and her vocal melody is presented in an extended form. When Peabody sees Lenore's hairclip lying on a rock the score briefly features an instrumental version of the motif. From this point on, Lenore's motif is heard regularly, both diegetically and non-diegetically. For example, brief hints of the motif are heard on wind instruments as Peabody accidentally hooks Lenore's tail when fishing. Tuned percussion instruments and orchestral strings take over the theme as Lenore's body and face come into view. The motif is heard again as Lenore dresses in a bikini top that Peabody has given her, and when her song wakes Peabody in the early hours of the morning after she is first taken to his house. The most extensive use of the motif occurs after Lenore overhears Peabody saying that he loves her. The score then highlights extended orchestral variations of the motif as the mermaid swims around in a state of bliss.[126] At the end of the film the orchestral soundtrack uses the motif as Peabody dives into the ocean in the hope of being re-united with the departed Lenore.

Cathy is also a persistent presence in the narrative and one of her most blatant gambits in flirting with Peabody is to sing a song about the Caribbean being "made for love" – with her rich, low alto tone suggesting sexual experience, in contrast to Lenore's higher, more innocent voice. Indeed, underlining the rivalry between the two female characters, Peabody's mere mention of Cathy while talking to Lenore is sufficient to prompt her to use her mer-vocality for a brief instant, making a sharp sound in disgust.[127] Aside from this sudden expressive flash, both Lenore and the overall film offer a restrained and somewhat demure representation of mermaid sexuality and desire (with emotional intimacy seemingly a more focal concern to Lenore than sexual congress). Physical interaction between the pair occurs – in the form of a kiss – but is markedly restrained. Lenore's undulating melodies are nonetheless represented as intensely seductive and expressive of an enchantment that transcends conventional human interactions.

The British feature, *Miranda*, was directed by Ken Annakin and adapted for the screen by dramatist Peter Blackmore from his eponymous stage comedy. While the original play script makes occasional reference to Miranda's vocal abilities it doesn't include any song sequences. In both the play and film Miranda is diametrically opposite to Lenore in that she is vocally articulate, speaking and understanding English with ease, rather than being mute. As discussed in the previous chapter, actress Glynis Johns uses her sensuous vocal huskiness in a flirtatious manner. The artfulness of her vocal interaction with human males is highlighted in a brief scene when she is taken to the seal enclosure at London Zoo. Shortly after catching a zookeeper's misdirected fish in her mouth and swallowing it down whole, she temporarily abandons her human voice in order to communicate with one of the seals, using loud, guttural, honking sounds.

In addition to the above-mentioned qualities of her speech, Miranda's singing voice is featured prominently throughout the film.[128] It is first heard as Paul regains consciousness

---

126 This underwater sequence, which stretches the film's realism by representing an aquatic space that seems far larger than that suggested by the space of the pool previously represented in the film, was shot at the newly-opened Weeki Wachee Springs aquatic attraction in Florida (discussed in Chapter 2).

127 The sound was produced by playing a recording of an ocelot snarl backwards (unattributed n.d.).

128 Johns was also an accomplished vocalist who appeared in various musicals and on a number of recordings. We have not been able to ascertain whether Johns contributed all the singing parts to the film herself but this issue is incidental to the representation of Miranda's voice in the film

after being dragged into the depths of the ocean, with Miranda singing a wordless ("oh-lee-ee-oh") melody in an operatic soprano style as Paul realises that he has been taken to her undersea grotto. The vocal melody features a prominent leap into the high soprano range and contains long, sustained notes that allow the listener to focus on her warm and rich vocal tone. Miranda sings again, unconcerned, as Paul attempts to escape from the cave, and her song is also used non-diegetically as Paul discusses the difficulties of taking her onto land with him. These performances are not so much seductive as assured and confident expressions of her position of power. Miranda's love of music is repeatedly emphasised in the film.[129] When she first asks Paul to take her back to land she says, "but most of all, I want to go to the opera". Her dream is realised when she attends a performance at Covent Garden with Paul. Taking advantage of the interval, she delivers an impromptu version of the main aria from a box, with the orchestra joining in and the crowd looking on in surprise. The identification of opera as Miranda's particular love is significant. As LaMay and Armstrong (2006) assert, prior to the advent of rock music, opera was the form of cultural expression in which women could deploy their vocality with greatest intensity. Developing this, the authors assert that "women's singing in Western culture has been inextricably linked to her sexualised body, a body whose ambition is to seduce" and comment that "early Modern theorists" contend that when a woman's "uvula was undulating in the act of producing song she was considered especially 'hot', her mouth open in an explicit invitation for sex, and her uvula in a rapturous state of 'excessive jouissance'" (ibid: 319). This characterisation is not inappropriate for Miranda in the film given her lascivious pursuit of men.

Music also functions in a subtly suggestive way in with regard to the film's surprising final twist. Like Disney's *King Neptune* (discussed in Chapter 1), *Miranda* utilises different musical styles to contrast mariners and mermaids. But whereas the Disney film uses a shanty to characterise its pirates, *Miranda's* score, composed by Temple Abady, utilises an instrumental version of the chorus from the patriotic anthem 'Rule Britannia' (1740[130]) as both a somewhat wry introduction to the film and as the element of score that accompanies Miranda swimming over to Paul's boat in an early scene. The lyrics of the chorus, which proclaim: "Rule Britannia! Britannia rules the waves/ Britons never, never, never shall be slaves" are somewhat ironic given that Paul is pulled into a grotto by a mermaid and subsequently obliged to indulge her whims.[131] Associated with Paul at the film's inception, the return of the chorus melody at the film's conclusion, at the very moment when Miranda is seen cradling her mer-child on a rock, suggests that Paul's engagement with Miranda during her time ashore went beyond what was shown on screen.

Music also played a prominent, if more diverse, role in the sequel to *Miranda*, *Mad About Men* (Ralph Thomas, 1954). This film involved Miranda impersonating her human cousin

---

129   During this first conversation with Clare, Miranda also recalls that, "We [i.e. Miranda and her sister] used to sing good duets though. I have rather a nice voice you know." Later, in an apparent reference to the Zennor mermaid tale, she tells her nurse that her great-grandmother had visited land when she was young and had sung at church.

130   Written by poet James Thompson and set to music by composer Thomas Arne.

131   This musical device is closely similar to one used in the popular Victorian Music Hall song 'Married to a Mermaid' (composed by Arthur Lloyd around 1865), which wryly alternates verses about a sailor and his bride with the chorus from 'Rule Britannia' to similar comic effect.

Figure 12 – Promotional poster for *Mad About Men* (emphasising its music aspects by showing Miranda singing into a microphone in the inset and surrounded by musical score on the right).

Caroline for two weeks (see Figure 12). Caroline discovers her mermaid relative in an early scene in the film, as she investigates strange sounds emanating from a cave pool in the basement of the coastal cottage in which she is staying. She is woken from sleep by a rendition of what develops as the mermaid's leitmotif in the film. This is initially heard as a distant diegetic melody with a sound quality reminiscent of a slightly distorted, highly reverberant trombone. The as-yet-unidentified instrument plays a lengthy, multi-phrase, major-key melody before Caroline goes to the basement and identifies the sound as being produced by a conch shell played by Miranda. This is an unusual inflection of mermaid lore as the conch shell is more usually played by mythological tritons, with mermaids more commonly represented strumming on lyres or harps. The melody appears regularly within the orchestral underscore (composed by Benjamin Frankel). It is played by French horns as Miranda-as-Caroline converses with Jeff, one of her love interests, and a diverse range of orchestral instruments articulate variants of the theme during the lengthy scene in which Barbara (the jealous wife of one of Miranda-as-Caroline's love interests) accidentally discovers Miranda in a cave while out swimming.

As might be expected, there are also strong similarities between the films in terms of mermaid vocality. Johns' speaking and singing voice is again one of the most distinctive aspects of the production, and her (previously discussed) idiosyncratic vocal timbre and delivery are ideally suited to the reprise of the flirtatious lead character. The principle difference between the films with regard to the portrayal of mermaid vocality relates to the introduction of an additional mermaid companion for Miranda, named Berengaria, played by Dora Bryan. Although Berengaria can speak English, she also makes distinctive, wordless utterances (such as high-pitched squeals and abrasive laughing sounds) that contrast markedly with Miranda's elegant and controlled diction. Unlike the standard representation of mermaids as mellifluous creatures, Berengaria's singing is high-pitched, shrill, out-of-tune and clumsily phrased, making it an effective comic foil for Miranda's more appealing singing. Jokes about Berengaria's unpleasant voice recur throughout the film. For example, when Berengaria asks Miranda's nurse if she would like to hear her sing, she comments that, "my high notes are so high that only a dogfish can hear them". It comes as no surprise that the nurse declines the offer. Later, Berengaria encounters an old sailor and asks, "Would you like me to sing for you?" When he declines, she pursues the matter, saying, "I've got a voice like a siren." Misinterpreting her meaning, the sailor responds, "I reckon you might have at that; no ma'am, that'd upset the mackerel, that would". The final musical joke occurs towards the end of the film, when Caroline appears in a wheelchair at a concert (effectively impersonating Miranda-as-Caroline). This causes a difficulty in that Caroline cannot sing. This is circumvented by Miranda singing through a microphone that has been dangled below the auditorium into her cave. However, Berengaria disrupts the illusion by grabbing the microphone and singing discordantly, to the audience's considerable discomfort. The comedy of these scenes derives from the well-established tradition of mermaids' melodiousness.[132] Deprived of this attribute, Berengaria lacks Miranda's seductive aura and appears far more human, despite her fish-tailed form.

II. Incidental Vocality

Following the trio of films discussed above, there was a thirty-year gap until the release of another film that featured a mermaid in a substantial character role.[133] But while the mermaid's return to prominence in *Splash* (Ron Howard, 1984) was a spectacular and popular one, Madison, a mermaid with transformative powers, appeared without the ability to sing (and, similarly, Lee Holdridge's lush orchestral score did not feature any obvious motifs suggestive of mermaid vocality). Despite this, vocality was a notable, if subtle, element of Madison's presence and character. Initially mute, when she swims ashore at Liberty Island in New York, having transformed to human form, Madison soon acquires (English) language speech after an afternoon spent in front of television sets at Bloomingdale's department store. A further element of surprise occurs when her love interest Allen (Tom Hanks) asks her real (i.e. mer-) name. This results in a particularly memorable moment in which Madison's mer-self is clearly indicated as fundamentally other to the human world when the high-volume sounds she utters resound around the room and prove intolerable for human hearing. Her mer-name takes the form of a short

---

132 An episode of the children's TV series *My Parents are Aliens*, entitled 'The Tale of the Knitted Map' (Tom Poole, 2005), also uses grating singing for similar comic effect. In the episode the family mother, Sophie (Barbara Durkin), who is an alien who can morph her physique, finds herself fixed in mermaid form after sprouting a tail to make swimming easier. Enjoying and wishing to show off her new physical attribute she visits a café and sings off-key, prompting her children to block her mouth and carry her out.

133 A mermaid character named Nya (played by Michelle Phillips) featured in three episodes of the TV series *Fantasy Island* in 1979–1984. In the first, entitled 'The Mermaid' (Earl Bellamy, 1979), she attempts to seduce a scientist into accompanying her into the ocean as her mate. Her seductive appearance is enhanced in the score by high, female, wordless vocals and evocative ascending string passages. Frustrated in her attempt to gain a human mate she featured in a further episode entitled 'The Mermaid Returns' (Earl Bellamy, 1980) where she was granted legs by the series' controlling figure, Roarke (Ricardo Montalbán), eventually falling for and being rejected by him. Her final appearance was in an episode entitled 'The Mermaid and the Matchmaker' (Philip Leacock, 1984) in which she unsuccessfully pleads with Roarke to give her a soul.

sequence of sounds, in which two loud, very high frequency, dolphin-like 'squeals' ("eee" sounds with a falling contour) are followed by an even louder, higher and longer screech that shatters the glass screens of the televisions that she has just been watching. Madison subsequently re-appeared in a low-profile sequel, *Splash Too* (Greg Antonacci, 1988), which was similarly bereft of sung vocality. These two films exemplify a tendency in cinema whereby transformative mermaids do not sing (either in their mer- or human forms), in contrast to 'fixed-form' mermaids who are highly vocal. The main exception to this duality is *Fishtales* (Alki David, 2007), which occupied a similar genre niche to the two *Splash* films, being a romantic comedy featuring a mermaid (Kelly Brock) falling for a mortal male (in the form of an American classics professor Thomas Bradley, played by Billy Zane). Set on Spetses island in the Aegean Sea, Brock's mermaid is represented as a nereid – one of the sea nymphs from Greek mythology known for their melodious singing voices. Her presence around the island is initially suggested by a repeated vocal motif embedded within other soft, sustained sounds in the score. When the professor encounters her for the first time she sings a louder, diegetic melody over the top of the score that features repeated third intervals based around notes from the major pentatonic scale. In human form, which she assumes between sunset and sunrise, her singing is not apparent.

While only incidental to the narrative, a striking representation of mermaid vocality was presented in John Williams's score for Steven Spielberg's 1991 film *Hook*, a live-action sequel to J.M Barrie's 'Peter Pan' (discussed in the previous chapter). The film features the adventures of an adult Peter (played by Robin Williams) and the mermaids feature in a sequence when he is pitched overboard into the sea. As he sinks into the depths, the loud music of the preceding sequence is replaced by the sound of bubbles (his escaping breath) and a soft, sustained major chord on strings and wind instruments. As he slides into unconsciousness he finds himself surrounded by mermaids, who swim to him, kiss him deeply (each in turn) and breath air into his lungs to sustain him. As the first mermaid appears, unison soprano voices begin a simple, sustained melodic line that weaves around the fifth and third notes of the chord. The voices are pure and without vibrato and as additional mermaids swim in to him the range and contour of the melody is expanded. The round, warm sound of the French horn is added to provide a final layer to the gentle and seductive musical texture that sustains him until he is pulled up from the water.

III. Predatory Mermaids in Early 21st Century Cinema

In contrast to the gentle mermaids of the 1940s and 1950s, early 21st Century cinema has been dominated by darker, more sirenic creatures. This tendency began to manifest itself in 2001, with the release of Sebastian Guttierez's horror-themed mermaid film *She Creature*.[134] Epitomising William Congreve's famous characterisation that "music has charms to sooth a savage breast",[135] *She Creature* opens with a scene that plays with conventions of the affective power of mermaids' songs. Set in a touring freak show in Ireland at the turn of the 20th Century, the sequence begins with a Caribbean zombie being

---

134   Although the film has a similar title to Edward Cahn's (similarly-themed) *The She-Creature* (1956), the earlier film does not feature a mermaid.

135   The opening line of his 1697 play 'The Mourning Bride',

brought on stage. Goaded by a member of the audience, it becomes enraged, breaks its chains and seems about to attack those in the room. It then suddenly pauses, apparently mesmerised by a sinuous vocalese melody sung in a soprano voice emanating from off-screen, and then rapidly exits the tent to seek the source. The song is found to be coming from a tank in another tent in which a beautiful mermaid is floating, her mouth apparently uttering the melody. While the zombie stares entranced at the creature the showmen manage to grab and restrain it. After ushering patrons out of the tent the illusion is revealed. The song cuts out as a gramophone is turned off and the mermaid in the tank is revealed to be a woman acting the role. This classic representation of hypnotic mermaid song is contrasted to the vocality of an actual mermaid (from the mythical 'Forbidden islands' of the mid-Atlantic) who is later found and abducted by the showmen. She turns out to be anything but soothing, issuing a range of indistinct speech-like murmurs, growls and shrieks as she begins to kill the crew of the ship she is transported on before transforming into a monstrous mermaid queen as the ship is drawn inexorably to her island home.

Of all the post-War filmic representations of the mermaid, the one with closest resemblance to the classic myth of the sirens (and, arguably with the most accomplished and effective combination of music and sound design in any of the films discussed in this chapter) occurs in the fourth episode of the *Pirates of the Caribbean* series, *On Stranger Tides* (Rob Marshall, 2011). The film features a plot line that involves pirates seeking to capture a mermaid in order to obtain a single mermaid's tear that is vital for a potion made from the fabled fountain of eternal youth. The scene occurs when Captain Blackbeard sends a boatload of sailors out in calm, misty weather as bait to attract mermaids. As the boat floats undisturbed, one of Captain Blackbeard's henchmen pulls a pistol on the crew and says, "They like to hear singing". His instruction reflects the mermaids' close association with song and musicality in general and also a more specific strand of mermaid folklore wherein mermaids are drawn to and seek to waylay men whose songs attract them. Prompted by the appearance of a loaded pistol pointed at him, one member of the crew named Scrum (played by Stephen Graham) commences singing the final verse of a traditional shanty that exists in several variants (and with several different names[136]) which is written from the position of a wealthy merchant's daughter who has fallen for a sailor and is resolved to forgo her inheritance in order to be with him. In a halting and untutored voice, Scrum sings the following lines from the song:

My name it is Maria, a merchant's daughter fair
And I have left my parents and three thousand pounds a year
My heart is pierced by Cupid, I disdain all glittering gold

And then, with fellow crew members joining in, continues:

There is nothing can console me but my jolly sailor bold.

---

136   Publicity materials for the film identify it as 'My Jolly Sailor Bold'. The song is more commonly known as 'Caroline and her Young Sailor Bold'. Its first written version appears to date from the 1840s and has been reported by folklorists who collected shanties and folk songs from Ireland, England, Scotland, Canada and the United States. See The Ballad Index (online) at: http://www.fresnostate.edu/folklore/ballads/LN17.html – accessed December 2013 – for further details on variants. A brief sequence from the song also features in an earlier scene in the film, being sung in a tavern where sailors are carousing before being recruited.

After a crew member splashes an oar in a further attempt to attract the mermaids' attention (prompting an echoing, non-diegetic bass note, as if the sound was resonating through the undersea realm), Scrum repeats the third and fourth lines before an ominous underscore rises during the repetition of the fourth line and precedes the arrival of a mermaid swimming to the boat.

The scene is cleverly designed to superimpose contrasting moods. While the sailors experience wonder and awe at the appearance of the mermaid and marvel at her ravishing beauty, they also dread her seductive power and her potential to lure them to their doom. Accordingly, Hans Zimmer's music is carefully constructed to support all of these elements. The underscore begins by enhancing the eerie atmosphere through the use of soft, sustained background sounds. These culminate in a very low-set brass chord before (non-diegetic) mer-voices enter in the form of high unison sopranos singing a wordless melody. The minor tonality of this melody, together with its emphasis on the semitone interval between the fifth and sixth scale degrees, provides a suitably eerie musical atmosphere.[137] The emergence of a string accompaniment that also highlights the semitone interval (this time between the second and third scale degrees) further enhances this atmosphere. Introduced by these tonalities, a beautiful young mermaid (named Tamara,[138] played by Gemma Ward) swims to the rowboat and holds on to its side, with her head and shoulders out of the water. Stunned by her presence, Scrum mutters "Lord Save Me" as the mermaid gazes fixedly at him while the evocative underscore continues. When one crewmember pulls a knife and stands aggressively, prompting Tamara to back off the bow, his colleagues restrain him while Scrum talks quietly to her, causing her to return. When he informs her that she is beautiful, she asks, apparently artlessly and innocently, "Are you the one who sings?" and then, smiling and more seductively, "Are you my jolly sailor bold?" After he bashfully answers in the affirmative, his fellow members try and hold him back from further engagement with her until he shakes them off, declaring that "there ain't much been given to me in my brief, miserable life, there's the truth in it but, by God, I'll have it said that Scrum had himself a kiss from a proper mermaid". Upon hearing this declaration, Tamara begins to sing the third and fourth lines from Scrum's song fragment, providing a striking contrast to the previous non-diegetic mer-vocals heard on the soundtrack by singing in a low-range, folk-style voice, with the camera showing a medium close-up of her face. Her voice is processed as she sings, through 'doubling', adding and subtracting reverb effects, and by moving the voice in and out of the background, adding two more lines of the song (not previously sung by Scrum), that (implicitly) call her sisters to the boat:

> Come all you pretty fair maids, whoever you may be
> Who love a jolly sailor bold that ploughs the raging sea

The previous two lines of the song are then repeated as other mermaids rise seductively beside the boat. Further tension is created in the score by bringing back the original (non-diegetic) mermaid melody as a strange-sounding string counterpoint to the diegetic

---

137   A sequence of similar music is heard briefly in the narrative earlier in the film, when the mermaids of Whitecap Bay are first mentioned.

138   As she is named in the film's promotional materials, rather than the film itself. See 'Tamara: Biography' at: http://pirates.wikia.com/wiki/Tamara – accessed December 2013.

folk melody and by adding new melodic elements (such as prominent major seventh scale notes). Tamara repeats her song lines about her heart being "pierced by Cupid" as she takes Scrum's head in her hands, pulling him down towards her as if to kiss him. As she completes the second line, she submerges her head below the water, then, as an instrumental passage and water noises create a moment of unease, her face transforms into a fanged (almost vampiric) one[139] as she attacks Scrum, uttering a scream that prompts the mermaids to mount a full-on assault on the boat.[140]

Similar combinations of seductive vocalese, murderous intent and monstrous transformation are also present in Milan Todorovic's film *Killer Mermaid* (2014), scored by Nikola Jeremic. The production's original Serbian title of *Mamula* refers to the location of much of its action on an (actual) Adriatic island that is infamous for being the site of a concentration camp run by Italian Fascist forces during World War Two. The film explains the origins of the predatory aquatic female who terrorises the area with reference to classic mythology. A character named Niko (Franco Nero) relates that the creature is one of an ancient race of sirens from the Sirenusas archipelago (off Italy's Amalfi coast) and explains that Mamula Island was a remote outpost of their marine empire. The film's plot involves a series of mysterious disappearances of young people. When a group of three locals and two American tourists visit the island they find a deranged man (Boban, played by Dragan Micanovic) feeding human body parts to a siren who lives there. Only two of the group survive their encounters with the siren and her aide and are rescued by Niko, who rows them to the mainland. A final confrontation between the siren and the three occurs just as they are about to tie up onshore, which results in the siren and her keeper being killed.

Female vocal sounds are used extensively throughout the film in scenes that initially allude to, and eventually show, the presence of mermaids. The first of these sounds occurs at the beginning of the film, during a scene involving a young couple at the water's edge. After the protagonists begin to undress and embrace, the camera moves to an underwater scene and the underscore introduces low, ominous, sustained rumbles together with the sound of human breathing. A melodic motif that previously accompanied the opening title sequence (and that becomes the main musical motif within the underscore) is recapped, using a pure sine-wave timbre. The underscore is removed as the camera returns

---

139 The figure of the vampire mermaid is also presented in a short series of low-budget video dramatisations of the *Scary Monsters* magazine graphic narrative series 'Destiny – The Vampire Mermaid' (which commenced in 1995). Following her appearance in related photo-shoots, singer and model Deborah Du Paul performed the role in the short video dramas *Crimson Currents* and *Death in the Dark* (Rusty Pietrzak and James Panetta, 2014). Despite Du Paul's singing abilities, this element is not developed in the productions. Du Paul also appeared in a similar, short low-budget video production entitled *Demon of Temptation* (2004) in which she played a mermaid who haunts a young woman and impels her to suicide. Fanged, predatory mermaids are also present as an incidental feature in the fantasy adventure film *SAGA: Curse of the Shadow* (John Lyde, 2013).

140 A variation of this type of aggressive transformative mermaid also featured in the 2006 pilot episode for an intended TV series (variously referred to as *Aquaman* and *Mercy Reef*) directed by Greg Beetman. The pilot provided an introduction to the series' titular character, who – as per his origins in the eponymous DC Comics' series – hails from Atlantis. While fully human in form he possesses special aquatic powers. The pilot involves Aquaman (Justin Hartley) being approached by an enticing young woman named Nadia (Adrianne Palicki). While swimming together, Nadia transforms into a mermaid with harsh facial features and vampire-like teeth. After he escapes her first attack she ambushes him again on a boat and fights him until he kills her by sticking a harpoon into her head.

to the young couple, and as the male becomes mesmerised by soft, distant female voices that his partner is unaware of. This scenario, in which a male is entranced by mermaid sounds that females are unable to hear, recurs throughout the film, emphasising the particular associations between human males and mermaids.[141] The eerie-sounding female vocal calls that attract the young man take the form of gentle breathing sounds, together with sustained moans with descending glissando tails. A single, pure, female voice then articulates the opening melodic motif of the film in the high vocal range. As the young man becomes increasingly mesmerised, these vocal utterances change to a cluster of soft, distorted, electronic sounds in a high pitch range (somewhat evocative of dolphin calls). An instrumental version of the main melodic motif is then played and the music rises to a crescendo as he leaps into the water. The drama is enhanced by the sudden removal of the underscore, briefly leaving only watery sounds, before he begins to swim frantically in an apparent effort to escape from an unseen presence in the ocean. The film's title then emerges in block capital letters on the seabed, signalling that he has been the victim of a mermaid attack.

The female vocal sounds introduced in the sequence described above (breathing, low moaning, downward glissandos, pure high sounds, clusters of distorted, dolphin-like calls) continue to serve as sonic indicators of the mermaid's presence during the lengthy sections of the film that precede her actual appearance. Similarly to the scene from *On Stranger Tides* discussed above, the siren represented in Todorovic's film alternates form between an archetypally lithe, attractive, young female with a fish tail (played by Zorana Obradovic) and a similar bodied creature with a monstrous face, sharp teeth and an array of horrific expressions. The alternations suggest the latter to be her true form and the former an appearance she generates to attract men. New sounds – including low guttural growls, agitated hissing, high screeching and sudden loud screams – are used to accentuate the frightening impact of scenes involving the monstrous version of the mermaid. As well as using a wide range of vocal sounds, the film also includes some explicit references to the overwhelming power of the mermaid's voice in its dialogue. For example, towards the end of the film, when the mermaid has been killed to the dismay of her heartbroken human lover/protector (Boban), Nico says, "someone might possibly have escaped from their singing, but from their silence certainly never", indicating that Boban has been totally possessed by mermaid song and will be unable to recover from its absence.[142]

---

141 It should be noted, however, that on one occasion late in the film a female character also appears to be mesmerised by a mermaid voice and subsequently closes her eyes and falls into the water.

142 In terms of cinematic realism, one of the problems with the representations of mermaid singing in *Killer Mermaid* (and some of the other films discussed above) is that characters are, at various points, represented as hearing song produced *below* the surface in the air *above* it. While the emergence of the mermaid's song from the depths of the sea gives it an innately otherworldly aspect, this is also a decidedly supernatural one in terms of the physics involved. Given that the films discussed above operate within the parameters of cinematic realism, this issue of sound source, transmission and perception merits some comment. Sound travels further and faster in water than it does in air. This is due to the very different nature of each. Put simply, air is a much more compressible medium than water. As a result, the surface of water, which comprises the barrier between the two mediums, acts as a reflector. As marine physicist Alec Duncan has identified, "only about 0.1% of the sound energy incident on the sea surface from either side will make it through to the other side" and therefore any mermaid singing below the surface would have to sing extremely loudly for her song to be heard above it (p.c. May 22nd 2015). There is a caveat to this characterisation, however, in that the hulls of boats can vibrate in response to sounds transmitted within water. But even in this case, Duncan has identified that "if the transmission occurred through the bottom of a boat then the song would be severely

A different take on the dangerously seductive power of mermaids' songs occurred in the short film *Heart's Atlantis* (Andrew Macdonald, 2008), scored by Siddhartha Barnhoom. This features Daniel (Samuel Wallis) as a young boy mourning his deceased mother and Hannah Fraser as a mermaid who appears in his backyard pool. Music plays a central role within the emotional narrative of the film. Sitting in his backyard the day after his mother's funeral, Daniel glimpses a beautiful mermaid before being called away by his father (Ty Hungerford). Skipping school, he returns to the pool and stares into it, with the underscore creating a magical atmosphere through a range of high, tuned percussion sounds. As the mermaid comes to the surface the score incorporates continuous arpeggios with harp sounds and rich low orchestral strings. A sudden, high sound occurs as she reaches out and touches the boy, followed by a section of quiet aural ambience, consisting of background pads and water sounds that continue as she begins to sing. Her unaccompanied song (performed by Daphne du Jong) is sung wordless (to "ah") and her vocal timbre is pure and lacking in vibrato, with extensive reverb added. Drawn by the sound, Daniel dives into the pool and swims with her. The pool space magically expands, allowing him to tumble blissfully underwater, wrapped in warm, lulling sound. Close to drowning, he is rescued by his father. Later that day he runs from the house and dives into the pool again. Once underwater, the mermaid's seductive song recurs in the score as they swim together again. His consciousness dims as the mermaid's vocal melody moves through a range of key centres and as he sees an apparition of his mother standing above the pool. Trying to reach the surface he is pulled back by the mermaid, as we hear more agitated, dissonant instrumental sounds and brief, dissonant vocal clusters. Glimpsing his mother again above the pool he finally manages to escape the mermaid and swims to the surface, implicitly choosing life over death and causing the sound and accompanying orchestration to recede from the soundtrack. The short film cleverly represents the dualistic aspect of mermaids' songs, evoking both the mother's lullaby and the siren's more deadly seductions. In Macdonald's film the lines between these blur and the mermaid's melodies primarily represent the option of the boy being reunited with his mother in death, an option he wisely declines.

More complex (although more idiosyncratic) representations of the dual nature of the mermaid as an alluring female and monstrous predator occur in *Harry Potter and the Goblet of Fire* (Mike Newell, 2005), scored by Patrick Doyle. The representations are complex in that they negotiate various versions of the mermaid myth, both in general and within the film. Hogwarts School, where Harry (Daniel Radcliff) and his fellow students reside, has a stained glass window that represents a conventional (i.e., young, slim and alluring) mermaid. Yet the mermaids that feature (later) in the film are far less human and more monstrous in appearance. Harry's introduction to the dualism of mer-folk occurs when he completes the first of his tournament tasks by retrieving a golden egg from a dragon's nest. Opening it back at Hogwarts, surrounded by his supporters, the egg emits loud hissing and screeching tones that deafen all in the room. Uncertain as to what these are,

distorted because the hull of the boat will respond much more strongly to some frequencies, and hence to some notes of the song, than to others" (ibid). While realist cinema's representation of fantastic themes is not bound to operate within the parameters of acoustic science, it is significant in the above regards that the mermaid's call in *Killer Mermaid* is often represented as much as a telepathic than an acoustic one.

what they portend, or how they might be interpreted, Harry closes the egg and goes on to consider how to comprehend its function as a clue. Revelation comes when another competitor suggests that he try opening the egg while taking a bath in the prefects' bathroom. After he fills the bath and climbs in, the mermaid in the window turns and looks at him and he, in turn, looks to the egg before opening it. As the stained glass image of the mermaid appears, a gentle underscore features watery sound effects blended with layers of simple melodic ideas based around a static C minor chord, including a three-note rising motif and a tonic arpeggio. When Harry opens the egg the gentle tone of the underscore is suddenly shattered as his ears are again assaulted by an intense, high frequency medley of screeching sounds, forcing him to close the egg again.

The intercession of 'Moaning Myrtle', the spirit of a deceased pupil, prompts him to open the egg under the water. At first, as he holds the egg down, the underscore shifts to a major key (B) and features very soft, reverberant female voices singing a simple melodic motif. Then, when Harry puts his own head underwater, a single female mer-voice singing a childlike song with a simple pentatonic melody replaces the earlier, screeching sound. Soft, reverberant female voices also provide a faint echo of the new melody – subtly conveying a sense of a mermaid sisterhood – and the words of the song inform Harry that his next task involves spending an hour underwater in the mermaids' haunt in nearby Black Lake:

> Come seek us where our voices sound
> We cannot sing above the ground
> An hour long you'll have to look
> To recover what we took

Appraised as to his task in the next stage of the tournament, Harry takes a potion that transforms him into a gilled and web-footed humanoid for his mission. The subsequent scene provides another engagement with the notion of mer-creatures as both seductive and dangerous, and the soundtrack is cleverly designed to reflect this duality. As Harry begins his underwater adventure in his modified form, a slightly ominous minor key motif highlights the semitone interval between the fifth and minor sixth scale degrees before a descending bassoon melody accompanies Harry's dive into the lake's depths. Faint mer-voices first appear in the form of wordless female vocal melodies, which subtly morph into a texture of gentle, overlapping major pentatonic motifs (based on the song that Harry heard when he opened the mermaid egg in the bath). Screeching sounds suddenly interrupt this gentle, seductive mood as a strange, octopus-like creature makes a fleeting appearance and the minor-key motif returns in a dramatic rhythmic form. The gentle major pentatonic theme appears again as Harry follows a mermaid-like creature, before the two main ideas (minor theme with semitone motif, overlapping major pentatonic motifs) are cleverly superimposed when Harry sees his classmates suspended in the mer-creatures' underwater lair. These creatures, with their frightening, inhuman faces, are markedly different from the mermaid figure Harry had seen in the stained glass window, and they make strange screeching and wailing sounds as they confront Harry with tridents.[143] More screeching sounds accompany Harry's battle with additional

143 Similarly monstrous marine humanoid creatures occur in an episode of the TV series *Primeval* entitled 'Underwater Menace' (Jamie Payne, 2008).

mer-creatures with octopus-like lower halves until he emerges, victorious, from the waters.

The brief sequences in *Harry Potter and the Goblet of Fire* discussed above suggest a range of mer-identities and vocalities that span the most conventional, in the form of the mermaid in the stained glass window (significantly only a representation, although apparently a sentient and animated one) through to the monstrous, tentacled creatures whose form more closely resembles Ursula, the sea witch in Disney's *The Little Mermaid* (Ron Clements and John Musker, 1989). The aquatic realm of the lake is emphasised as intractably other and as hostile to humans, with Harry only able to access it by taking on a semblance of mer-form (with gills and webbed feet) through a painful transitional process that invites comparison to the Little Mermaid's reverse transformation in Andersen's original short story. This transformation (male to quasi-merman) is relatively unusual in Western popular culture and is notable for being far briefer and far more precarious than the series of transformations of mermaids to human form described in the following chapter.

Conclusion

The mermaids represented in the films discussed above are slippery creatures. They slide between oceanic and terrestrial environments. Their voices cruise smoothly between notes in song, glide into human speech or, on occasion, flip into inhuman, mermaidic modes. Mermaids promise erotic bliss for terrestrial males but elude their possession as they remain inexorably in between realms of fantasy, desire and material existence. The mermaids of 1940s' and 1950s' cinema resemble the glittering femmes fatales of film noir in that their existence in the patriarchal (read 'terrestrial') order is tenuous and tantalising. However, unlike classic cinematic femmes fatales, who have no fluid, feminine realm outside patriarchy to escape to, Lenore and Miranda have access to their own autonomous spaces where they may variously recover from their terrestrial adventures or return to spawn. The 21st Century mermaids discussed in the later sections of this chapter exercise dominion over their aquatic realm with either a far more aggressive approach to the human males they encounter or else live a separate mer-life without apparent need for interaction with humans (*Harry Potter and the Goblet of Fire*). But whatever the outcome of their narratives, vocality is key to their engagement with humans. Their voices announce them as sensual, alluring creatures outside the realm of everyday human existence, initiate engagements with men that bypass linguistic courtship and, instead, offer a direct connection with an essential (albeit inhuman) feminine sensuality that is as fluid as the realm from which they emerge. In many ways, the impossibility of conventional coupling with the mermaid creates her voice as a fetish entity that appeals and stimulates in its own right, promising an alternative route to erotic rapture that bypasses genital sexual expression (and thereby avoids the problematic nature of such activity).

Chapter Four

Making Out: Sexuality and the Transformative Mermaid

On another night, one of the women, a Columbia University student who called herself Naiad after a water nymph from Greek mythology, floated around the room in an airy silk robe over matching undergarments. It was her second night at the club. She asked men, "What's your story?" When they asked her the same in turn, she told them she was a mermaid from the waters of Riverside Park. "I only grow limbs in the nighttime," she said. "And I enjoy what being a woman below the torso offers, because I don't take it for granted as much." A man asked her to go to a private room after a couple of dances. (Secret 2104: online – reporting on an evening at Manhattan's Bliss Bistro club)[144]

The anecdote related above encapsulates a particular development of mermaid media-lore that draws on a long-established association. Intentionally or not, the identity 'Naiad' chose to project to potential clients was one that was established in the European sex industry as early as the 1500s. In this period the term 'mermaid' became an English language euphemism for a prostitute, drawing on the use of the mermaid in medieval churches as a symbol of lust (or, rather of lust to be avoided). As the preceding chapters have elaborated, the perception and representation of mermaids as both sexually-motivated and as objects of human desire is a key (if complex) element

---

144 For a discussion of a range of New York based-women who identify with and/or perform aspects of mermaid culture see *Mermaids of New York* (Ilise Carter and Mica Scalin, 2015) and the related website: http://mermaidsofnewyork.com/tag/micawave/ – accessed January 27th 2016. A transformative mermaid (played by Katrina Cunningham) also features in Don Downie's short film *Pepper and the Salt Sea* (2015), set around Red Hook in Brooklyn in the aftermath of Hurricane Sandy.

in the figure's history and contemporary representation. Mermaids' sexual charisma relies on a number of aspects, including: most prominently, their representation as having the upper body of a young, attractive human female; their representation as variously amenable to and/or actively in pursuit of human male attention; their seductive vocal skills; and their most complicated sexual aspect, the allure and symbolism of their tails. As discussed in Chapter 2, the mermaid's tail can be understood as both a fetish attribute and as a physical feature that precludes the possibility of conventional penetrative sex. In this, the tail is somewhat of a provocative 'tease' to those who desire sexual interaction with mermaids. One way that this impasse has been circumvented is through the figure of the transformative mermaid. While the protagonists of Andersen's original story and Disney's film experienced traumatic and irreversible transitions to human form, the transformative mermaid present in late 20th and early 21st Century audiovisual culture switches with relative ease. This allows her to both enjoy genital pleasure (and/or more fully-rounded relationships with humans) and return to her original form. The representations of the transformative mermaid considered in this chapter include mainstream audiovisual productions, independent erotic features and overtly pornographic material. The latter, in particular, has provided a number of illuminating deconstructions and reconfigurations of the mermaid's form and its potential sexual functions.

I. *Splash* – Establishing a Template[145]

In one of the several synchronies in the production of mermaid films, two similarly-themed projects were in development in the early 1980s. One initiated at Columbia Pictures resulted in a script written by noted screenwriter and occasional director Robert Towne. Entitled *Mermaid*, the project concerned a middle-aged sailor developing a local marina who is approached by a mermaid who lives around a rock scheduled for removal. After meeting with the mermaid, who shows him how to perform water magic, he falls in love with her and resolves to spare her home.[146] But, unbeknownst to him, his wife is planning the demolition and tensions unfold until a happy resolution is reached.[147] Despite consid-

---

145 While *Splash* can be seen to have set the template for subsequent screen representations of transformative mermaids, it was not the first live-action film to explore this topic, being preceded by *Ondine* (also released as *Undine 74*), a Western European exploitation feature made by German director Rolf Thiele in Austria in 1973. Thiele's film drew on previous literary and dramatic interpretations of the myth of the water sprite Undine and on themes from Andersen's 'Den lille Havfrue' and featured a mermaid named Ondine (Angela von Radloff) arriving on land and assuming human form in order to gain love and, thereby, a soul. Events don't go as she plans and she returns to the sea when she fails to win the love of Hans (Ingo Thouret), the human she desires. Returning to land after five years in the sea (and a narrative ellipsis), she resumes contact with Hans. This is far from productive for either of them as he is about to marry Berta (Gundy Grand), who takes exception to his interaction with Ondine and murders him. Things go from bad to worse for Ondine as she is subsequently raped by a group of Berta's acquaintances. Despite her dire experiences onshore, her mother blocks her return to the sea and instead requires her to remain on land and to seek interactions with friendlier humans. Ondine appears in human form for the majority of the film and her mermaid identity is essentially a 'back story' that provides an explanation for the naive manner in which she behaves in the harsh social situations she encounters. Despite superficial similarities to *Splash* and to subsequent films featuring transformative mermaids it is effectively an isolate in terms of the textual cycle discussed in this chapter.

146 This element of the film is similar to the plot of the German film *Undine* (Eckhart Schmidt, 1992) which features Isabelle Pasco as a beautiful, fish-tailed water nymph living in an Alpine lake scheduled for development. Her charms prove so persuasive to the surveyor sent to map out the site that he colludes with her to sabotage the project.

147 See Scriptshadow (2013) for a critique of the script: https://www.facebook.com/permalink.php?story_fbid=1504478709768572&id=1496046613945115 – accessed July 16th 2015.

erable efforts to realise the project, which was slated at various times to include Herbert Ross as director, Warren Beatty as the male lead and Jessica Lange as the mermaid, it was eventually shelved. The other film, provisionally entitled *Wet*, was initially conceived by producer Brian Grazer in 1978. Grazer has identified that his interest in the project stemmed from frustrations he had in forming relationships with young women during his early career in the film industry:

> *Los Angeles is an industry town, and a lot of the good looking girls here are in the business and have all these phony bullshit standards. So I thought, wouldn't [it] be great to go out with a girl that was uncluttered, and didn't have all that phony junk in her. Then I thought, 'What about a mermaid?' I imagined that a mermaid would be an extraordinarily beautiful girl with an unblemished outlook towards life, and the story grew from here.* (Mayo 1984a: 15–16)

This frank statement of thwarted heterosexual ambition is notable for the different personalities Glazer attributes to "good looking" Los Angeles "girls" and his fantasy mermaid. He uses the term "phony" twice to refer to the former, emphasising his perception of them as insincere or deceitful. These vague and pejorative descriptions are contrasted to the (ambiguously) "unblemished outlook towards life" that he imagines that a mermaid would have (suggesting her as pure, sincere and amenable to male attention).

Following on from the initial impetus outlined above, Grazer and Fishman described the project as being based around 'kernel' questions:

> *What happens when a mermaid comes out of the ocean on to dry land? What would her impressions be, what would her life be like? What would happen if I got to meet that mermaid? What would it take to win her love – what would she have to give up? What would a man wooing her have to give up?* (2015: 103)

Grazer had a series of rebuffs for the project idea, which he initially pitched as a comedy, and then as a fantasy, before concluding that his initial treatment was too orientated to the mermaid's perspective. This resulted in a significant shift in his pitch:

> *So I thought, Okay, this isn't a mermaid movie – it's a love story! It's a romantic comedy with the mermaid as the girl. I recontextualized the movie. Same idea, different framework. I started pitching a movie that was a love story, between a man and a mermaid, with a little comedy thrown in.* (ibid: 104)

Provisional interest from United Artists' executive Anthea Sylbert (who, Grazer recalls, had a penchant for "mythology, fables, for a fairy-tale kind of thing" [ibid: 105]), led to the company employing screenwriter Jay Friedman to rework the original project. Grazer recalls this process as relatively straightforward, "it wasn't too hard to make the mermaid movie into a mermaid–man love story, and from that into a mermaid-man-love-story-fairy-tale" (ibid). Sylbert also required "rules" for the mermaid, with regard to "how she behaved in the ocean and how she behaved on the land (what happened to the tail, for instance?)" (ibid). Grazer also describes that Sylbert "wanted the audience to be in on the rules … She thought it would add to both the fun and the fairy-tale element" (ibid: 105–106). United Artists' interest ceased however when news of the rival Columbia film reached the company. Grazer then approached Disney. The company were interested but were concerned about brief nude scenes in the treatment and aspects of the sexual interaction between the lead characters, regarding these as being unsuitable for Disney's traditional family demographic. Despite this, the company perceived that the project – now entitled *Splash* - had likely box office appeal and agreed to release it through a newly-established adult-orientated division named Touchstone Pictures.

I detail Grazer's account of the lengthy gestation of his film project to give some context to synch-sound cinema's first extended representation of what is now a well-established media-loric trope: the transformative mermaid.[148] As Grazer has identified, the final product was "a romantic comedy with the mermaid as the girl" but – particularly for its decade – it also represented a highly sexualised inflection of the genre.[149] With director Ron Howard on board, Tom Hanks and Daryl Hannah were cast as the focal (male/mermaid) couple (named Allen Bauer and Madison) and the film's scenario explored the 'kernel' questions that Glazer had initially outlined.

Following Sylbert's suggestion, the audience were made aware of Madison's nature as a mermaid who can assume human form long before Allen realises the true nature of his lover and were also privy to extended representations of Madison swimming underwater. One of the most distinctive aspects of Madison's appearance – both in the film and in the broader history of screen representations of mermaids – concerns her tail and the manner in which Hannah uses it to swim in a convincing manner. Special effects designer Robert Short initially favoured a "dolphinesque mermaid, with a smooth gray skin that would be biologically real and make zoological sense" (Mayo 1984b: 93) but Howard preferred a more sensuous, "tropical" look (ibid). In order to realise this, Short provided a revised tail design based on the appearance of ornamental koi carp. Retaining his determination to give the tail a credible biological function and appearance, the tail was made out of a partially translucent urethane material named Skin-Flex (a material also used in the manufacture of prosthetic limbs), with supporting plexiglass inserts that helped the wearer exert leverage when kicking with it. The choice of material and the decision to use various hues of red and orange gave the tail a highly sensuous appearance.[150] Complementing the tail's colouration, a blonde wig was made for Hannah that allowed her long hair to float in the water in a sensual and 'un-clumped' manner (ibid: 94).

Hannah's convincing performance as a mermaid (particularly in the film's underwater sequences), derived from the firmness and flexibility of her tail, her agility as a swimmer and her empathy for the character. Hannah had a particular affinity for her role since she had strongly identified with the protagonist of Andersen's story as a child (and had even experimented with tying her feat together while wearing flippers and swimming like a mermaid in her family's backyard pool [Jerome 1984: online]). Indeed, her attraction to Andersen's story initially disinclined her to read Glazer's script as she aspired to produce her own, modernised version of the tale (Mayo 1984a: 16). Although Howard initially

---

148　I stress, *synch-sound* representation since both Méliès's *La Sirène* (1904) and the lost film *Neptune's Daughter* (Herbert Brenon, 1914) also featured transformative mermaids.

149　While graphic sexual themes are common in 21st Century rom-coms, 1980s' genre productions were far less explicit in representing sexual activity. (See director Rob Reiner's comments on the topic in Miller 2015: online.)

150　Which evokes the vivid descriptions of the mermaid's tail in the novel 'Peabody's Mermaid', discussed in Chapter 2.

conceived that the majority of underwater action shots of the mermaid would feature doubles, Hannah's swimming abilities caused him to reconsider:

> *It wasn't until he asked her to watch an audition of aquaballerinas for underwater double work that he knew he had a perfect catch. "I asked her to jump in just for size and shape," he recalls. "She started dolphin kicking, smiling and gliding. It was lyrical and beautiful. I told her, 'Do yourself, the movie and me a favor. Get in shape with the tail and do as many of the shots as you physically can.'"* (Jerome 1984: online)

While *Splash's* creative team have not acknowledged Andersen's 'Den lille Havfrue' as a direct inspiration, there are a number of close parallels in both plot and thematics. The most obvious elements of this include the film's male protagonist being rescued by a mermaid (twice in *Splash's* case, once as a child and once as an adult). Like the Prince's dim memory of his rescuer in Andersen's tale, Allen retains a vague memory of his first encounter with a mermaid. Like Andersen's female protagonist, Madison's time onshore in human form is limited. While she isn't threatened by the prospect of turning into sea foam, she is nevertheless stressed by the prospect of having to return to the sea without the human she desires. In this manner, the poignancy of Andersen's story, with its protagonist's heartfelt love for a human male and his struggle to find and recognise the female who rescued him, resounds in *Splash*. There is, however, one clear difference. Madison's ability to switch between mer- and human form with relative ease distinguishes her from the protagonist of Andersen's story[151] and is a defining aspect of her persona.

Splash opens with a brief flashback sequence set in Cape Cod "twenty years ago" (i.e. 1964)[152] that sets up the subsequent narrative and presents two distinct male approaches to romance and sexuality. The sequence represents its main protagonists' first brief meeting when a young Allen jumps overboard from a cruise boat after seeing something alluring in the water. The mysterious presence turns out to be a similarly-aged mermaid who sustains him until he is rescued. In contrast to this magical moment, his older brother, Freddie, is shown dropping coins on the ship's deck in order to gain the opportunity to look up women's skirts. Later, in present-day (i.e. 1984) New York, an adult Freddie is shown arriving at his family grocery business loudly proclaiming that he has had a letter published in *Penthouse* magazine and handing out copies to his employees. The extended nature of this sequence (together with mention of the magazine later in the film) strongly suggests product placement.[153] Since the repeated mentions and on-screen images of the magazine are largely incidental to the narrative they would appear to serve two, interre-

---

151   Indeed, Short deliberately tried to make transition scenes as un-horrific as possible, so as to prevent audiences feeling alienated from the character, aiming instead for transitions that would be "lyrical and dramatic" (Mayo 1984b: 96).

152   In the film Cape Cod stands as a remote and pre-modern counterpart to New York, much as Cornwall does to London in *Miranda* and *Mad About Men*. While Cape Cod doesn't have as marked an association with mermaid mythology as Cornwall does it has a number of relevant associations, including the use of Western mermaid folklore as a minor element of local maritime culture. There is also an aquatic female figure in regional First Nations' folklore (see Reynard 1934).The area's strongest contemporary association with mermaids derives from the paintings of celebrated native Cape Cod artists Martha and Ralph Cahoon, who produced a number of representations of mermaids and their interaction with young men around the coast of Cape Cod during the 1960s–1990s.

153   While I have been unable to locate documentation that establishes this, Boyle identifies that magazines such as *Penthouse, Playboy* and *Hustler* have historically secured product placement in Hollywood films (2010: 140).

lated purposes: to promote the magazine in the film and, thereby, to associate Freddie with the male sexual swinger scene that the magazine was associated with (in distinction to Allen, who is represented as less sexually pre-occupied). Shortly after the initial grocery depot sequence the film introduces the adult Madison when she arrives naked, in human form, at Liberty Island where she is (with no little irony) promptly seized by police and led away.

Madison arrives at Liberty Island as a result of her second encounter with Allen in the sea. After attending a wedding, Allen gets drunk and maudlin about his inability to find love and decides to take a taxi to Cape Cod (which holds a mysterious appeal for him). After meeting an irascible marine biologist named Dr Kornbluth (Eugene Levy), he sets out across the bay in a boat, falls overboard and is knocked unconscious, with his wallet tumbling to the sea floor. The viewer sees him rescued by an adult mermaid who brings him to shore. Upon waking he sees a beautiful young woman with luxuriantly tangled blonde hair peering at him from behind vegetation and calls to her. She then tries to run past him to the sea but stops, approaches and kisses him, before diving into the water and swimming away, leaving him, somewhat dazed. As he turns away, Madison breaches the surface and displays her (regenerated) fish tail to the camera and audience. She then swims down and retrieves Allen's wallet (with his ID and address in it). After looking up the location of New York on a map in a sunken ship, she swims south to pursue him on land.

Since he was unconscious when Madison rescued him in mermaid form, Allen recalls the incident on the beach as one where he encountered a mysterious, nubile young woman. Like the prince in 'Den lille Havfrue', this memory tantalises him. Shortly after his trip to Cape Cod he gets a call from the police telling him that they have found a mute young woman who has his ID with her. Guessing her identity, he rushes to meet her. Upon his arrival the female gazes fixedly at him and then commences kissing him in the police station. Taking her back to his apartment building, she can barely contain her desire and kisses him passionately in the lobby. The couple are then shown entering the lift, with its external indicator subsequently showing that it has stopped between floors (suggesting that the couple have paused to engage in congress). After a fade, the scene shows Allen elated in his apartment, about to leave in order to return to work for the afternoon. After initially trying to resist Madison's attempts to re-commence sexual interaction by declaring, "please, no, you're gonna put me in a hospital", he quickly acquiesces. These scenes present a particularly pro-active form of female sexuality (of a type common to porn cinema in the period) in which a woman engages insatiably with a male without the necessity of contemporary courtship rituals and/or progressing through stages of intimacy. In this context it is Madison's lack of implication within particular morals and mores, which makes her so appealing to Allen. She is both socially naive and 'liberated', in that she has not learned to restrict her behaviour or expectations. Her fixation on Allen is unrestrained and unconditional in both emotional and sexual terms. In this regard she directly represents the previously discussed fantasy figure born from producer Grazer's perceptions of and frustrations at dealing with Los Angeles women. As *Movieline* magazine expressed it five years after the film's release, this aspect appeared to resonate with a particular demographic, "playing Madison, the innocently randy mermaid in *Splash*, thrust Hannah into the collective fantasies of a good percentage of America's male population" (1989: online), with the result that "Hannah became the blonde of the moment, among the first to get a crack at "A" scripts, with covers of Life, and People to attest to her visual appeal" (ibid).

Once Madison miraculously acquires English Language competence after a day watching TV broadcasts in Bloomingdale's Department store, the narrative revolves around two aspects of her secret identity: her attempts to find the right time to inform Allen that she is a mermaid temporarily transformed into human form, and Dr Kornbluth's attempts to prove that very identity in order to claim her as his scientific discovery. Kornbluth first encounters Madison underwater shortly after she rescues Allen. Despite the scepticism of his scientific peers, he becomes obsessed with finding her again, thereby proving that mermaids exist. Suspecting that she can transition to human form, he locates a woman he believes to be her in Manhattan, stalks her and attempts to reveal her true identity by soaking her legs in an attempt to get them to revert to tail form. After mistakenly dousing a wrong woman (twice) and having his arm broken by her enraged partner, he finally ambushes Madison and succeeds in 'outing' her while Allen looks on, aghast.

The sequence in which Madison involuntarily reverts to mer-form invites audience sympathy. She is represented as clearly distressed and is surrounded by flashing cameras before she is led away by security staff while Allen looks on without attempting to intervene. This scene, and a subsequent one where he initially recoils from her when he sees her in a large water tank, is notable in terms of the corpus of mermaid films discussed in this book. While many male characters (such as Paul, in *Miranda* [1948]) are initially startled when they realise the identity of the females they are with, they quickly become comfortable with and appreciative of their mermaid's anatomies. Allen's unease persists until his compassion for Madison's deterioration in captivity prompts him to collude with Kornbluth and facilitate her escape. Love then revives and the film ends with the couple evading pursuit and diving into the Hudson River together and setting off for a new life in the ocean – represented as a realm of pure delight away from the restrictions of metropolitan existence.

Hannah's performance as Madison is key to the film's impact. Her physicality and agency are striking. She is represented as powerful and empowered in underwater sequences, rescuing humans and even fighting off military divers (in the final moments of the film). This aspect also carries through into her alternative human form, where she is assertive and determined in pursuing her desires. This is cleverly combined with her representation as romantically direct and vulnerable (echoing Grazer's initial imagination of a mermaid as "unblemished" by opportunism and/or pretension). In these contexts her (not inconsiderable) libido is shown to reflect her simple and uncomplicated desire for a committed monogamous relationship with a human male (who also desires the same). In these regards, while she embodies many of the aspects originally imagined by Glazer, her mer-identity is so vividly and convincingly rendered that she has a coherent individuality and credibility as a character. While she may have been an attractive fantasy figure for male viewers (as identified in the above *Movieline* quotation) she was also, as detailed in Chapter 6, a significant inspiration for later generations of female mermaid aficionados who were attracted to her capacity for autonomous action and her mastery of the aquatic environment.

Splash's box office success[154] resulted in the production of a follow-up, *Splash Too* (Greg Antonacci, 1988), made with different actors playing the lead roles established in the original. The film returns Madison (Amy Yasbeck) and Allen (Todd Waring) to Manhattan for further adventures. Unlike the original film, which was consciously made for an adult audience, the follow-up was produced for and first screened on the Disney Channel and, unsurprisingly, had a markedly lower sexual emphasis than its predecessor.[155] The film was set four years after the original (although the new lead actors, somewhat confusingly, look younger than Hannah and Hanks in the original film). The plot involves Allen becoming bored with living on a tropical island with Madison and returning to New York. Back onshore, Allen works on reviving his family grocery business while Madison, Allen and his brother Freddie manage to liberate a dolphin from an aquarium where a crazed scientist is conducting experiments on cetacean brains. After various trials and tribulations Madison agrees to live onshore and to raise a family with Allen rather than return to the sea. The thin plotline, re-casting of leads and lack of appealing new elements resulted in muted reviews and audience indifference. As a result, Disney decided against releasing the film on VHS format in North America and it has not subsequently been released on DVD.[156]

II. *Splash's* Porn Parodies

While *Splash Too* toned down the sexual orientation of the 1984 original, this aspect was amplified as the central feature of two porn parody films,[157] *Talk Dirty to Me Parts III* and *IV* (Ned Morehead, 1984 and 1986). These productions were instalments in a series that commenced with *Talk Dirty to Me* (1980), written and directed by Anthony Spinelli. The film, about a man convinced that he can seduce any woman, was commercially successful and received some (albeit begrudging) praise from critics for its combination of a narrative frame, convincingly written character roles (at least for a porn feature) and spirited performances by leads Jessie St James and John Leslie.[158] *Talk Dirty to Me II* (Tim McDonald, 1982) also starred Leslie and had a similar plotline and characters to its predecessor. A major deviation from the series' format occurred in 1984 when director Ned Morehead took over to direct a porn parody script inspired by *Splash*, written by producer Jerry Ross.

Talk Dirty to Me Part III (henceforth referred to as *TDTM III*) opens with images of the sea and a deserted beach accompanied by a classic fairy tale introduction, "Once upon a

---

154 The film took just under US$70,000,000 at the US box office on initial release. (Source: http://pro.boxoffice.com/statistics/movies/splash-1984 – accessed April 15th 2015.)

155 The only overtly sexual element takes the form of a visual double entendre that occurs when Allen ducks under a dining table in a restaurant to dry off Madison's mermaid tail, which has sprouted following an accidental water spill. Madison's wriggles, Allen's position and the bemused reaction of another couple eating at a nearby table might be considered to suggest that he is engaging in cunnilingus with her.

156 Elements of the *Splash* formula were blended with aspects of *The Little Mermaid* in an episode of the TV series *Hercules: The Legendary Journeys* entitled 'Love on the Rocks' (Rick Jacobson, 1999) in which Angela Dotchin played a mermaid named Nautica who falls for a human. The mermaid returns in a subsequent episode, entitled 'My Best Girl's Wedding' (Andrew Merrifeld, 1999), where her human lover rescues her from a forced marriage and is rewarded by being turned into a merman.

157 See Chapter 1 section VII for an introduction to the nature of porn parody as a form.

158 See Hampton (2007: 393–393) and Taylor (2009: 260–263)

time in a land not too far away", spoken by a young female. The narrator then goes on to describe the plight of a restless young woman intent on finding a man in a location where "men were in very short supply", requiring her to "look elsewhere". The "elsewhere" is immediately represented as the shore, where – in an echo of the openings of the 1948 films *Mr Peabody and the Mermaid* and *Miranda* – a fisherman snags (what appears to be) a naked young woman on his line (played by Traci Lords in the original version and by Lisa De Leeuw in a subsequently modified one[159]). The voiceover continues, referring to the protagonist in the third person:

She knew that finding someone to love wouldn't be easy, it never is. But in her case it would be doubly hard because she was different from the rest. You see, she was a mermaid.

The latter characterisation is reinforced on screen by the image of a mermaid swimming, with her long, golden tail fully visible. The film's opening is relatively unusual in that a female voice functions as an *acousmêtre* (see Pisters 2003: 181, referring to Silverman 1988). Chion defines the *acousmêtre* as a "character whose relationship to the screen involves a specific kind of ambiguity and oscillation" that is "neither inside nor outside the image":

It is not inside, because the image of the voice's source - the body, the mouth - is not included. Nor is it outside, since it is not clearly positioned offscreen in an imaginary "wing", like a master of ceremonies or a witness, and it is implicated in the action, constantly about to be part of it. (1990: 129)

There are a number of ambiguities and oscillations to the voice-over in *TDTM III* that are related to the mermaid who is central to the narrative and, in particular, with her assumption of human form. While the young and innocent-sounding narrator's voice suggests itself as compatible with the image of the young mermaid we see on screen it is displaced from the temporal moment of the mermaid's arrival onshore in a significant manner. After introducing the mermaid and her mission, the *acousmêtre* continues:

Considering the circumstances, she decided she better look up some friends she knew - and fast - but not knowing the language made it a little difficult for her to ask directions. Luckily she stumbled upon a place that made her feel right at home.

This comment signals that language (and language acquisition, in particular) is a key issue for the mermaid and for the film. The place the mermaid chances upon turns out to be Ocean Park Naturalist Club on its 'Ladies' Day'. This involves a variety of naked young women participating in keep fit exercises and sunbathing, watched by two men (one of whom is Jack, played by John Leslie, reprising his role in the earlier *Talk Dirty* films). Suspecting that Jack and the Club's female fitness trainer are about to engage in intimacies, the mermaid instantly, and seemingly effortlessly, transforms to human form and comes ashore to spy on them. From a concealed position she hears Jack uttering various profanities about genital anatomy and sexual activities before the trainer falls for his advances and fellates him before he penetrates her vaginally and then ejaculates over her breasts. The couple's interaction arouses the mermaid and prompts her to stimulate her

---

159   Twelve years after the film's production it was discovered that Lords was sixteen when the film was produced and a second version of the film was produced in which Lords' scenes were re-shot with actress Lisa De Leeuw.

newly acquired genitalia. As Jack departs the scene of his congress he encounters her and they briefly kiss and caress before he becomes distracted and she slips away. The scene is significant for two main and fundamentally connected reasons. The first is that the couple's classic porn-film-style sexual interaction is understood by the mermaid to represent typical human sexual interactions and, second, that the couple's verbal interactions – in which they 'talk dirty' to each other, as per the film's title – is taken by the mermaid as a standard linguistic description of and accompaniment to sexual activity.

The film's principal plotline brings Jack and the mermaid together for a sex scene after a number of delays and digressions. There are also various subplots that facilitate dramatic interactions and sex scenes between other characters, including a trio of other mermaids (in human form) who reside together in a beach house as they attempt to form relationships with human males. In the mermaid's initial interaction with her friends she visits their house and remains in the water, fish-tailed, while they tease her about her lack of any human speech aside from the basic phrases she has picked up from watching her first sexual interaction. Their principal assistance is to instruct her as to colloquial names for parts of the female anatomy. Throughout the film these are the main terms she recalls and can repeat, ensuring that her interaction with human characters is somewhat limited.

Following their initial brief encounter at the resort, Jack and the mermaid meet again at a villa where she tries out her newly acquired skills in 'talking dirty'. Jack is clearly attracted to her but is disconcerted and makes a rapid exit after she is accidentally knocked into a swimming pool, with the result that her legs transform into a tail. Jack subsequently broods on the encounter and visits an occasional lover, a marine biologist named Helen Spangler (Amber Lynn), in order to learn more about mermaids. She is sceptical, declares that mermaids don't exist and compares his description of a mermaid who alternates mer- and fully-human form to a movie she once saw (implicitly *Splash*). But she also states that "according to folklore they are one of the most amorous creatures alive" and that they are also "extremely loyal". While this is a somewhat selective interpretation of mermaid folklore it is broadly congruent with a number of traditional themes concerning mermaids' interactions with human males and appears to whet Jack's appetite for further interactions with her.

Unbeknownst to Jack and Dr Spangler their interaction has been overheard by a visiting salesman who invites Jack to provide him with proof of the mermaid's existence in return for cash. After initially cooperating with him, Jack becomes uneasy when the salesman announces his intention to catch the mermaid and sell her to Ocean World and withdraws his cooperation. Jack then seeks her out, just as she is about to return to the ocean. Finding her sad, disillusioned and now more fully in command of the English language, Jack persuades her to come back to his house to hide. In the course of discussing their emergent relationship Jack comments on her newfound linguistic development, stating, "I liked you a lot better when you talked dirty". She replies, "What good did it do me? You're afraid of me anyway". He replies that he just needed time to get used to things. Warming to him, she smiles, her lower body instantly transforms to a human one and she returns to uttering short, sexually explicit phrases, leading Jack to comment "I love the way you talk" and to commence sexual interaction with her.

When the salesman subsequently arrives and attempts to seize her the couple escape underwater. The film concludes with a return of the voice-over, providing a synopsis of the story:

> So the mermaid finally got Jack and everybody lived happily ever after. And the moral to our story? To stay wet on dry land you have to learn the language [laughs]. Good talking to you.

The film's final comment (which might also be taken to allude to Madison's acquisition of English language skills in *Splash*) can also be seen to represent the manner in which the mermaid's transformative interaction on land involves her eschewing the affective phallic vocality of the mermaids discussed in Chapter 3 in order to enter the masculine/hetero-normative speech world of human society. One of the paradoxes of *TDTM III* as a porn parody is that it closely parallels aspects of its referent text. *TDTM III's* mermaid may have 'talked dirtier' than Madison but it was the latter who actually initiated and enjoyed sexual interactions earlier in her film's narrative. Rather than a porn parody, in the established sense, *TDTM III's* representation of the mermaid was more of an imitation of aspects of its referent text, framed by a group of sex scenes that were essentially similar to *TDTM I* and *II*. *TDTM III's* mermaid falls for a specific human, Jack, and – throughout – exhibits the quality Dr Spangler attributes to her species (and the quality Madison manifests), namely loyalty in the face of adversity.

Talk Dirty to Me Part IV (henceforth *TDTM IV*) followed in 1986, drawing loosely on aspects of its predecessor[160] and featuring Leslie back in role as Jack. The film dispensed with the language and language acquisition issues of its predecessor and instead added a science fiction element. The film opens with a group of young women in a room being briefed that they only have three days before having to leave their locale because the water has become so polluted that it could be fatal to them. It soon becomes apparent that the three women are mermaids in human form. Another problem they have is that one of their number has gone missing. Showing an awareness of Jack's interests in mermaids (as demonstrated in *TDTM III*) they approach him and ask him to assist them. In the course of his mission Jack discovers that there are no mermen where these particular mermaids come from, with the result that they have to visit land in a "mating pilgrimage" in order to breed. Jack eventually finds the missing mermaid working in a sushi restaurant, has sex with her and persuades her to leave with him. The final scene takes place back in the room shown in the film's opening, with the women in ceremonial costumes as they prepare to depart. When Jack asks where the mermaids' home is he receives the somewhat puzzling reply that they will blink a light for him. The film ends with the top of the building lifting off into the night sky, transformed into a spaceship that is returning the mermaids to their home planet.

III. Erotic Deconstruction and Reconfiguration

Subsequent to the two *Splash* porn parodies in the *TDTM* series, the most notable utilisation of mermaid imagery for pornographic purposes in live-action media occurred

---

160 One variance from *TDTM III* concerns the nature of the mermaids' bodies in the fourth film. In an innovation, when Jack asks one who visits him in human form to undress in order to prove that she is a mermaid, her breasts are shown to be concealed with flowers that are seamlessly interwoven with a green body garment that morphs into a fishtail that she can, somewhat surprisingly, stand erect on.

in three of the four scenes in Madison Young's 2013 video *Mermaids and Unicorns*.[161] Young, an erotic film performer, director, author and educator who co-ordinates the Feminist Porn Network, has described her overall approach as:

> *expanding the conversation about the complex identities of people in LGBTQ, kink, sex worker, and sex-positive communities ... The work I do is about creating space for people to feel confident and safe in exploring their full and complete identity without judgment. If we are able to expand this to a mainstream level, it breaks a wall of isolation that individuals might feel when they are discovering parts of their identity that might set them apart from the people they see around them.* (Martin 2012: online)

Made a quarter of a century after the *TDTM* films discussed above, *Mermaids and Unicorns* is very different in tone and style. The video features four sex scenes with a thematic (rather than narrative) linkage. Each scene involves a female couple interacting in a role-play scenario where one or both of the characters are in role as mermaids (in three instances) or as unicorns (in two). The three mermaid-themed scenes differ considerably with regard to the prominence of the mermaid motif and the means of its dramatisation. The opening scene is the only one shot out of doors and features the (suitably named) Lorelei Lee as a mermaid and Baretta James as a sailor. The action takes place on rocks at the edge of the sea and the sequence's soundtrack is dominated by the sound of wind buffeting the microphone and the noise of crashing surf (giving the scene a far more realist sonic element than many of the films discussed in this volume). The mermaid, initially wearing a purple fabric tail, a turquoise bikini top and string of pearls, beckons the sailor over and starts kissing and caressing her. Three minutes into the scene the couple remove the mermaid's fabric tail and then commence an extended erotic interaction that occupies the remainder of the scene's 30-minute duration. While Lee retains a blue tasselled mini-skirt and shell belt throughout the scene, this and the coastal locale are the only markers of the scene's mermaid theme after the initial scene-setting sequences.

By contrast, the video's second scene – the longest in the production, running for 49 minutes – features a sustained and concentrated exploration of mermaid media-lore and of aspects of Disney's *The Little Mermaid* in particular. As the following discussion identifies, the women play with conventions of mermaid form and function as part of their sexual–emotional interactions. The scene takes place in a bedroom decorated with metallic mermaid wall ornaments and a framed mermaid painting. Young and actress Ela Darling are shown reclining next to each other wearing pearl and shell necklaces and bracelets, seashell bras and luxurious fabric mermaid tails (Young's in white silk and pale blue edgings, Darling's in light brown with crimson edgings, see Figure 13). The couple begin kissing, caressing each other's genitals through the fabric and then remove each other's shell bras. Their increasing arousal leads Young to pick up a knife and slice open the tail material around Darling's buttocks. After licking and fingering her exposed genitals, Young places a dildo on top of her own tail and Darling first fellates and then straddles this. Darling then reciprocates by stimulating Young's clitoris with a vibrator through

---

161 There are also other short, erotic videos available online that include elements of basic mermaid costume play – such as *Lesbian Mermaids* (director unknown, 2014) – but none have the complex and varied aspects of *Mermaids and Unicorns*.

Figure 13 – Production still from *Mermaids and Unicorns* shoot (scene 2) (Young to left of image, Darling to right) (reproduced by permission of Filly Films).

her tail fabric before taking the knife and cutting through the rear of Young's tail (and then stimulating her orally, digitally and with a vibrator). As Young's arousal becomes more marked, the couple engage in verbal role-play that draws on mermaid media-lore and gives it lesbian inflections, with Young repeatedly characterising herself as Darling's "mer-slut". After Darling pulls the remnants of Young's tail off, the couple indulge in further verbal role-play that derives from the scenario of *The Little Mermaid*. Young comments, "I feel like I'm becoming more human" to which Darling replies, "usually you have to give up your voice for this". Young then offers to do this but Darling instead requests Young to sing, which she does, wordlessly approximating aspects of the melody of 'Part of Your World' from the Disney film to the best of her abilities (given that she appears close to orgasm). After removing the remnants of her tail, Young again characterises herself as a "mer-slut" for her lover as she approaches a further climax, only for Darling to correct her and remind her that she is now a "human slut" (now that her legs are revealed). Initiating the final part of the scene (and referring to the lyrics of the aforementioned song) Darling asks, "Shall I grow legs and become part of your world?" When Young agrees, Darling removes her fishtail and Young pleasures her for the remainder of the scene.[162] The scene ends with Young saying "I don't know whether I can put you back in the sea" to which Darling replies "Just keep me forever".

The third and fourth scenes of the video feature variations on the practice known as *equus eroticus*, a fetish role play in which one individual takes on the role of trainer or rider while the other plays the pony.[163] The video presents a variation of this with female characters wearing ornamental unicorn horns on their foreheads (providing obvious phallic symbolism). After a scene between two women, involving one in role-play as a unicorn being dominated by another, which doesn't involve any mermaid role play, the final scene

---

162 Further verbal role play occurs when Darling refers to the coolness of a metallic dildo that Young is using on her, saying that, "it doesn't get any warmer at the bottom of the sea" and later urging Young to "eat me up like a sea monster".

163 See http://www.submissiveguide.com/encyclopedia/pony-play/ – accessed August 21st 2015 – for a summary of this practice.

features Baretta James, as a unicorn, and Missy Minks, as a mermaid. Their costumes are fairly perfunctory, James's role being signified by her silver horn and Minks's by a sparkly blue-green top and a red fabric tail that is removed some three minutes into the 28-minute-long sequence. Mermaid-related role-play activity mainly occurs in the final part of the scene when James asks Minks to go into the shower because she wants to see her "grow a tail". Switching to the bathroom, James sits in the bath with her red fabric tail back on while James showers her before the couple use the shower nozzle in extended genital play. The shower scene ends with James delivering a line that appears to tie the video compilation's fairytale themes together, declaring that, "the little mermaid fell deeply in love with the unicorn and they lived happily ever after".

While Jung (1968) identified the mermaid as a primordial archetype of the female configured within male consciousness (and subsequently disseminated through mythology), scenes 1, 2 and 4 of *Mermaids and Unicorns* engage with the symbols and scenarios of mermaid folk- and media-lore in exclusively female erotic game-playing scenarios. Reflecting this, the DVD's promotional material describes its contents as "an orgasmic array of femmelicious fantasies come true". The term "femmelicious" originated in the late 2000s and refers to aspects of femme lesbian identity (often somewhat reductively characterised as being the opposite of butch [i.e. a stereotypically masculinist] lesbian identity). In the context of the DVD, the term "femmelicious" appears to refer to various aspects of erotic interactions between femme women and a broader sex-positive attitude that informs Young's Filly Films' productions in general. But while the material featured in the DVD may appear to operate outside of the usual parameters of heterosexual desire it is also conducive to what Williams identifies as a pervasive "male heterosexual pleasure in lesbian spectacle" (2005: 205) that most usually manifests itself with regard to representations of femme lesbian interaction. In this regard, the DVD can be seen to offer figures of erotic appeal to both heterosexual male spectators and to female spectators attracted to representations of "femmelicious" sexuality.

One of the most distinctive twists on the sexual identity and activity of the transformative mermaid occurs in the five-minute-long video, *The Mermaid: The Siren of Seduction* (2011), produced by TSSeduction, a company that specialises in high production value short films featuring transsexual performers. Evoking the opening sequence of the atmospheric, mermaid-themed *Night Tide* (1961), shot around Santa Monica Pier, with Denis Hopper playing a sailor, the video opens with a mermaid (Yasmin Lee) floating in a seawater pen in the lower section of a pier at night, swaying with the motion of the sea. Pulling herself out of the water, she sits on a rail, swaying her glittery, blue tail. The soundtrack then features heavily processed and sustained electronic vocal tones, causing a sailor who has wandered in to turn and look at her. Her tail is shown, audibly flicking the ground, drawing him towards her. As he approaches her, the music cuts out and in the shadows, accompanied by the sounds of lapping waves, she smiles and lets him kiss her. After a fade to black, the scene shows the mermaid transformed into fully-human form, with her middle body covered by an elaborate loincloth, in an 'Arabian Nights' style boudoir constructed in the pier space. The sailor is shown unconscious, bound in white cord, until she awakes him by ardently fellating him. After this awakening, the mermaid reveals another facet of her identity, a large erect penis. The remaining two thirds of the video shows the transsexual mermaid anally penetrating the sailor and being fellated by him, to his apparent pleasure. The video provides a novel representation of the mermaid as a phallic female who transforms the appeal of the large twitching tail in its opening sequence to that of an actual penis. In control, and in avaricious pursuit of 'her' orgasm throughout, the mermaid is represented as fluid in her gender identity and role. In her transformed state she retains the upper body beauty of her female mer-form but replaces her phallic tail with a human phallus. She is also, significantly, the active (stereotypically masculine) participant in the sex scene. She does not offer herself for anal penetration and the scene ends with her ejaculation, rather than his.

The TSSeduction video represents one of the most radical representations of the mermaid discussed in the volume with regard to her human form being that of a 'shemale'. The latter term is commonly used in the sex industry to refer to a biological male with secondary female characteristics (usually augmented breasts) who presents as female in all but genital functionality.[164] Lee, who is one of the highest profile transsexual actresses in the United States,[165] is known for her exotic inter-racial appearance (being of Cambodian, Thai, Chinese and Brazilian descent). Her role in the film represents the most striking 'queering' of the mermaid to date, suggesting a latent element of the appeal of the mermaid to ostensibly 'straight' heterosexual males that has only hitherto been expressed through the *symbolism* of the mermaid's tail (as discussed in the Introduction and elsewhere in this chapter). In combination with the film's representation of the mermaid's seductive voice, the transformed mermaid in TSSeduction's video is triply phallic – with her tail, her voice and the actual penis she gains and deploys in her interaction with her submissive sailor partner. In terms of the discussions advanced in this volume, she is as 'out there' as a mermaid can go, intervening in the phallic order and engaging with masculine desires through deployments that transcend any characterisation of her form, essence and appeal as being premised on the lack of a phallus.

If the TSSeduction's shemale mermaid represents an ultra-phallic interpretation of the mermaid and her sexual symbolism, the Permaid, a woman fully covered in skin-tight, black latex complete with fish tail, represents an opposite polarity, a *reductio ad absurdum* of the mermaid's absence/concealment of genitalia. The Permaid is a creation of two Los Angeles-based artists, fashion designer Nicolette Mishkan, who performs the Permaid role, and photographer Aeschleah De Martino, who documents her public appearances. The Permaid's social interactions are communicated via social media applications such as Instagram and Tumblr and in the short film *Brentwood Manor* (De Martino, 2015). Unlike the transformative cinematic mermaids discussed above, or the mermaids featured in *Mermaids and Unicorns* (whose tails can be sliced through or otherwise removed to access concealed genitals), the Permaid's all-embracing body suit remains in place throughout her performances. She is as she appears on the surface; her black skin is not so much a covering that veils her physique as it is a body without orifices that is openly presented to the spectator. She is a complex erotic manifestation. She is an impossible object of desire

164 Despite their titles, the Brazilian transsexual porn films *Exotic Blonds – Mermaids with Dicks* (director unknown, 2002) and *Recruits in Training: Mermaids with Dicks* (M. Wax, 2002) do not actually feature mermaids, the term being used allusively.

165 She has also appeared in mainstream cinema, such as *The Hangover Part II* (Todd Phillips, 2011).

Figure 14 – Set-up photo – 'She thinks his name is Danny' (reproduced by permission, Aeschleah DeMartino and Nicolette Mishkan, 2014).

for males, with regard to the conventional satisfaction of heterosexual desire, in that she is manifestly unavailable for penetrative sex. At the same time she is highly sexual, with the tight black 'skin' of her suit adhering tightly to her slender, curvaceous body. The mermaid suit worn by Mishkan derives from a well-established sexual fetish practice involving the wearing of tight polyester fabrics (such as PVC or latex), whose constriction can be interpreted as a form of bondage. Clad in an all-embracing 'second skin' (often in black), the body and persona of the wearer can assume different guises, distanced from the wearer's usual personality. The Permaid represents one particular version of this practice that also engages the symbolism of the mermaid's tail.

One of the duo's regular performance activities in 2014–2015 involved them seeking male partners for the Permaid via the dating application Tinder. The duo then interacted with men who responded via the application and invited some to meet them and, if agreeable, participate in a date with the Permaid. As the Permaid's online visual documentation indicates, many have been more than willing to accept such invitations and have agreed to have their interactions visually recorded. Several of the images presented on the Permaid's Instagram site (idpermaid.com) such as Figure 14, show the Permaid and one or more partners in what appears to be post-coital repose, tantalising the viewer through the ambiguity of what might have occurred. The Permaid's presence in these, and other scenes, is often awkward. Many of the situations she is represented in recall the little mermaid's frustrations in Andersen's and Disney's stories. In mer-form, the otherness of the little mermaid's physique precludes her from bonding with her prince and entering the world of human society. Similarly, in her transformed state she is mute and also excluded from a social order. Many of the photos of the Permaid and sequences in the film *Brentwood Manor* show her in situations where she is going through the motions of interactions but is unable to fully participate in and enjoy them. The ambiguous imagery of Figure 14 captures this. The Permaid's hand upon her brow may signify frustration and despair (rather than the relaxation of sleep) and might be read as a further manifestation of the absurdity of the mer-form within the context of the expression of heterosexual desire.

While the Permaid is a highly original figure in contemporary media-lore, the duo has identified that they had a particular point of reference and identification for her that derived from watching Disney's *The Little Mermaid* as children:

> *We were both more interested in Ursula when we were young girls. She embodied a more accurate and attractive version than Ariel did for us. Perhaps, it was our innate darkness that we could relate to. But ultimately, she was so much more powerful and exciting. Ariel was too sweet, naïve and slightly daft. Ursula was beautiful and ugly. She was dominant, intelligent, charming, calculated and magical. Today, we understand and appreciate her ability to embrace her true (evil) self.* (p.c. October 19th 2015)

Further aspects of the Permaid's darkness were emphasised in an interview conducted (in persona) for the online magazine *Issue* (unattributed 2014) in which the Permaid identified Jonathan Glazer's science fiction film *Under the Skin* (2014) as her favourite film. The film features Scarlett Johansson as an alien dressed in human skin who seduces and consumes lonely human males before being revealed to have a black body devoid of orifices or bodily details. The sight of her body is so repulsive to a man who finds her that he douses her in petrol and kills her. The photographic scenarios produced by the duo have avoided any such representation of masculine hostility but nevertheless play upon the troubling nature of the blackness of the Permaid's bodily silhouette amidst the warm landscapes of Los Angeles and the warm bodies of the men who date her.

IV. Alternative Transformation

In contrast to the smooth transformations that facilitate the sexual attraction and congress between mermaids and men discussed above, an episode of the early 1970s' US television series *Night Gallery* represented a more problematic outcome. The episode, entitled 'Lindemann's Catch' (Jeff Corey, 1972), centred on a fishing boat captain (played by Stuart Whitman) whose crew catch a (stereotypically young and pretty) mermaid (Anabelle Garth) in their nets. The captain finds himself attracted to her and decides to keep her on board despite her discomfort and deterioration out of the water. Seeking a solution to her malaise, the captain obtains a potion from an eccentric old seaman who promises that it will transform the mermaid's physique. It does, but not in the way the captain anticipated. While it turns her tail into legs it also turns her upper body into that of a fish. Dismayed at her transformation the mermaid dives overboard and swims away. Bewildered by the turn of events the captain dives after her and the episode ends with their subsequent fates remaining a mystery. A more positive response to a similar figure occurred in an episode of the TV science fiction comedy series *Red Dwarf* entitled 'Better Than Life' (Ed Bye, 1988), where a reverse mermaid appears as a virtual reality companion for the feline-humanoid character Cat. When his ship's computer avatar expresses surprise at the reversal of usual bodily arrangements, the Cat expresses his preference for the combination he has chosen.[166]

107

Figure 15 – Rene Magritte's painting 'Collective Invention' (1934).

The two programs evoke and parallel a minor strand of visual representations of mermaids whose physiques are inverted. The best-known example of this approach occurs in French Surrealist Rene Magritte's 1934 painting 'Collective Invention' (Figure 15). The painter's inversion of the regular form of the mermaid serves to remind the viewer of the anatomical absurdity of the conventional figure by depicting a human lower form bizarrely comple- mented by a fish's head (which is manifestly unsuited to being out of water). A similar figure also appears briefly in an impressionistic collage of imagery in Saul Bass's 1974 horror/science fiction film *Phase IV*. The collage sequence represents the experiments made by a mad scientist and the 'reverse mermaid' is a symbol of his crazed vision, a sign that he is truly unhinged. Evoking William Blake's famous epigrammatic verse from 'Several Questions Answered',[167] these images serve to draw attention to how the line- aments of desire are conventionally rendered in the body of the traditional mermaid and how awkward and aberrant her inverted form appears – offering the possibility of genital intercourse but without the essential humanity of the conventional mermaid's upper form. Indeed, this aspect provided the humour for one of the few explicit cultural acknow- ledgements of the problematic aspects of the gratification of male desire with mermaids. The lyrics of Shel Silverstein's 1965 song 'The Mermaid' concern a young man who goes to sea, falls for a mermaid and subsequently lives with her under water. While he loves her, he finds her fishly lower-half decidedly frustrating. His problem with regard to the

166   An episode of the pirate-themed TV comedy series *Captain Butler* entitled 'Desert Island Dick' (Iain McLean, 1997) also explores aspects of a reversed-form merman. The program involves Captain Butler (Craig Charles) being rescued from the sea by a mermaid named Tray-sea (Elizabeth Anson). Falling in love with her, due to a spell she has cast on him, he marries her only to find that his upper body becomes fish-like, in a reverse mirror of her form. In order to escape this condition he flees his marriage and returns to his crew.

167   *What is it men in women do require? The lineaments of Gratified Desire. What is it women do in men require? The lineaments of Gratified Desire.*

latter is solved when he meets her sister, who has a reverse physique (similar to that of the creature represented in Magritte's painting). The song concludes with a reductive expression of the satiation of male desire: "And I don't give a damn about the upper part/ That's how I end my tale ('cos now I'm getting tail[168])".

Conclusion

Whereas the mermaids discussed in Chapter 2 possess phallic powers and attractions that they are ready to flaunt and exploit in their interactions with terrestrial men, the majority of transformative mermaids discussed in this chapter are more equivocal about revealing their true identities.[169] The transformative mermaids represented as achieving sexual interaction with human males secure that activity by temporarily suspending their essential attributes *as* mermaids. The protagonists of *Splash* and *TDIII* behave strategically. After gratifying their (and their human partners') conventional heterosexual desires and establishing relationships with them they transform back to mer-form and return to the sea with human partners in tow. Notably, no film to date has represented this stage of mermaid–human relations as anything but a fleeting phase. The depiction of the interactions of such couples in a marine environment in which the humans can only survive through their close interactions with their mer-partners is less inviting and viable than the land-based transformative interactions frequently represented in cinema.

The role-play aspect of being represented as a mermaid is most fully explored in *Mermaids and Unicorns*, where there is no pretence of the mermaids shown on screen being viable physical creatures. In this way, the video is illuminating since it suggests that the representation of mermaids, their impossible bodies and/or impossible transformations might be considered as a more general exercise in role-play that explores sexual desires premised on their symbolism. In a very different manner, *The Mermaid: Siren of Seduction* provides a radical reduction of the implicit queerness of the straight male's attraction to the mermaid by taking this to a particular logical conclusion. Similarly, the Permaid signals the absurdity of the mermaid's form in a markedly opposite manner, as an impenetrable representation of female form. In these regards the various films discussed in this chapter represent attempts to work through the complexity of the mermaid's erotic charge and symbolism, making sense of its absurdities by delivering scenarios that visualise various possibilities for the manifestation and gratification of desire both within and outside of normative heterosexuality.

---

168 'Getting tail' being slang for men having penetrative vaginal sex.

169 This is also the case in the Russian comedy *Chudesa v Reshetov* ('Wizards of Reshetov') (Mikhail Levin, 2004), which features a mermaid, named Inka (played by Tatyana Arntgolts), hiding her identity along with a group of similar magical characters in a small Russian town. She is only shown briefly in fish-tailed form, when emerging from a bath, with her legs regenerating as they become exposed to the air. A very different approach to identity concealment and transformation is presented in 'Waves' (2014), an episode of the TV series *Lost Girl*, which has a plot line about an evil merman and mermaid obtaining human legs in order to stay on land after visiting during temporary transformations in their late teens.

Chapter Five

Channeling the Anima: Inspirational Folklore in The Mermaid Chair

T he opening chapters of this volume have analysed a series of representations of mermaids as living beings. This chapter complements these by considering two associated texts – Sue Monk Kidd's novel 'The Mermaid Chair' (2005a) and its eponymous film adaptation (Steven Schachter, 2006) – which draw on mermaid folklore to provide motifs that enable their lead (human) protagonist to negotiate a mid-life crisis. In this regard, the texts bear some comparison to Guy and Constance Jones's 1946 novel 'Peabody's Mermaid' and its 1948 film adaptation (discussed in Chapters 2 and 3). But whereas the mermaid in these 1940s' texts is a physical manifestation of an anima that tempts and tantalises a male protagonist, the mermaids in Kidd's novel and its screen adaptation are figurative ones. By internalising an aggregation of mermaid folklore, Kidd's female protagonist effectively channels her own 'inner mermaid' and experiences life from that position (for a fleeting phase, at least).

Kidd's novel draws on spiritual reflections pursued by its author over an extended period. After growing up within a conservative Baptist milieu, Kidd began to explore broader notions of spirituality in the 1980s, including Christianity's points of connection with pagan traditions. Her 1996 work 'The Dance of the Dissident Daughter' represents her attempt to move discussions of female spirituality from theological contexts to a broader public arena by relating her journey from mainstream Christianity to the pursuit of sacred femininity. As she details in her book, this was accomplished through her engagement with various approaches, including Jungian analysis. She moved into fiction with 'The Secret Life of Bees' (2002), a story set in South Carolina in the early-1960s. The novel is centred on a young (Caucasian) girl who has lost her mother and who interacts with a group of African-Americans as she matures and finds a life path. It also includes substantial references to the Black Madonna tradition.[170] In an interview in *U.S. Catholic* magazine, Kidd explained her interest in and reading of the topic in the following terms:

> Their history suggests that there may have been a kind of underground nerve-center for worshipping the divine feminine within the medieval church, and it often came through in the Black Madonna. If that is the case, we've got a very powerful amalgamation going on, a blending of the Christian Mary and these old earth goddesses. And there's an amalgamation going on not just in her history, but in her spirituality, in her mythology, in the stories that evolve around her and in the way that people relate to her ... In the case of the Black Madonna, I think we can begin to see reflections of the sacred feminine. (Schlumpf 2003: online)

The focus of Kidd's debut novel, and of the aspect emphasised in the final line of the quotation above, is strongly reminiscent of aspects of Irigaray's essay 'Divine Women' and, in particular, her claim that:

> as long as woman lacks a divine made in her image she cannot establish her subjectivity or achieve a goal of her own. She lacks an ideal that would be her goal or path in becoming ... If she is to become woman, if she is to accomplish her female subjectivity, woman needs a god who is a figure for the perfection of her subjectivity. (1996: 476)

The combination of such spiritual considerations with well-drafted characters and an intricate plot set in a tense period in modern United States' (US) history contributed to the novel becoming a critical success. After being promoted on the popular US television program *Good Morning America*, it sold over eight million copies internationally and was adapted into an eponymous film in 2008. Kidd's second novel, 'The Mermaid Chair', was published in 2005. Like its predecessor, it topped the *New York Times* bestseller list and was adapted for the screen. Similarly to 'The Secret Life of Bees', 'The Mermaid Chair' utilised motifs from European religious folklore and considered aspects of female subjectivity and identification with regard to aspects of the divine. Unlike its predecessor, it utilised elements of Christian theology and Jungian theory, particularly those concerning the anima, to represent a female subjectivity in which the sacred feminine is entwined with a far more corporeal exploration of female sexuality.

In addition to these elements, Kidd's novel also explores aspects of the Electra complex with regard to its female protagonist's relationship to her dead father and of how her memories of him and of his demise inform her adult identity and relationship patterns. Kidd's approach to this topic has parallels to a number of confessional poems written by Sylvia Plath and Annie Sexton in the 1960s and 1970s and Chung's (2008) analyses of these works provides insights that are also pertinent to Kidd's novel. Drawing on Freudian theory,[171] Chung identifies the manner in which several of Plath's and Sexton's poems attempt to overcome their author-protagonists' inhibiting Electra complexes by revisiting and reconstructing memories of the past in a manner that enabled them to achieve greater

---

170 The Black Madonna is a figure that appears in European Christian statuary, with various explanations as to its origins and significance – see for instance, Begg (1989) and Moss and Cappannari (1982).

171 Primarily on essays included in Freud's study 'Sexuality and the Psychology of Love' (1963).

psychological autonomy in the present.[172] She characterises such representations as attempts to shake off troubling remnants of the complex and to attain a mature subjectivity. In these situations, the figure of the mother is present as both a rival and as a rival repository of memories of the father. In the case of Kidd's novel, further depth to this rivalry is created through its central protagonist's misapprehension of the means of her father's death (blaming herself as the unwitting cause) and her mother's long-held suppression of the actual circumstances (which involved her mother assisting in her husband's suicide). The revelation of the latter, towards the end of the novel and film, removes the protagonist's sense of guilt and provides a closure that she utilises to reconsolidate her relationship with her husband. The mermaid weaves through these explorations as a figure cued by the protagonist's memories of her father's stories but also as an anima that appears to exercise its own agency at various phases and offers alternative options for female behaviour. As the following sections identify, the folkloric sources that Kidd employs in the novel are complex with regard to their symbolism and their development in the film precipitates particular aggregations of association and meaning.

I. Zennor, Saint Senara and Cornish Mermaid Folklore

Although Kidd's novel and its film adaptation are set in the US both texts draw substantially on aspects of folklore associated with the English county of Cornwall. The particular themes that proved inspirational to Kidd are derived from Zennor, a village located six miles south west of the seaside town of Saint Ives.[173] One prominent aspect of Zennor folklore concerns a mermaid who has come to be closely associated with its church, dedicated to the (obscure) Saint Senara.[174] The name 'Senara' appears to derive from 'Asenora', the name of a Breton princess who was sealed into a barrel and cast into the sea.[175] Legends attest that during her time afloat she gave birth to a baby boy and was sustained by angels until she washed ashore in Cornwall. Settling in the county she led a virtuous life that somehow resulted in her elevation to sainthood (the latter being a more locally-determined category in the pre-medieval period than in latter times).[176] Senara's story has become closely associated with a local tale that was first documented by folklorist William Bottrell in 1873 (also see James 2015). The tale concerns a young male, named Mathey Trewella, who possessed a particularly melodious singing voice. This attribute

---

172 Chung also contends that the poems attempt to reconcile aspects of the author-protagonists' "infantile traumas" with "sweet childhood memories" in order to reflect upon their relationships with their deceased fathers and the profound influence the latter had on their later life (2008: 88).

173 Cornwall occupies the southwestern tip of a peninsula and is separated from its neighbouring county of Devon by the River Tamar. Prior to the development of roads and bridges, the Tamar was a substantial barrier to cross-county travel, allowing the county to maintain a distinct cultural identity for an extended duration. A key aspect of this identity was its status as one of the five Celtic regions of the British Isles (along with Ireland, Scotland, Wales and the Isle of Man). Many of the county's folkloric traditions have persisted through to the present despite the county's close integration into the United Kingdom.

174 The village's name also reflects local folklore (with 'Zennor' being commonly regarded as a derivation of 'Senara').

175 See Monaghan (2004: 26) for instance. (My caveat around attribution derives from the lack of early sources for this linguistic explanation.)

176 Saint Senara's Church in Zennor dates from the 1100s (although it is unclear whether the church was initially dedicated to its present designate).

113

Figure 16 – St Senara's Church mermaid chair, with a mermaid carving on the right side panel (author's photo, 1990).

caught the attention of a mysterious and beautiful woman who led him away, never to return. The disappearance was later explained when a ship's captain came across a mermaid in nearby Pendower Cove. The mermaid asked him to move his anchor as it was obstructing access to the underwater home where she dwelt with a husband named Mathey and their children.[177]   Bottrell goes on to elaborate that, after learning of this, local residents decided to warn young men of the perils of being led astray by mermaids by having a mermaid's image carved into a wooden pew end in Saint Senara's Church that was subsequently re-utilised as the side panel of the church's so-called 'mermaid chair' (Figure 16). The carving (Figure 17) is more obviously sexual than many representations of mermaids present in churches in a similar period, by virtue of showing her tail commencing just above her pubic area (rather than around her waist) and hanging (skirt-like) off her torso, suggesting genitalia barely concealed by a tail. In combination with her standard accoutrements of comb and mirror (whose symbolism is discussed in the Introduction to this volume) she is an erotic figure whose allure is evident.

The linkage between the tale and the carving in Bottrell's account is somewhat problem-

177   This story combines several elements from items in the Arne-Thompson Index, including B81.13.1, a mermaid asking a captain to move a boat that blocks access to her dwelling and an inverted variant of B81.3.2, a mermaid singing in church and enticing a young man to follow her.

atic. While the story of Trewella's disappearance and of the sea captain's role in uncovering this is relatively self-contained, the motivation for the carving appearing in church might be considered as an attempt (either on Bottrell's part and/or on his local informants') to give a reason for the mermaid image's appearance in a church during a mid-Victorian period characterised by its prudish religiosity. The attempt to tie the particular image to the local tale is also less than entirely persuasive given that mermaids feature in a number of English churches that do *not* have associations with local mermaid folklore. The mermaid iconography that has survived to the present in Cornish churches is that which either escaped the iconoclasts of the mid–late 16th Century and/or has subsequently been restored. During the period in question, Protestant zealots defaced and/or removed artefacts and images from churches across England in an attempt to enforce the Second Commandment that, in Protestant theology, was deemed to forbid idolatry (i.e. the worship and/or veneration of images as things-in-themselves).[178] In these regards, the Zennor mermaid carving is chiefly notable for its survival to the present.

Figure 17 – Mermaid chair side panel carving (author's photo, 1990).

The standard explanation for the presence of mermaid images in churches across Europe in the Middle Ages is that they were intended to represent temptations of lust and vanity to be avoided (see Berger 1985 42–43). While there is a degree of plausibility to this, it does not preclude significantly different local adaptations and/or subversions of this function. In the case of mermaids in Cornish churches there is another interpretation available, namely that such images had a similar function to an analogy in the late 14th Century Cornish *Ordinalia* mystery plays, where the dual nature of Christ as both human and divine is compared to the mermaid (as half human and half fish).[179] There is a degree of plausibility in this.[180] Indeed, as the title of Betcher's 1996 article on early Cornish mermaid images suggests, it is "a tempting theory". However, as Betcher goes on to argue, while Cornish mermaid images may have been open to interpretation in this manner, they have such a close resemblance to similar images elsewhere that the analogy can be regarded more as a local interpretative tradition than as the explanation for their presence (ibid). Indeed, the varying interpretations of the mermaid's meaning and rationale in St Senara's church are part of its folklore and the lack of any decisive explanation for her presence is a key element of her enigma and appeal.

---

178   The Roman Catholic version of this commandment is similar but less prescriptive. See Aston (1989) for a detailed account of the iconoclasts and their motivations.

179   See Peters (2015: 30).

180   And the representation of mer-*men* in pew ends in St Buryan Church (that were subsequently adapted into a desk) could also be interpreted as representing such an allusion.

II. Senara in the Carolinas: The Novel and its Location

Kidd's novel is centred on the mid-life crisis experienced by Jessie, a 42-year-old married, middle-class woman who lives in South Carolina, on the mid-eastern seaboard of the US, where she works as an artist. As the book's prologue, written in first person, specifies, she perceives her malaise as being due to her having "never done anything that took my own breath away" (2005a: 1). Reflecting on the tale she is about to relate, she observes, "Some say I fell from grace, they're being kind. I didn't fall – I dove" (ibid: 2). The narrative opens with a phone call from (the fictional) Egret Island, off the Carolina coast. The call draws Jessie back to the place she grew up in to help her mother, who has deliberately cut off one of her fingers. As the novel later details, Jessie feels a profound ambivalence towards the island. She remembers it as a quasi-magical place before her father died in (what she had always understood to be) a boating accident. After that, however, it became more fraught and problematic as her mother became obsessed with religion and began to behave increasingly bizarrely. Jessica's ambivalence is also caused by an enduring perception that she had inadvertently caused her father's death by giving him a pipe as a gift, embers from which sparked an explosion that killed him. Once on the island, she seeks answers as to the reasons for her mother's self-mutilation and, somewhat to her surprise, embarks upon a brief, passionate affair with Whit, a trainee monk (who has the religious name of Brother Thomas[181]). These two plot elements are interconnected as Jessie's mother works as a cook at the island's abbey, a Benedictine establishment dedicated to Saint Senara that features an ornate mermaid chair in its chapel. This aspect overlaps with Jessie's preoccupation with the mermaid stories that her father told her as a child and her sense that mermaids are calling to her and offering her an escape from her current life situation.

While the notion of there being an abbey devoted to an obscure Cornish saint on a remote island in the US is a somewhat fanciful one, the Carolina Barrier Islands at least have an element of credibility as a location. The region was the site of the first (short-lived) English colony in the Americas, a settlement established in 1585 on Roanoke Island in the (present-day) state of North Carolina. The group of settlers transported there included four Cornish men, one of whom fathered what has been described as "the first Cornish child born in America" (Payton 2005: 31). Kidd does not, however, draw on this aspect of local history but rather presents the abbey as a 20th Century institution, stating (through Jessie's narration):

> It had started as a simple outpost – or, as the monks said, "a daughter house" – of an abbey in Cornwall, England. The monks had built it themselves in the thirties on land donated by a Catholic family from Baltimore, who'd used it as a summer fishing camp. (2005a: 33)

Jessie describes the abbey as a tourist attraction:

> Mostly because of the mermaid chair that sat in a side chapel in the church … a replica of a very old, somewhat famous chair in the abbey's mother house. (ibid: 33-34)

---

181 Kidd refers to the character as both Whit and Brother Thomas at various points. In order to avoid confusion I refer to the character as Whit throughout the chapter.

Recasting Zennor Church as a "mother house", Kidd manages to both specify the contemporary nature of the Egret Island abbey (i.e. as not associated with patterns of Cornish settlement in the Americas) and to give it symbolic weight and credence by directly associating it with a Cornish referent.

Jessie remembers her early years on Egret Island as innately connected with the aquapelagic spaces and experiences generated by her father's livelihood activities as a fisherman and from her youthful fascination with his mermaid stories:

> *Long ago, when my brother and I used to row his small bateau through the tangle of salt creeks on the island, back when I was still wild and went around with Spanish moss braided into my hair, creating those long and alarming coiffures, my father used to tell me that mermaids lived in the waters around the island. He'd claimed he'd seen them once from his boat ... The mermaids swam to his boat like dolphins, he'd said, leaping through the waves and diving ... I believed any and every outlandish thing he said.* (2005a: 2)

As the above passage suggests, Jessie's association of the island with mermaids during her childhood derives more from her father's (somewhat generic) expositions of mermaid folklore than the specific images and associations of Egret Island abbey and it is only upon her return as an adult that the abbey's saint and her iconic chair play a more significant role in her perceptions and experiences.

Kidd's use of the Zennor mermaid myth was not the first occasion in which the Cornish tale had been utilised in contemporary popular culture. As discussed in Chapter 2, English dramatist Peter Blackmore used the legend as part of the back-story for his stage-play and subsequent film adaptation of *Miranda* (Ken Annakin, 1948), a comic tale of an amorous Cornish mermaid at large in post-War London. But unlike Blackmore's utilisation of the folkloric theme, Kidd's novel is both more serious in tone and is set in a location far from Zennor. Kidd's relocation of the legend to the US is noteworthy. While some traditional folkloric entities took root in the locations in which early waves of Anglo-Irish migrants settled in North America (such as faeries in Newfoundland[182]), the mermaid does not seem to have been amongst them.[183]

Kidd's version of Saint Senara is one that synthesises various strands of the saint's mythology, based on her research on Senara, Asenora and related Zennor folklore (aspects explicitly acknowledged in her Author's Note to the novel, 2005a: 333–335). As she has also explained in her author's website:

> *In the novel, the mermaid saint, then, is a figure that is part historical and part mythical. She is St. Senara, the godly patron saint of the monastery and the one to whom The Mermaid Chair is dedicated. Ah, but she also has this completely other aspect – before she was a saint, she was Asenora, the mermaid.* (2005b: online)

Kidd draws the various threads of Senara, the chair and mermaid lore together through the fictional device of having these documented by the abbey's Father Dominic in a publication entitled the 'The Mermaid's Tale' (which appears to express Kidd's synthe-

---

182   See Narvaez (1997).

183   See Hayward (2015b) for reference to one of the few accounts of mermaids being glimpsed across the Atlantic.

sised version of the tales), allowing Jessie to quote the following passage from Father Dominic's book in the novel:

> *According to the legend recounted in Legenda Aurea: Readings on the Saints,*[184] *in 1450 a beautiful Celtic mermaid named Asenora swam ashore on the coast of Cornwall where a Benedictine monastery had recently been established. After removing her fish tail and hiding it among the rocks, she explored the area on foot and discovered a community of men. She made many clandestine visits. Suspicious that Asenora was no ordinary woman but a mermaid, and greatly alarmed by her presence, the abbot of the monastery hid himself by the water and waited. He witnessed Asenora swim ashore, remove her fish tail and hide it inside a niche in the cliff.*
>
> *When she wandered off in the direction of the abbey, the shrewd abbot retrieved the fish tail, bundling it into his robe. He tucked it inside a secret compartment hidden underneath the seat of his chair, in the church. Without her tail, the poor mermaid could never go back to the sea, and soon the wildness of it drained out of her. Asenora was converted and eventually became St. Senara ...*
>
> *An interesting footnote to the legend states that after her conversion Asenora sometimes missed the sea and her former life so strongly that she prowled the monastery at night in search of her tail. Conflicting stories exist about whether she ever found it. One story suggests she not only found her fish tail but donned it whenever she wanted to revisit her lost life, always returning, however, and replacing it inside the abbot's chair.* (ibid: 95, 98)

While aspects of this account resemble elements of Cornish folklore they also depart from it in several notable ways. One is the close association and interaction of the mermaid with Benedictine monks. Despite the presence of a number of Benedictine monasteries in Cornwall during the medieval period (including the famous St Michael's Mount), there appears to be no (surviving) folklore concerning Benedictine interaction with mermaids. Another is the novelty of a mermaid who could easily remove and subsequently re-attach her tail, as if it were a garment. The latter facility is not a common element of traditional Anglo-Celtic mermaids but *is* part of related selkie (seal/human) folklore (see Thomson 2001). As the middle paragraph of the quotation emphasises, the mermaid's separation from her tail deprives her of (its) phallic power and drains her autonomy and agency (i.e. her "wildness"), allowing her to be "converted". The latter term is a significant one. She is "converted" in various associated senses, to human form, to Christianity and to the phallocentric order that dominates these.

As Kidd has also explained, she took considerable liberties with the mermaid chair itself, imagining a far more ornate version than the actual Cornish artefact:

> *The idea for The Mermaid Chair began one day quite unexpectedly. While talking with a friend about her trip to Cornwall, England, she casually mentioned that she'd seen a "mermaid chair" in a small church. She described it as a chair with a mermaid carved on its side which had been in the church for centuries though the reason seemed to be a mystery ... I went around for a while after that with*

---

184   While *Legenda Aurea* (written by Jacobus de Voragine in 1275 and published in English translation by William Caxton in 1483) is an actual reference work on the lives of Christian saints (and related topics), the Index of the seven-volume set does not include references to Asenora or Senara – see http://www.fordham.edu/halsall/basis/goldenlegend/ – accessed October 10th 2015

the image of a mermaid chair vividly planted in my mind: not like the actual chair in the Cornish church, rather a chair whose arms were formed by the carved bodies of two winged mermaids. (2005b: online)

In marked contrast to the somewhat basic wooden chair in Zennor church (Figure 16), the novel describes the Egret Island "copy" of the (re-imagined) Cornish one as ornate and bejewelled, with the mermaid arm carvings painted in red, blue and green, with garnets inlaid as nipples on the mermaids' exposed breasts and with the back "carved with an intricate Celtic knot design" (ibid: 108). The chair, and the particular presence Kidd ascribes to it, play a prominent role in the novel. It is represented as having a spiritual power that allows visitors sitting on it to pray to Senara and to obtain answers to questions concerning their direction in life (ibid: 34). The chair also has other connotations, particularly in terms of an idiosyncratic interpretation by Father Dominic that is particularly pertinent to Jessie's experiences of it:

Some scholars suggest that the story of Saint Senara may have been created to help people choose the path of godly delight over that of sexual delight. But might it also be a way of emphasising the importance of both? (ibid: 99)

And it is indeed this message that Jessie takes from the chair at a significant moment during her sojourn on the island. Chapter 15 of the novel describes the intense reverie she falls into while sitting in the chair in chapel during which she decides to follow her inclinations and consummate her relationship with Whit.

Jessie's lucid, reflective narrative also contains a number of references to particular artworks that complement Father Dominic's reflections.[185] One of her first references occurs as she is beginning to imagine a relationship with Whit:

I had always loved Chagall's Lovers in the Red Sky,[186] *his painting of an entwined couple soaring above rooftops, above the moon. The image would come to me each time I sank into the water, the couple sometimes flying through a red sky but more often swimming in searing blue water ... Other times I would think of the mermaid Chagall had painted, suspended above the water, above the trees, a flying mermaid, but without wings, and I would think of Thomas saying he envied mermaids who belong equally to the sea and to the sky.* (ibid: 129)

Whit's comment alludes to the siren's form in early literature as a winged female creature and, more specifically, to the compound (winged and finned) form carved into the (fictional) mermaid chair's two armrests. It also suggests Whit's desire to reconcile and conjoin two distinct impulses and associations. One of his particular duties at the abbey is to monitor the island's populations of egrets, creatures of the sky who can transcend both the earthly and the aquatic spheres, just as the spirit and religious inspiration can be seen to transcend the material and sensual realms. The sky, in this manner, can be regarded as Whit's associative space. This aspect is explored when Jessie and Whit meet at an isolated beach to share their first intimate time together. She takes her easel with her and

185 Jessie also reflects on mermaid symbolism in a more down-to-earth manner by producing paintings of mermaids for her friend Kat to sell in her mermaid-themed gift shop. Weary of the "typical thing – mermaids on rocks, mermaids under the water, mermaids on top of the water" she produces a series of humorous works that attempt to reconcile mermaids' otherness with the everyday mundanity of the terrestrial world (ibid: 185).

186 A 1950 painting also known by its French title, 'Les Amants au ciel rouge'.

starts to paint before he arrives, producing an image of a diving woman that feels intuitively right to her, one that "captured the moment when her arms and head first pierced the water, cutting cleanly into the emptiness below" (ibid: 186). In terms of the previous discussion, her dive places her briefly in (his) aerial space before she dives deep into her medium. Shortly after she completes the painting Whit arrives at the beach, considers the image, embraces Jessie and goes on to make love with her for the first time. After another sexual encounter, Jessie returns to the Chagall imagery that had presaged her affair by discussing this with him:

> Lying in his arms, I told him once about Chagall's Lovers in the Red Sky, how the pair – some thought Chagall and his wife, Bella – were wrapped in a glorious knot, how they floated above the world. (ibid: 236)

His response, "But they can't stay up there forever" (ibid: 237), unnerves her and underlines the brief and unstable nature of their budding affair.[187] Jessie's own engagement with such imagery occurs in paintings that represent her and Whit enraptured and entangled in an aquatic realm. The latter provides her with a more intense and visceral sense of the sublime, a place innately involved with cycles of life rather than the reified aerial spaces of Chagall's imagination, a place where mermaids dive and swim rather than soar:

> it was the water I reveled in. Traveling water. It was filled with decay and death, and at the same time with plankton and eggs and burgeoning life. It would recede, stripping everything in its path, then turn into a brimming, amniotic estuary. I needed it like air. (ibid: 234)

The waters of the island provide Jessie with a space that she can explore instinctively – an emotional aquapelago where boundaries and rules ebb and flow with the tides of her passions. She expresses her fascination with this environment in a series of paintings that represent her as floating deep in sensual seas (ibid: 236). One representation of a couple immersed in this is so explicit in its symbolism that it has an instant effect on her husband when he visits the island and finds the painting in a room:

> Hugh was staring at my underwater couple – Lovers in the Blue Sea, I called them ... He turned around, parting this night from all other nights, letting his eyes, bruised and disbelieving, come slowly to my face, and I could feel the air around us blaze up with the terrible thing that was about to happen ... "Who is he?" he asked. (ibid: 265)

---

187 Kidd's invocation of Chagall's work is illuminating. Marc Chagall (1887–1985) drew on a range of mythical and folkloric sources and frequently represented animal–human hybrids in usual circumstances, including mermaids floating in the sky (e.g. 'Sirène et le poisson' [1957] and 'La Baie des Anges' [1962]). 'Lovers in the red sky' (1950) has similar imagery to his mermaid paintings but is distinct from them by virtue of the blood red background that fills the canvas around a pair of entwined lovers hovering in the air, suggesting the carnal nature of their passions. In an analysis of Chagall's early work Schneider (1946) refers to Freud's characterisation that preoccupations with flight represent the "concealment of another wish", namely "the longing for the ability of sexual accomplishment" (1932: 107–108). Considering a number of Chagall's paintings of flying figures Schneider notes that their most distinct aspect was that they expressed the act of flying "as the act of love" itself (1946: 120–121) and notes that individual paintings illustrated lovers "flying in the sky in an embrace and a posture clearly suggestive of the sexual act and yet combined with the poetic phrases of the soaring sensation of being dizzily in love" (ibid: 121)

III. Gullah and Inuit Motifs

Along with the Cornish traditions reconfigured in her novel, Kidd blends in other cultural themes through the presence of an old friend of Jessie's mother's named Hepzibah, a resident Gullah "culture keeper" (ibid: 31). The Gullah are descendents of West Africans who were brought to the South Carolina/Georgia Lowcountry as slaves in the 18th and early 19th centuries. The forced migrants, who belonged to diverse cultural/language groups in Africa, interacted and developed a creole language and syncretic forms of music, dance, ritual and folklore. When the states' rice cultivation industries declined in the mid–late 1800s those groups who lived on the states' Barrier Islands were left in isolation and many have retained strong elements of their culture and language through to the present. One of the main inscriptions of the vitality of Gullah culture in the novel concerns an annual May Day feast held on Bone Yard Beach (a name that suggests its connection to an ancestral past) that Hepzibah participated in with Jessie's mother and her friend Kat. At these events the women made bonfires out of beach wood and danced on the sand to Hepzibah's drumming. As Jessie recalls, on the last occasion the feast occurred (directly before her father's death), the three women also enacted an unusual ritual together. Waist-deep in water, they tied threads of wool together to symbolise enduring friendship and then threw them into the waves. Emerging from the sea, Hepzibah found a turtle skull in the shallows and held it aloft, declaring, "Look what the ocean has sent" (ibid). The description of the annual feast, the specific friendship ceremony and the finding of the turtle skull represent elements of Gullah culture adapted (and thereby perpetuated) in an inclusive and multi-cultural context. Upon her return to the island it strikes Jessie that she lacks such an intense engagement with female networks and their expression through spiritual traditions connected to the sea:

> *Something struck me then: I'd never done any of these things my mother had done. Never danced on a beach. Never made a bonfire. Never waded into an ocean at night with laughing women and tied my life to theirs.* (ibid: 91)[188]

While there is no expectation – let alone requirement – for cultural producers to comprehensively represent aspects of the locales in which their fictions are set, Kidd's references to Gullah culture eschew (or, at least, miss) an opportunity to ground the novel's mermaid motifs in local folklore. Gullah culture contains a number of mermaid themes or, rather, syntheses of African female water spirit folklore and Western mermaid forms. Brown (2012) has provided an account of these that identifies that the blending of African spiritual figures and mermaid form represents "a point of cultural connection and exchange" between cultures (ibid: 259).[189] But despite this, this aspect is entirely absent in

---

188 This incident, and Jessie's reflections on it, represent a fictionalisation of an episode from Kidd's own life (as recounted in her 1996 memoir) where she observed women dancing by the sea at a Jungian retreat but felt unable to join in.

189 Brown links this to African simbi legends, concerning powerful water serpent spirits. As he describes, the transition of the legend to the Americas, through the oral culture of the slaves taken there, affected changes to the simbi's representation and perceived function: "African-descended people often chose to talk about these spirits as mermaids ... With their stories of mermaids, they remembered slavery, renewed their relationships with the simbi, and asserted understanding of the immorality of captivity and domination that had both spiritual and political meanings" (2012: 253).

the novel. Instead Kidd weaves a thread of Inuit mythology into her (otherwise Eurocentric) mermaid themes.

The Inuit element, concerning the tale of Sedna, a woman transformed by violence, is dovetailed with an aspect of medieval Christianity. Helping Jessie in her attempt to understand her mother's motivations to mutilate herself, Whit informs Jessie that her mother had read accounts of a 12th Century prostitute named Eudoria who cut off a finger after being converted to Catholicism and planted it in a field where it miraculously grew into a sheaf of wheat (ibid: 221). Kidd cross-associates this element of Christian folklore with Inuit mythology by noting that Jessie's mother had also consulted a reference book on indigenous traditions before mutilating herself. Jessie describes the page her mother bookmarked as featuring an image of a mermaid whose fingers take the form of the bodies of dolphins, whales, seals and fish (ibid: 222). Sedna's tale is an actual Inuit myth that has a number of variants (see Kennedy 1997). The version presented by Kidd is as follows:

> A young woman sends word to her father to come rescue her from a cruel husband. They are fleeing in his boat when her husband pursues them. Fearing for his life, the father throws his daughter overboard, but she grabs on to the side of the boat and refuses to let go. Panicked, her father cuts off each of her fingers. One by one... Sinking into the ocean, Sedna becomes a powerful female deity with the head and torso of a woman and the tail of a fish or a seal. She came to be known as "Mother of the Ocean", her severed fingers becoming sea creatures that filled the waters. (2005a: 222)

This story has a complex relationship to the novel's narrative, evoking comparisons to aspects of Jessie's experiences and to those of her mother. The first part of Kidd's rendition of Sedna's tale might be seen to allude to Jessie's embrace of her father's memory (and his tales) as a means of escaping a husband that she has grown tired of. Her husband also pursues her after she flees by boat to Egret island. But here the analogy breaks down as Jessie retains warm memories of her father and successfully fends off her husband's intrusive contacts. The story's account of mutilation more clearly parallels Jessie's mother's severing of her fingers. The finger motif can be read in classic Freudian terms, in that Freud contended that concern over the possible amputation of a finger represented a displaced castration anxiety.[190] Within this context, Jessie's mother's amputations of her fingers can be read as acts of symbolic castration to atone for her having exerted (phallic) power by aiding her husband in his demise. Sedna's transformation into a mermaid-like figure releases her from her abjection in a manner akin to that of Jessie's embrace of the mermaid, but is not an identity that resonates with Jessie's mother's experiences as she more gradually comes to terms with her past actions.

Unlike the general stories of African-American experience that Brown perceived as key to Lowcountry mermaid folklore (2012: 253), Kidd uses her transplanted Cornish mermaid folklore to explore a highly individual theme. Her novel explores a woman's search for identity and satisfaction at a point in mid-life when her mothering function is waning, when her artistic practice as a painter is providing her with little solace and when her marriage is giving her little emotional or sexual satisfaction. Jessie's immersion in

---

190   See, for example, his analysis of a dream of one of his most famous patients, 'The Wolf Man' (Freud, 1971).

mermaid folklore does not so much serve to reconnect her with any Cornish/Celtic heritage (aspects of her European ancestry are unspecified in the novel) as to a fluid, spiritual space of female experience constructed outside the constraints of patriarchy. Jessie's experience of the mermaids' realm, and of the abbey and its religious theme, essentially involve fantasy spaces – ones located on the edge of the Carolina Coast, on the edge of mundane modern experience, on the edge of Christianity, on the edge of Gullah culture and (with regard to Jessie's mother's experience) on the edge of sanity itself.

IV. Pacific Northwest Translation[191] – The Film

In 2006 a feature-length screen adaptation of Kidd's novel was made for the Lifetime television channel and was subsequently released on DVD. Directed by Steven Schachter, with a score by Rolf Løvland, the film starred Oscar-winning actress Kim Basinger as Jessie Sullivan, Alex Carter as Whit, Lorena Gale as Hepzibah, Ken Pogue as Father Dominic and Roberta Maxwell as Jessie's mother, Nelle. The film opens with soft string sounds and an atmospheric minor key piano motif accompanying a dark screen that slowly transitions to show blurry, underwater images. The name of the film's star (Kim Basinger) appears as the image resolves to show kelp fronds waving underwater. The film's title (*The Mermaid Chair*) then takes centre screen as a pale-skinned mermaid emerges from the middle-distance to the right of the image, followed by another. A wordless female vocal melody enters the mid-ground of the sound mix, as if heard from far away. A voice-over then commences, with an adult female stating, "My father used to tell me that mermaids lived in the waters around the island." The narrator recalls that she used to ask him, "did they sit on rocks and comb their hair?" The camera position then shifts, pointing up at the mermaids, now silhouetted against the sunlit surface of the sea, as the voiceover answers its question, "he said 'yes, but their main job is saving people'". Following a sequence where the mermaids glide effortlessly above, tumbling and turning with each other to the score's atmospheric accompaniment, the voiceover returns, "I know this much, the mermaids finally came to me and I welcomed them." A rushing noise then presages a change of scene. The screen shows a ferry crossing a narrow strait, sounding its horn, before the narration adds, "I'm going home ... the woman who wanted to swim with the mermaids ... the woman who wanted to be free".

---

191 While still set in a place identified as Egret Island on a jetty sign featured in the film's opening sequence, the film's location is markedly different from the low-lying Carolina Barrier island described by Kidd in her novel. The underwater kelp thickets and pine-clad shores shown on screen indicate the film's location in the Pacific Northwest. This relocation did not result from any artistic decisions but, rather, reflected the lower costs of film production north of the Canadian border and the cluster of production facilities operating in south western British Columbia (see Coyle 2012). While there is no specification in the film that the Pacific Northwest is the location for the drama enacted on screen; the inexplicable manifestation of Gullah culture in a location on the opposite coast of North America is tacitly acknowledged in the film's narration, which refers to Hepzibah as being a "*transplant* from South Carolina, bringing the Gullah culture along with her" (my emphasis). The island represented on screen comprises a composite of locations around Victoria, on Vancouver Island. As Kidd subsequently related:*Adapting a novel into a movie is not the easiest task in the world – some things have to be changed, others sacrificed. The only time this created a problem for me was when it became clear the movie would not be set in South Carolina like the novel. I could not fathom The Mermaid Chair without marsh grass, tidal creeks and pluff mud. But at some point on my second and final day on the set, I look around at the mist on the mountains, the water and rocky coastline of the Pacific Northwest, and I get over it ... I would still have preferred the novel to be set in the Low Country, but I can honestly say now that the setting ... is on my list of "Favorite Things In The Movie That Were Not In The Novel."* (2006: online)

As identified above, the film's credit sequence commences by providing the name of its star. In this position, preceding the identification of the film itself, Basinger's presence and identity is established as pivotal to what follows. As the narratorial protagonist of the novel, Jessie's appearance is rarely foregrounded in Kidd's text. The film reverses this situation, representing Basinger-as-Jessie as both the narrator of her drama and as its central visual figure. As John O. Thompson emphasises in his essay 'Screen Acting and the Commutation Test' (1978), the choice of actors to play roles is crucial in that actors are far from interchangeable. They bring with them particular qualities, appearances and (if familiar to audiences) sets of associations. After working as a model in New York and gaining a series of small roles in television dramas, Basinger gained her first lead role in *Katie: Portrait of a Centerfold* (Robert Greenwald, 1978) before going on to appear in sexually provocative roles in films such as *9½ Weeks* (Adrianne Lyne, 1986). In 1997 she won an Oscar as best supporting actress for her role in *L.A. Confidential* (Curtis Hanson, 1997), where she played the part of Lynne Bracken, a prostitute who modelled her appearance on 1940s' film noir star Veronica Lake. This career trajectory provides a particular set of associations that media-familiar audiences can deploy in interpreting Basinger's performance as Jessie in *The Mermaid Chair*. While Kidd's novel is vague as to Jessie's appearance, Basinger brings her statuesque beauty to the role in a manner that gives the character a strong presence. Indeed, her appearance proves eye-catching for Whit on their first encounters, with his gaze lingering on her in a manner somewhat unbecoming for a trainee monk. Her appearance is also carefully crafted for her role, particularly with regard to her long blonde hair, which is coiffured into sensuous, unruly tresses and braids that evoke Madison's similarly sensual hair in *Splash* (Ron Howard, 1984). Basinger's initially demure portrayal of Jessie is thereby offset by the above factors, which suggest a more passionate and less socially conformist identity lurking below the façade of a conventional, dutiful wife. In these regards Basinger-as-Jessie's presence is a powerful one even before the character strays from marital fidelity and hooks up with Whit.

The association between Jessie and mermaids is made explicit in the film's opening credits, where her narration recalls her father's mermaid stories as the screen shows images of two graceful mermaids swimming underwater. Similar images of a single mermaid occur at key points in the narrative, accompanying and emphasising her narration. The first occurs just before Jessie joins Whit on a boat trip that advances their affections. Weaving a line from the book's preface into a later point of its screen adaptation, Jessie's voiceover states, "Some say I fell from grace, they're being kind. I didn't fall – I dove" as a mermaid is shown swimming underwater. A similar image occurs in a flashback sequence when Jessie recalls her father telling her that mermaids bring messages of healing. These associations are also present in a painting she made as a child, shortly after her father's death. The juvenile composition shows a boat, broken in two and consumed by flames, lying on the seafloor. A blonde-haired mermaid hangs in the water above it to the right, looking on helplessly. Reacquainting herself with the painting decades after her father's death, she rips it up, overwhelmed by its representation of the tragedy and of her assumed role in it.

In addition to the three short sequences that feature images of mermaids swimming underwater, the version of the Asenora/Senara legend that Father Dominic's booklet relates is also visually represented in the film. Jessie's voice-over recounts the tale of

Figure 18 – Ornamental chair created for *The Mermaid Chair* film by Renaat Marchand.

Asenora's attraction to a monk as Jessie is shown walking along a rocky shore past the abbey, where monks are mending nets. Her voice-over cues a brief narrative insert that shows a mermaid with long blonde hair swimming away from a rock where she had left her tail. Returning to an image of Jessie, with her own long blonde hair, the film reinforces the link between Asenora's tale and Jessie's own by cutting to a shot of Whit on the abbey lawns. These associations are further emphasised in a sequence where Jessie visits the mermaid chair. Standing before it and touching it, her reflective moment is interrupted by Whit's arrival. He talks with her about the chair (significantly referring to it as *she*) and its power, "she saved Egret Island, not only from storms but from golf courses". He also comments that tourists make wishes to the chair. As the monks begin chanting Jessie sits in the chair, feeling the materiality of its carved arms (see Figure 18), and slips into a reverie. The scene effectively visualises the relevant passage in the novel by cutting between images of Jessie's distracted, dreaming face, Whit's visage as he sings and details of the chair. As this sequence intensifies, Jessie's voice-over makes her experience in the chair explicit "I felt a sensation of floating, of being distant from my life … It scared me".

125

In synch with the last phrase, Jessie leaps up, disturbed, and exits the chapel, with the camera lingering on the image of the mermaid carved in the back of the chair.

The aforementioned scene, in particular, provides a strong impression of the mermaid chair as imbued with spiritual power rather than merely representing it – the factor that was central to the medieval iconoclasts' rationale for destroying and defacing such images and artefacts. The mermaid chair's strong affectivity provides an effective representation of the emotional/spiritual resonance that particular religious icons and artefacts have been perceived to possess. In marked contrast to the actual bench-chair in St Senara's Church in Zennor (Figure 16), the film's rendition (partially derived from the book's descriptions) is both more throne-like and more detailed in its representation of a mermaid (on its back panel) and on carved arm rests that represent mermaids with additional wings[192] (see Figure 18).

The chair also features prominently in a sequence in the film that is only suggested in the book and which provides a tangle of imagery and associations that are barely constrained by their narrative context. As Jessie, her mother and friends gather in order for Jessie to be told the truth of her father's death, the annual Saint Senara parade is shown reaching its climax outside. As Jessie learns, the two events are deeply connected, as her father drank the potion that killed him while sitting in the mermaid chair, basking in its holiness. Intercutting between Jessie's mother's account of past events and the external spectacle, the film shows images of a marching brass band (similar in style to a traditional Cornish band) playing an instrumental version of the Lutheran hymn 'A Mighty Fortress is Our God'. While the performance of this composition may appear to be an incidental aspect of the procession's soundscape, it is so incongruous (for those aware of the significance of its lyrical text) that it emphasises the strangeness of the event. The composition is one of Luther's best-known hymns, and is widely known in its English language translation. Its opening line summarises a solid, intractable (and somewhat militaristic) version of Christianity ("A mighty fortress is our God, a bulwark never failing") that is the antithesis of the more fluid, tolerant version of Christianity practiced by the monks at the island's abbey. The hymn's second line offers a further pointed rejoinder to the island and its fluid, liminal spaces, identifying God as pitched against "the *flood* of mortal ills" (my emphasis). But despite the tenor of the band's hymn, fluidity prevails on Saint Senara's Day.

Upon reaching the dock, the mermaid chair is placed with its back to the sea while seawater is raised from the dock, poured into a large clam shell and first flicked over the chair and then into the harbour by means of a sprig of fir. This ceremony is ambiguous both in itself and in relation to the mermaid chair's role in the assisted suicide of Jessie's father. There are several distinct Christian traditions that involve the sprinkling of holy water. Christenings are perhaps the best-known example and in certain Catholic contexts, sprigs of herbs, such as rosemary or basil, are used to flick holy water on the child being baptised. There are also obvious allusions to Christian blessings of fishing fleets, such as those currently held in Cornish locations such as Newlyn and Mousehole and a range of other harbours in various continents (without any of the elaborate artefacts or icons featured in the film). But despite these various practices, the chair seems a greater focus of attention

---

192   See Holford-Stevens (2006).

than the fleet. Indeed, rather than a blessing, the ceremony might almost be considered as one of annual re-consecration, of (re-)conferring a Christian spiritual status on a somewhat unstable artefact, one whose multiple meanings and associations are always liable to escape their binding into Christian purposes (such as inspiring Jessie to violate her marriage vows and seduce Whit away from his religious calling). Similarly, the blessing can be interpreted as an attempt to exercise spiritual control over the sea, an unstable and capricious medium that is innately associated with Senara and the chair that commemorates her.

There is a similar ceremonial aspect to one of Jessie's last acts on the island. After having said her farewells to Whit, she visits a deserted beach and wades into the water. Accompanied by elegiac music performed on piano and strings, her first steps are slow and contemplative as the voiceover reflects on the journey of self-discovery she has undertaken, "all my life I tried to complete myself with someone else". Picking up a long frond of kelp she wraps it around her neck as her voice-over states "first my father ...". Loosening the kelp, she holds it aloft in her outstretched arms, turning back to the shore as she states "then Hugh", before wrapping it around her neck again and walking on as she states, "even Whit". Literally and metaphorically moving on, she loosens the frond, trailing it behind her, and walks further out into the bay as her voiceover adds, "I don't want that anymore". After she exits screen right, the shot lingers on the water, showing the ripples that follow in her wake. The short sequence evokes the mermaid imagery of the film's opening as her green-toned skirt darkens and clings to her legs, tail-like, as it wettens. Her movement out into the water also symbolises her embrace of an environment that she "reveled in" as a child (Kidd 2005a: 234). As she moves deeper into the "brimming amniotic estuary of her memories" (ibid) she consciously identifies her life of constraint within the Electra complex (with her father, husband and lover) and states her sense of no longer needing their completion of her identity, having achieved the goal that her voiceover identified in the film's opening sequences, her desire to "swim with the mermaids" in order "to be free".

Conclusion

Kidd's adaptation of Zennor folklore to 21st Century popular cultural contexts has brought increased attention to the Cornish religious folklore that inspired it, particularly from aficionados of Celticity imagined within various New Age contexts.[193] Despite these factors, the novel and film fundamentally utilise the Zennor/Senara element and a more general background of mermaid folklore to provide their central protagonist with an inspirational motif that she can deploy during a mid-life crisis. After indulging her passions she sets her anima aside and returns to her marriage. Her performance of elements of an imagined mermaid identity can be read as an attempt to access and experience particular aspects of female experience and agency symbolised by the figure. As in Jung's 1968 characterisation, the mermaid can be taken to symbolise a pre-modern period when

---

193   Indeed, a number of web pages and blogs identify that Kidd's representation of Senara/Asenora have influenced their own interest in, representation of and/or visits to Zennor – see, for instance, MissMerFaery (2012). Senara/Asenora has also been represented in manners that strongly suggest that Kidd's version and interpretation has been formative on their perceptions. Recent texts, such as artist Imogen McCarthy's 'Saint Senara's Prayer' (2012), for instance, offer readings of the legend that are more congruent with Kidd's modern interpretation than with the original tale.

"moral conscience" had not established itself. Jessie's sense of being possessed by the mermaid's unrestrained nature moves her to slip the bonds of marital fidelity and seduce Whit. But whereas Jung posited that men's resistance to "terrifyingly chaotic" phenomena such as mermaids might allow them to gain moral strength and purpose (ibid: 31), Whit's willing acceptance of Jessie's advances turns him away from his spiritual vocation. While Whit heads off into an uncertain future, Jessie's engagements with various facets of mermaid folklore during her period on the island facilitate her return to her husband. The truth of her father's death, and of the role that the mermaid chair and the abbot played in facilitating it, remove a deep sense of guilt. Similarly, her successful application of quasi-mermaidic powers of seduction during her island sojourn engages and exercises her frustrated libido. Her embrace of the anima proves to be an enriching one in these regards and provides her with a temporary escape from social mundanity. The novel and film conclude uneasily, showing Jessie re-united with Hugh and with an awkward and gradual rekindling of trust and affection between them. The book also adds an Epilogue that explains Jessie's resolve to refresh and reformulate her relationship with her husband while also retaining her engagement with her anima:

> I talk to him instead about the mermaids. They belong to themselves, I told him once, and he frowned in the way that he does when weighing something he's unsure of. I know at times he's afraid of the separateness, my independence, the abiding loyalty I have to myself now ... I tell him, smiling, that it was the mermaids who brought me home. I mean, to the water and the mud and the pull of the tides in my own body. To the solitary island submerged so long in myself, which I desperately need to find. But I also try to explain they brought me home to him. (Kidd 2005a: 328)

This final reflection provides the novel with its most assertive aspect. Rather than indulging her mermaid fantasies for a brief fling that she can later explain away as the product of temporary delusion, she embraces the anima as a means of reconnecting with a lost sense of self and of agency. Unlike Asenora's "conversion" to a passive figure drained of her "wildness" by a contriving abbot, Jessie maintains the right to retain her autonomy and agency, choosing to stay in her marriage rather than being marooned there. In this manner, the film's images of her wading out into the waters of an island bay symbolise her embrace of a fluid realm that affirms her senses of female selfhood and of spiritual wholeness.

Chapter Six

"Mermaid-like a While": Juvenile Mermaids and Aficionado Culture

T he last two decades have seen a significant increase in the representation of juvenile mermaids in live-action films and television series, many, if not all, targeted at pre-teen[194] and early teenage audiences. This has been closely associated with another phenomenon: the rise of a mermaid aficionado culture amongst young girls apparent in Facebook pages, blogs, social networks and through the production of amateur video dramas. This chapter analyses the nature of the representations offered in these audiovisual productions. While I draw on various aspects of the discussions advanced in preceding chapters, I am also concerned to provide insights into the distinct nature of recent representations of young mermaids and of the aficionado culture that interacts with them. For all that adult mermaids have been represented as variously sexually avaricious and/or hostile to humans (usually men), there is also a substantial strand of media production that represents younger mermaids who are not directly implicated in adult socio-sexual milieu. This aspect is considered in this chapter with regard to aspects of what Driscoll (2002) terms "feminine adolescence", a life-stage that she disassociates from any specific age category, deeming it to refer to girls who are "not necessarily teenagers and not exclusively young women either; rather, they are defined as

---

194   The terms 'pre-teen' and 'tween' refer to children in the later stages of pre-adolescence. There is no clear consensus as to the precise age range of this group but it is usually taken to refer to children in the age range of 9–13.

in transition or in process relative to dominant ideas of Womanhood" (ibid: 6). As she goes on to elaborate, adolescence (in general):

> *functions as an explanation of the indispensable difficulty of becoming a subject, agent, or independent or self-aware person, as well as a periodization that constructs both childhood and adulthood as relative stabilities. Understanding this difficult adolescence as universal trauma is a twentieth-century Western idea that retrospectively constructs childhood as a period of stability, heightening both the crucial intensity of adolescence as [a] transformative passage and the distance between childhood and maturity.* (ibid)

These issues were also approached in Pipher's study 'Reviving Ophelia: Saving the Selves of Adolescent Girls' (1994), which delivered a popular exposition of the traumas of female adolescence. In her volume, Pipher, a clinical psychologist with a background in anthropology, characterises a range of social pressures on adolescent females in the United States (US). In particular, she explores the manner in which intense senses of female selfhood developed prior to puberty are subject to extreme societal pressures during a period in young women's lives when they feel disempowered and, consequently, fragile. Her study postulates that teenage girls develop false senses of self as ways of attempting to negotiate the social construction of adulthood that they feel impelled to conform to in various ways. Pipher uses a particular spatio-folkloric metaphor to crystallise the theme:

> *Something dramatic happens to girls in early adolescence. Just as planes and ships disappear mysteriously into the Bermuda Triangle, so do the selves of girls go down in droves. They crash and burn in a developmental Bermuda Triangle ... They lose their assertive, energetic and "tomboyish" personalities and become more deferential, self-critical and depressed. They report great unhappiness with their own bodies.* (ibid: 19)

Pipher's book takes its title from the story of Ophelia, as related in Shakespeare's 'Hamlet'. She asserts that Ophelia's story shows "the destructive forces that affect young women" by initially depicting her as "happy and free" before she transitions to early adolescence, where "she loses herself" (ibid: 20). While she does not comment on it, the play represents Ophelia as undone by her failure to negotiate the Electra complex. Instead of disentangling herself from her father and transferring her affections and allegiance to her suitor, Hamlet (as per standard transitions within the complex), she remains conflicted and, as a result, is spurned by both. As Pipher characterises it, Ophelia responds to this situation by becoming "mad with grief" and, dressed in "elegant clothes that weigh her down", "drowns in a stream filled with flowers" (ibid). While this adequately summarises a strand of the play's narrative, the characterisation does not acknowledge that the specific incident that provides her book with its title is a complex and ambiguous one. In 'Hamlet', Ophelia's final moments are not represented onstage. Instead, our knowledge of the incident derives from a description provided by Hamlet's mother, Gertrude, who characterises the moments before Ophelia's demise in the following terms:

> *Her clothes spread wide,*
> *And mermaid-like a while they bore her up,*
> *Which time she chanted snatches of old lauds*
> *As one incapable of her own distress,*
> *Or like a creature native and indued*
> *Unto that element.* (Act 4, Scene 7, lines 172–177)

Gertrude's description represents Ophelia at the fleeting moment when she has escaped from the maddening world of patriarchy and is floating (and singing) like a mermaid upon the waters, displaced from the terrestrial word and its restrictions. In her discussion of the significance of mermaids to the production of knowledge in Early Modern England, Pedersen interprets Gertrude's characterisation of Ophelia's final moments as a "profound rhetorical and artistic response" that goes beyond representing the picturesque death that inspired subsequent painters and poets (2015: 135). Pedersen argues that in her brief, water-born moments Ophelia is represented as embarking on a voyage away from the terrestrial/phallocentric order that has severely stressed her adolescent sense of self towards an unknown/alternative realm. Pedersen further characterises this in terms of the broader project of interrogating "self-unified epistemological boundaries" (ibid: 136) and indicates the complexities of unpacking the combination of "the queer and the ordinary" (ibid) in the moments during which Ophelia floats on the surface of the stream, immersed in song.

While Pipher did not utilise the mermaid as a motif in her reflections on adolescent identity and self-esteem issues, I take up that thread in this chapter with regard to the popularity of the mermaid as a media-loric motif in films and television programs targeted at young girls and by young girls acting in and/or producing representations of themselves as mermaids. As previous chapters have established, the mermaid has been used in a variety of ways in recent decades. Writers such as Williams have characterised that US media culture has utilised the mermaid to symbolise "female rites of passage", "pubescent change from girl to woman" and the "painful 'growth' experiences" involved (2010: 194). While this is clearly apparent with regard to individuals such as the titular protagonist of Disney's *The Little Mermaid*, who transforms from one form to another to affect a key shift in the film's narrative, other audiovisual productions have significantly different orientations. The analyses offered in this chapter point to the temporary spaces and/or pauses offered by identifying with and/or performing mermaid identity. I engage with aspects of Pipher's (1994) and Driscoll's (2002) studies by asking to what extent aficionado productions might represent, reflect and/or otherwise re-interpret aspects of the problematisation of teenage girls' senses of selfhood. In particular, I discuss the extent to which mermaid-themed productions might offer escapism through mermaids' impossible bodies and the environmental and social contexts that they inhabit.

My findings concur with comments made by Dinnerstein in 'The Mermaid and the Minotaur' (1999), a volume addressing the negative impact of asymmetrical gender roles on both women and men. In her introduction she contends that folk-/media-loric figures such as the mermaid "have bearing not only on human malaise in general ... but also on our sexual arrangements in particular" (1999: 2) and further characterises that:

> our species' nature is internally inconsistent ... our continuities with, and our differences from, the earth's other animals are mysterious and profound; and in these continuities, and these differences, lie both our sense of strangeness on earth and the possible key to a way of feeling at home here. (ibid)

This subtle characterisation provides substantial insight into the material discussed in this chapter. The mermaids (and, in occasional instances, mermen) represented in the productions analysed in the following sections are figures that allow their audiences to feel comfortable with them and with (terrestrial or aquatic) realms in which standard socio-sexual pressures are displaced and/or reconfigured. The visible lack of genitalia on mermaids' and mermen's tails is emblematic in this context, suggesting that they are not implicated into sexual relations with each other and/or other humans or, at least, those involving and/or pre-occupied with genital/penetrative interactions. In the productions discussed below, the world presented is a safe zone in terms of sexuality. Desire occurs but largely within a romantic framework. Kisses can be exchanged but anything further is barely suggested.

Given that the productions discussed in this chapter were produced after the successful launch of Disney's *The Little Mermaid* franchise in 1989 it is not unreasonable to assert that the latter acted as a substantial catalyst for the imagination and production of a body of subsequent films and TV programs. For this reason, and on account of the pronounced parallels of many aspects of the productions discussed in this chapter to the original Disney film (and/or aspects of Andersen's original story), it is worth reprising my earlier characterisations of these texts. Drawing on a body of psychoanalytic interpretations I referred to in the Introduction to this volume, I identified how the story of *The Little Mermaid* could be read as a manifestation of the Electra complex. As I also elaborated, Ariel's traumatic transformation into human form could be interpreted as a representation of her transition to womanhood and to her access to the world of sexual interaction, in which she successfully secures a relationship with the man of her dreams. But while this may be eminently credible as a Freudian reading of the film's overall narrative, this characterisation does not necessarily identify the key aspect of the film's appeal to audiences. One clue as to the latter concerns Ariel's representation in a slew of audio-visual, visual and literary representations produced by authorised merchandisers and unauthorised commercial and fan producers alike over the last twenty-five years. These overwhelmingly concern and represent Ariel in her mer-form rather than in the human form in which she successfully secures a relationship with her princely object of desire. In this regard it is not the travails of the humanised, young adult Ariel that appear to appeal and resonate but rather the image of the playful, adventurous 'tomboyish' mermaid who inhabits and explores a wondrous oceanic realm prior to her transformation. It is significant in this regard that Disney's spin-off television series featured this aspect exclusively, representing Ariel before she developed her fixation with transforming herself. While some of the productions discussed below concern mermaids transitioning to human form these do not directly shift the transformed individuals into realms of sexual congress and tend to leave them in a transitional zone, anatomically and sexually enabled but not yet ready or inclined to deploy their physical forms in sexual interactions.

I. Teen-Oriented Productions

(a) Feature films

Although Sam Irwin's *Magic Island* (1995) featured a young mermaid transformed into human form as the partner to a 13-year-old boy experiencing a fantasy adventure,[195] the

---

195 The film features Lily, a young mermaid (Jessie-Ann Friend), first shown rescuing the film's male protagonist, Jack (Zachery Ty Bryan), from drowning and then transforming (apparently effortlessly) into human form to accompany him on his adventures.

body of work discussed in this chapter is primarily a 21st Century phenomenon. The first live-action film to feature a teenage mermaid in lead role was Elizabeth Arden's (2006) eponymous screen adaptation of Alice Hoffman's (2001) novella 'Aquamarine'.[196] Hoffman first gained commercial and critical success with her novel 'Practical Magic' (1995) and subsequent works developed a vein of magical realism within popular, women's-oriented fiction. 'Aquamarine' concerns a brief, pivotal moment in the lives of two girls. Set in late summer around a decaying beach resort, in the final hours before its demolition, the novella concerns Claire and Hailey, two 12-year-old girls savouring their close companionship before Claire relocates to Florida with her grandparents. Claire is also concerned that the destruction of the club's facilities will weaken her memories of the time she spent there with her deceased parents in previous years. This poignant scenario is given a further twist when a storm swamps the club pool overnight, filling it with seawater, seaweed and sand. As the girls soon discover, it has also delivered a 16-year-old mermaid named Aquamarine, the youngest of seven sisters, who was swept away from her family during a storm. Hoffman provides a vivid description of the mermaid's delicate beauty:

> Her voice was as cool and fresh as bubbles rising from the ocean. She was as beautiful as a pearl, with a faint turquoise tinge to her skin and eyes so blue that they were the exact same color as the deepest sea. (2001: 31-32)

While palely beautiful, the young mermaid is also grouchy and capricious and stuns her new human accomplices by instantly falling in love with Raymond, a handsome male resort attendant, whom she has only glimpsed from the pool. Despite suffering from the chlorinated pool water, Aquamarine refuses to leave until she can meet Raymond. When the girls agree to facilitate this they make the condition that the mermaid will have to leave the next morning, a deal she reluctantly agrees to: ("Aquamarine begged and cried until the pool was awash with blue tears that stained the moon jellyfish turquoise and indigo, but the girls would not change their minds" [ibid: 51]). This resolved, the girls then devise a way of engineering a date between the two without Raymond realising Aquamarine's true identity.[197] Hailey adapts one of her mother's old blue dresses in order to provide Aquamarine with a garment long enough to cover her tail and the girls deliver her to a café in a wheelchair the next afternoon (together with a story about a recent accident she has had). After Raymond and Aquamarine enjoy a romantic dinner the girls return, wheel her away and leave her overnight in the pool. When they arrive the next day she is weak and her body is rapidly deteriorating. The girls get her into the seawater just in time ("her skin gave off puffs of greenish dust, as if she were already turning to ash, right there in their arms" [ibid: 90]). After watching her revive and return to the sea, Claire departs for Florida and Hayley prepares for the bulldozers to move in on the resort.

Aquamarine resembles the protagonist of Andersen's story and Disney's film adaptation in several regards: in (approximate) age, in being the youngest of her sisters and in falling

---

196 A brief sequence of mermaid imagery also occurred in the marine adventure film *A Ring of Endless Light* (Mike Schondek, 2002), when the film's female teenage lead, Vicky (Mischa Baron), dreams that she is a mermaid who gets caught in a fishing net.

197 Raymond realises her true identity towards the end of the novella when he glimpses her in the pool and the story ends with references to him meeting her again out at sea, suggesting the possibility of a future relationship developing.

deeply in love with a human male at first sight. But she also differs in significant ways, most notably in that she neither seeks nor gains the ability to transform into human form and in that she is not the principal focus of the narrative. Instead, Aquamarine figures as a personification and foreshadowing of the world of romance and of transition (and of stress and fragility) that the two 12-year-olds will enter in adolescence. The girls' own tentative admiration of Raymond is displaced into their assistance in arranging his date with Aquamarine, who is effectively their surrogate in developing an amorous relationship with an unattainable, older male. Strong female relationships are thereby the core of the narrative.

Hoffman's novella was adapted for the screen by Jessica Bendinger and John Quaintance. The writers specialised in scripting teen-oriented female-themed productions (in this period at least), Bendinger having previously written the cheerleader feature *Bring it On* (Peyton Reed, 2000), starring Kirsten Dunce, and Quaintance having written the Hilary and Haylie Duff vehicle *Material Girls* (Martha Coolidge, 2006). These films share similarities with director Elizabeth Arden's adaptation of 'Aquamarine' (2006) in featuring personable and attractive teenage actresses involved in negotiating the transition to adulthood. While ostensibly set in Florida, *Aquamarine* was an Australian-American co-production shot in Queensland, with a trio of young American female leads and a supporting cast of mainly Australian actors affecting US accents. The film's titular mermaid was played by Sara Paxton, with Hailey played by Joanna 'JoJo' Levesque and Claire by Emma Roberts. The major change affected by the screenwriters concerned Aquamarine. Unlike the novel, the film gave its mermaid the power to transform to fully-human form (during daylight hours). The narrative differs from the novella in that the girls are able to interact with the mermaid in human form during the day, with much of the narrative concerning attempts to keep her mer-identity secret by concealing her whereabouts at night. There are also other small but significant differences. Whereas the novella's mermaid was washed ashore by an unexpected storm, the filmic Aquamarine has come ashore in order to escape her father's attempt to get her to marry a merman. Much of the action and humour in the film concerns the girls' attempts to educate Aquamarine in appropriate behaviour and courtship protocols (entirely sourced from magazines, as the girls have minimal experience of such things). They also have to negotiate their way around Cecilia (Arielle Kebbel), the bitchily assertive girl who is attempting to cultivate a romance with Raymond (Jake McDorman) and who comes to suspect Aquamarine's identity.

Like the novella, the film explores the close commitment between the girls and the mermaid as they co-operate to overcome adversity and manoeuvre around adults who are unaware that there is a mermaid in their midst. In contrast to the fragility of the novel's mermaid, the filmic Aquamarine is a more robust and likeable individual who fits more easily into the girls' world (in both human and mer-form). The central plot element of the novella, concerning Aquamarine's desire for one date with Raymond before she returns to the sea, is substituted in the film for a scenario in which Aquamarine has to prove to her father that she can find love onshore in order to escape the marriage he has planned for her. Despite an opening that makes it clear that the two girls also have a crush on Raymond, they rally round and support Aquamarine when she becomes similarly smitten and help her to date Raymond and to fend off Cecilia's attempted interventions. Played with kooky charm by Paxton, Aquamarine's attempts to gain a statement of love from Raymond during her brief time onshore are rendered with pathos, underlining the extent to which she doesn't understand the nature of courtship and romance. Failing to obtain the statement she requires, she is fated to return to the sea. At the end of the film she is pushed off a pier by Cecelia and is swept out by currents that her father has generated to drag her home. Help arrives in unexpected form as Hailey and (the previously aquaphobic) Claire jump in to try and assist her. Clinging to a buoy together, Aquamarine asks them why they have their risked their lives for her. When they answer that they have grown to love her, she cries a tear of joy that falls into the sea, immediately calming the waters. Paddling out on his board, Raymond perceives Aquamarine's mer-form and, undaunted, asks whether they might meet again in future. The film ends with the girls embracing on the beach, affirming their friendship and vowing to reunite the following year. This focus on the girls' deep commitment saving the day and resolving the narrative distinguishes *Aquamarine* from Disney's film and presages the production of the sororally-themed productions discussed in following sections.[198]

(b) Television series

While young mermaids featured in individual episodes of youth-oriented shows in the early 2000s,[199] the first TV series dedicated to them was *H₂O: Just Add Water* (2006–2010). The series was developed by Australian producer Jonathan M. Shiff, drawing on elements of his earlier *Ocean Girl* (1994–1997), a series based around the adventures of an alien teenager with highly developed aquatic abilities. *H₂O* was successful internationally, screening on the Disney Channel in the US, on Discovery Kids in the United Kingdom (UK) and on a range of other international broadcasters. Identifying the combination of effective drama and characterisation with extensive underwater sequences as being key

---

198 Similar themes of collaboration between a girl and young mermaid were explored in *Roxy Hunter and the Myth of the Mermaid* (Eleanor Lindo, 2008). The film featured Hunter (Aria Wallace) trying to ascertain the identity of an amnesiac girl (who resembles a junior version of Madison in human-form in *Splash*). A number of clues, such as her ability to sing haunting, wordless melodies, lead Hunter to identify her as a mermaid temporarily transformed into human form. Following the resolution of a criminal plot to illegally dispose of toxic waste, which endangers the lives of the female duo, Hunter helps the girl to return to the water (and presumably to change back to mer-form). While she is never represented in fish-tailed form in the film her identity as a mermaid is crucial to the narrative and its resolution.

199 Mermaids featured in several episodes of the (revived) dolphin-themed aquatic series *Flipper*. In an episode entitled 'Submersible' (Peter Fisk, 1995), the series' two teenage leads glimpse a mermaid while out swimming and then search for her in an undersea vehicle before getting into difficulties. A subsequent episode entitled 'Mermaid Island' (Donald Crombie, 1997) features more sustained representations of a transformative mermaid (played by Rachel Blakely) who - somewhat ambiguously - appears to be both a human confidence trickster and a transformative mermaid. A mermaid named (played by Marliece Andrada) featured in an episode of *Baywatch* entitled 'Rendezvous' (Gus Trikonis, 1997), interacting with a character named Cody (David Chokachi) after she encounters him underwater and mistakes him for a human male she had met a hundred years previously. A double episode of US series *Power Rangers Lightspeed Rescue* broadcast in 2000 (entitled 'Neptune's Daughter' and 'Ocean Blue' - both directed by Jonathan Tzachor). Marina first acts as lure to allow Vypra, a demon princess, to capture Chad, the Blue Lightspeed Ranger, and later grows to love him, assist him to escape and seek his help in securing a trident stolen from King Neptune. A double episode of US series *Charmed*, featuring the adventures of three American witches, entitled 'A Witch's Tail' (James Conway, 2002), also included a mermaid on the run from an evil sea hag. In order to assist her, Phoebe (Alyssa Milano), one of the program's core trio of young witches, transforms into a mermaid and experiences the charms of the ocean.

Figure 19 – Rikki (Cariba Heine) swimming underwater, promotional still from H_2O (2006, courtesy of Jonathan M. Shiff Productions).

elements of *Ocean Girl's* international appeal (Urban 2007: 7), Shiff developed H_2O as a teen-orientated production that features a trio of girls becoming mermaids. The latter aspect is significant in that the transformations discussed in previous chapters concerned mermaids assuming human form. The spontaneous transition from human to mer-form represents both a novel element in media-lore and one rarely present in folklore. Shiff identifies the central element of his series' appeal as the manner in which "the girls are real characters" experiencing this transition, with the intention that "kids can identify with them" (Urban 2007: 11). The producer's perceptions appear to have been correct in that the program was even more successful than *Ocean Girl*, being screened in over 120 countries and being accompanied by a dedicated Wiki site[200] and a series of spin-off novellas published by Simon and Schuster (2009–2011).

The program developed over three series. Series 1 (2006) introduced three mid-teen girls living on Australia's Gold Coast, Rikki (Cariba Heine, see Figure 19), Emma (Claire Holt) and Cleo (Phoebe Tonkin), who wash up on the mysterious, uninhabited Mako Island after the motor on their inflatable boat cuts out. While exploring the island they fall down a shaft and find a pool that is open to the sky via a narrow aperture. As the moon passes overhead and shines down the trio are bathed in a strange light. Upon their return to shore they discover that they transform into mermaids when they get wet and that they have also acquired the ability to manipulate water. In mer-form they share a similar appearance with orange-brown, scaled tails and matching bikini tops (both of which have a carp-like quality and patterning). The first series concerns the girls juggling the vicissitudes of adolescence, the difficulties of keeping their mer-abilities secret and their desire to enjoy the sea in mer-form. The trio's close relationship, forged by their unique shared attributes, is a key element of the drama, as is the pleasure they take in their powerful aquatic abilities. The second series (2007) retained these basic elements and also added a temporary adversary for the trio in the form of Charlotte (Brittany Burns), another girl who has gained (short-lived) mermaid powers from the pool. The third series, produced in 2009, included a variation in casting, replacing Emma with the similarly-aged Bella (Indiana Evans) and introduced novel plot elements. The latter include a water tendril that draws the girls to Mako and a Science Fiction plot element that culminates in the girls using their special

200   http://h2o.wikia.com/wiki/H2O:_Just_Add_Water_Wiki – which has been maintained and expanded to incorporate the series' sequels – accessed August 7th 2015

powers to deflect a comet from crashing into the Earth. As these summaries suggest, the majority of the series involves the girls interacting as adolescents with extra powers and alternative identities (rather than becoming mermaids full-time and relocating to an aquatic realm).

The success of H_2O led its producer to develop a related program entitled *Mako Mermaids*[201] (2013–), which reversed the premise of its predecessor by being based around three mermaids who transition to human form.[202] The mermaids' appearance and inter-action with high school students suggests them as being in their mid–late teens (in human years[203]) and the trio resemble the similarly-aged human protagonists of the preceding program by virtue of being young, slim, attractive and of European-Australian appearance. The first episode introduces Sirena (Amy Ruffle), Nixie (Ivy Latimer) and Lyla (Lucy Fry) as members of a pod of (around a hundred) mermaids who live around Mako island. The episode shows the pod preparing for a full moon ritual that requires the trio to stand guard over the island while (similarly beautiful) adult mermaids float in circles, holding hands in the sea, looking upwards and bathing in the light of the full moon. This scene marks an original contribution to mermaid media-lore, showing the participation of groups of mermaids in cultural activities (aside from singing on rocks or swimming underwater together). The trio's neglect of their guard duties allows a human boy, Zac (Chai Romruen), to fall into a magical moon pool and gain the ability to transform to mer-form.[204] Expelled from their pod for neglecting their guard duties, the trio follows Zac back to land where they use a magic ring to transform into human form and attempt to remove his enchantment. The extensive onshore sequences allow the trio to interact with their human peers as conventional teenagers and initially generate humour from their lack of knowledge of human codes and customs. Similar to the protagonists of H_2O, the three mermaids and other teenage characters in the series are represented in a fundamentally wholesome manner, in that there is no suggestion of consumption of alcohol or drugs and the teenagers are represented in what might be termed a pre-sexual phase where heterosexual interactions are limited to hand-holding and chaste kisses.

The Mako mermaids are represented as powerful in a number of ways. Their ability to swim at high speeds over great distances is frequently represented in the program and they are also shown to possess a range of magical powers, including various forms of telekinesis and the ability to be invisible. Sirena also possesses a particularly melodious singing voice, which she frequently uses in human form in featured sequences (in addition to singing the program's theme song 'I just wanna be'). In a similar manner to the main protagonist and supporting characters of the popular US series *Sabrina: The Teenage Witch* (1996–2003), the trio are not always shown as fully adept at using their magical mer-powers and are often unsure as to how and to what extent they should deploy them. Similarly to

---

201   Screened in Australia as *Mako: Island of Secrets*.

202   A theme also explored in an episode of the teen comedy series *A Pair of Kings* entitled 'A Mermaid's Tail' (Andy Cadiff, 2010), which featured four teenage mermaids coming ashore to become converted to human form.

203   In common with many mermaid films and television series, mermaids are represented as living longer and ageing more slowly than humans.

204   See Chapter 7 for a discussion of Zac and the representation of mermen in audiovisual media.

137

Figure 20 – Lyla (Lucy Fry) after an unwanted transformation onshore in Series 1 Episode 4 of *Mako Mermaids* (courtesy of Jonathan M. Shiff Productions).

H₂O, they also have to negotiate the perils of reverting to mermaid form if they get wet (see Figure 20). While the world of human teenagers is initially shown as somewhat tricky for the mermaids to come to terms with it is also one in which the mermaids-as-girls can exercise considerable autonomy. As discussed in the following chapter, the most severe challenge to their power occurs when Zac discovers and becomes attracted to a magical trident produced by an ancient merman and the mermaids have to combat him and a human accomplice in order to destroy the weapon and preserve the sanctity of their "island home".[205] The theme of sisterhood is constant throughout and the trio overcome a series of internal tensions and personality clashes in order to rise above adversity.

II. Mermaiding – Aficionado and Cosplay Communities

The success of the series discussed above, and of *H₂O* in particular, created an aficionado culture that has been manifest in blogs, social networks and through the production of amateur videos. The latter range from singular representations of young girls in mermaid costumes through to multi-part narratives, often inspired by aspects of the TV series. These video productions have been facilitated by parallel and partly overlapping developments concerning the availability of commercially-manufactured mermaid tails and a related diffusion of information about how to make such tails. The life-like appearance and functionality of Madison's tail in the 1984 film *Splash* (discussed in Chapter 4) is generally regarded as having initiated interest in the possibilities of wearing such an appendage and/or swimming in role as a mermaid.[206] A number of women who developed skills in swimming with mermaid tails in the 2000s have emphasised the significance of

---

205   Commemorated in the second line of the program's theme song ('I just wanna be'): "You know I love my island home."

206   Indeed, special effects designer Robert Short has been celebrated by mermaid aficionados for his creation of Madison's tail in the film (see Raja 2015).

Figure 21 – Hannah Fraser in a sequined mermaid tail
(2010, reproduced from HannahMermaid.com).

Madison as a figure that enabled them to combine their attraction to the mermaid with the possibility of physically enacting her role. Actress and model Hannah Fraser (see Figure 21), generally considered to have been the first successful commercial mermaid performer internationally,[207] has identified that:

> *Ever since I could remember, mermaids seemed fascinating and romantic to me. The flowing lines of weightless form, the beautiful tail, and long hair – as a child, I spent hours drawing fantasy artworks ... Mermaids are alluring, yet independent ... I think young girls especially identify with mermaids because they exemplify eternal youthfulness and a symbol of freedom inherent in the energy of the oceans.*

> *When I saw* Splash, *my visions turned to reality with Daryl Hannah's perfect portrayal of a mermaid. I realized I could do the same thing. I made a tail with the help of my mother and swam around for months in it. When I grew up to become an artist, photographer, costume designer, model, and professional mermaid, all my skills and passions combined to give me the talent to create tails and perform underwater successfully.* (Peterson 2013: online)

In addition to *Splash's* continuing appeal, interest in mermaid tails and related costumery resulted from and entwined with the continuing success of Disney's *The Little Mermaid*

---

207 Fraser's performances as a mermaid have been represented in a range of photo-shoots, short films and music videos produced over the last decade. Many of these have represented the mermaid as an intermediary between the mythological-folkloric realm of the sea and living species and eco-systems and have attracted strongly positive responses from female viewers. See, for example, *Dream of the Siren*, a stills montage accompanied by narration and music (and posted viewer responses), online at: https://www.youtube.com/watch?v=zdngeRvMYI4 – accessed September 11th 2015.

Figure 22 – Cosplay performance for a photo session (Vancouver, 2014) –
Mimi Reaves in role as Ariel and Madeline in role as Vanessa (Ursula
transformed into human form) (Note that Reaves's costume combines
elements of Ariel in mermaid and human form and both cosplayers are
depicted wielding tridents, which are traditionally symbols of male power)
(2014, photo by Megan Ives – ZC101.

franchise, which was launched in 1989 and exploited throughout the 1990s and 2000s. The decade following the release of Disney's film also saw the rise of the phenomenon known as 'cosplay', a practice involving the role-playing of fictional characters in appropriate costume. This first appeared at aficionado conventions during the 1970s and 1980s, when fans impersonated live-action characters (such as Darth Vader and Princess Leia from the *Star Wars* films). The practice became more widespread, and more ambitious and elaborate in terms of make-up, costume and accessories, through its development in Japan, where it is known as *kosupure*. The latter practice involves individuals modelling (and thereby 'bringing to life') drawn characters from manga publications, anime films and/or video games. *Kosupure* fed back into US/European cosplay culture in the 1990s and 2000s, and given that Disney productions have been an enduring object of interest for cosplayers, it was unsurprising that Ariel began to be enacted by cosplayers in the 1990s and continues to be regularly performed. As Gn identifies, such performances are complicated, since the gendered entities in drawn media are not ones whose gender is defined by any actual anatomy but rather represent a "synthesized performance of gender" (2011: 585). As he elaborates:

> *Animated bodies, despite being visual figures, are also embedded within the narrative of the text. To that effect, they are always endowed with a sense of artificiality that complicates any theoretical attempt to simplify the distinction between subversion, difference, and pleasure. Reading animated bodies along the same lines as a 'living subject' would thus negate the ways in which they will always 'fall inside quotation marks'; they are, essentially, virtual objects capable of shifting between different systems of representation. (ibid)*

This characterisation is singularly appropriate for the mermaid, as a figure whose lower body can only be approximated and interpreted by cosplay performers.[208] As Figure 22

---

208   While the cosplay realisations of Ariel clearly operate within these parameters it can also be asserted that any attempts to imitate the fictional body of Madison in *Splash* is similarly an artificial performance of an illusory screen body.

illustrates, this aspect also allows cosplay performers to synthesise and adapt characters and their interplay.

In her discussion of Disney cosplaying at US conventions in the early 2010s, Amon characterised that one distinguishing aspect of the cosplayers she surveyed was their "nostalgia for characters encountered in childhood", accompanied by a related sense of pleasure and gratification when children responded to their appearance by expressing a deep attachment to the characters portrayed (2014: 6). This is borne out in the experience of Traci Hines, one of the most successful mermaid performers to emerge from the cosplay convention circuit. Hines, then a young, aspirant pop singer, attended an Anime Expo in Los Angeles in 2008 in character as Ariel and was videoed singing an impromptu unaccompanied version of 'The World Above' (from the stage musical version of *The Little Mermaid*) that went on to register over two million views on YouTube. She followed this up in 2013 with a music video performance of Ariel's signature song 'Part of Your World'. Her version of the song differed from the original by being a 'stand alone' number showcasing her vocal abilities rather than weaving the song's delivery into a narrative context. Her wide dynamic range, extensive rubato, dramatic vibrato at phrase endings and gospel-style melismas are complemented by Adam Gubman's arrangement, which features a variety of textual and timbral elements and rhythm section accenting the drama of the chorus.[209] Complementing the sonic 'gloss' of the music track, the video was a high quality production (see Figure 23) that combined a live-action reworking of the song's visual setting in the original film with other sequences that director Raiya Corsiglia deemed as the most iconic and memorable (such as Eric's coming-to onshore, Ariel's transformation and her dancing with Eric in human form).[210] Hines's accomplished vocal performance and her charisma in role as Ariel resulted in the video receiving over five million views, further boosting her profile as a fairytale character entertainer. Hines has identified her attraction to Ariel as based on her perception of the character in the original film as an empowering and positive role model:

> *She's bubbly and vivacious, fun loving* and inspiring, and many of those qualities are ones we strive for ourselves: her fearlessness, her likability, her passion, her ambition and her true heart. Like so many other girls out there, I not only see myself in her, but see who I want to be ... And she doesn't wait around for things to happen. She has big, almost impossible dreams, and doesn't let anyone stop her in going after them. (Turgeon 2011: online)

She has also reported that her perceptions have been affirmed and boosted by children's responses to her appearances in-role:

> *The children's faces light up when they see me dressed as their favorite mermaid princess – usually I'm swarmed with a flurry of instant hugs, and when I start to sing, the reaction is indescribable! Seeing those kids be so mesmerized and happy that the character is singing just for them is so special – and a lot of times, even the parents get excited too! I love it when they sing along! It's got to be the most wonderful job in the world!* (ibid)

---

209 Thanks to Jon Fitzgerald for his comments on the music track.

210 See Corsiglia's comments in her *Making of Traci Hines' "Part of Your World" Music Video* (2014), online at: https://vimeo.com/61242754 – accessed January 20th 2016.

Figure 23 – Image of Traci Hines as Ariel from her music video *Part of Your World* (2013, Raiya Corsiglia).

This sense of children's appreciation motivating adult cosplay performers was one factor that fed into a practice that developed in the US in the late 2000s and expanded significantly in the 2010s. This involved a number of adults (some of whom were also participants in aspects of cosplay or other costumed performance practices) working as mermaid entertainers at pool parties, usually held for young girls. In these contexts the mermaid performers would entertain by appearing as mermaids and by leading appropriately themed activities, sometimes including dressing up girls in tails. In addition to these activities, some performers, such as Virginia Hankins, a mermaid model and underwater performer who operates the Sheroes Entertainment Company in Los Angeles,[211] also provide sea swimming experiences for girls, supplying tails, appropriate swim-training and video records of the activities. Hankins has provided the following account of her early inspiration:

> I remember being a child and seeing the movie 'The Little Mermaid' from the Walt Disney Company. I was struck by the character's love of adventure and similar appearance to myself. When I was growing up there was very little diversity in the appearance of cartoons or other fictional characters so seeing another adventure-loving redhead was something that I was able to relate to as a child. I would pretend to be Ariel in the pool for months after the movie came out and try to swim while keeping my legs together to be a mermaid too. While playing make believe I would let my mind daydream that my pool was actually the ocean and of the wonderful animals that I would meet there. (p.c. October 30th 2013)

She developed this interest into a professional identity as 'Catalina Mermaid':

> I have found my live entertainment niche with children. I love working with kids. They have a fresh outlook on life and aren't burdened down yet by what they

211   See: http://www.sheroesentertainment.com/ – accessed September 10th 2015

"should" be or believe in. I often appear as a specialized "playmate" to many of them, hired by their parents to bring a magical day in to their life. (ibid)[212]

One of the results of this social practice, and of its recording on video cameras, was the development of amateur video productions by participants, their friends and/or family showing young girls in role as mermaids that were often uploaded to platforms such as YouTube.[213] This activity has flourished in recent years and has resulted in a significant number of productions, many made in serial form.

III. Aficionado Productions

A survey of the variety of series available online suggests that the usual age of on-screen participants is around 8–14. Productions span a range between tightly scripted dramas and more semi-improvised ones. The videos appear to reflect a young audience's interpretation of contemporary mermaid media-lore, their artistic engagement with and reinterpretation of that, and their use of this approach to represent aspects of their own lives and preoccupations. Reflecting this body of production there's even a wikiHow website entitled 'How to Make a Good Mermaid Show on YouTube'.[214] The site contains advice that reflects the number of online mermaid productions produced over the last five years and opens with a question that refers to some of the best-known amateur mermaid aficionado dramas:

> *Have you ever seen Secret Sea Life by Niki, The 3 Tails, Truly H₂O, Mermaid Miracles, or Secret Life of a Mermaid on YouTube? Have you ever thought, "Wow, I want to make a mermaid show, too!" Well, here you have it. You can learn how to make one with easy steps!*

While some of the comments on the website are generic tips on video drama production others reflect specific aspects of filming mermaid dramas. These include technical advice, such as point 5, which emphasises that a waterproof camera should be used if video-makers are planning to shoot underwater sequences, and discuss some more aesthetic matters, including Item 2, 'Decide on how you will get your mermaid tail':

> *The show always has a special way to make you and your cast become mermaids! Maybe you went swimming in a special lake and you came out to be a mermaid! Or, if you are a fan of H2O, you could get lost and have to go to a Moon Pool for safety, and the Moon Pool turns you into a mermaid. Make it unique. Don't just touch water and magically become a mermaid without any real reason for being one. Be creative and make sure it goes smoothly and make sure it makes sense!*

> *Try not to copy other shows too much, or people will not like the show. Be*

---

212   Also see the discussion of Hankins' career in Hayward (2013).

213   It is probably far from coincidental in this regard that a number of the animated television films produced under the Barbie franchise in this period included representations of mermaids. Following an earlier film, *Barbie Mermaidia* (Walter Martishius and William Lau, 2006) (in which a flower fairy visits Mermaidia to rescue a prince and teams up with a mermaid to accomplish this), a more concentrated exploration of mermaid themes followed in the 2010s in the form of *Barbie in a Mermaid Tale* (Adam Wood, 2010), *Barbie in a Mermaid Tale II* (William Lau, 2012) and *Barbie: the Pearl Princess* (Ezekiel Norton, 2014). These films parallel *H₂O* and aficionado series by featuring attractive, assertive and sympathetic young women and/or mermaids battling adversity and maintaining strong relationships with their peer groups. Similarly, a number of programs in the *Dora The Explorer* series featured mermaid themes, including 'Dora Saves the Mermaids' (director unknown, 2007) and 'Dora's Rescue in Mermaid Kingdom' (2012, director unknown).

214   http://www.wikihow.com/Make-a-Good-Mermaid-Show-on-YouTube – accessed September 9th 2015.

original! ... There are so many mermaid show[s] on YouTube, try to make show [sic] stand out and be different from the others! Don't worry, just think outside of the box![215]

A number of the series were produced over extended durations and are marked by an increase in production and acting skills as the girls involved matured and gained greater experience. One of the first extended series to be produced was *Secret Life of a Mermaid* (2009–2014), initiated by Christine Davis when she was aged 9. The series' website provides the following introduction:

When I was younger, my best friend (Claire aka Brenna) and I decided to do a little home movie on my mom's old video camera about how we magically turned into mermaids when we touched water because of a star. When we made this film, we didn't have real tails or anything, just a sheet of green fabric. A while later, my sister (you may know her as Tess) got bored, so she decided to see if she could find a mermaid tail for sale. She couldn't find a cheap one though, so we decided to make our own. After we made the tail (which took a couple of tries until we finally got it right) my sister wanted to find an underwater camera so we could film it. After she purchased one, she filmed me swimming in the tail and put it up on youtube. I then got a comment from someone saying that I should make a series. So I filmed a short, raw episode calling the series "Secret Life of a Mermaid". I didn't think much would come of this show, but I kept getting comments asking if there was going to be more episodes. So, Bridget and I made more and then decided to get my friend from the original movie to co-star in my series. People were responding positively to the episodes and pretty soon, the once small, unknown "Secret Life of a Mermaid" series turned into what it is today. (Davis n.d.: online)

Shot in Florida, the web series developed a significant fan-base, and YouTube viewing figures indicate that individual episodes routinely achieved viewing figures of around 500,000 with some receiving significantly higher numbers.[216] The series also spawned spin-off items, such as the *Teenie989 Newscasts* in 2010, which provided spoof TV news coverage of the series.

The initial episode of *Secret Life*, entitled 'Flip Flop' (1.43) comprised a short sequence showing Christine (in role as the series' main protagonist, Amy) being caught in the rain in a pool. Later, back at her house she finds that she sprouts a pink mermaid tail when water gets splashed on her legs. The second episode, 'Heat Wave' was longer (3.01) and included the series' first scenes of swimming with a mermaid tail in a pool. The episode also included the series' first use of music (via an off-screen sound source recorded live). Subsequent episodes in Series 1 continued to expand the potential of the drama and went on to introduce other young female characters who had the ability to assume mer-form. Subsequent series developed the girls' personalities and inter-personal relationships as a key aspect. The concluding series was uploaded in 2014 and culminated in episodes in which the girls ran away from home, fearing capture by men who had discovered their identity. The final (13.49-minute-long) episode closed the narrative with the girls tiring

215 Item 7 also offers practical advice around obtaining mermaid tails for cast members to wear, suggesting purchase from identified online tail retailers (such as Mermagica.com or Finfun) or means of making them.

216 Series 1 Episode 2, *Heatwave*, for example, showing 6.5 million viewers (as of September 2015).

of being "mermaid-like a while" and growing weary of being outsiders. A rare 'blood moon' event allows them the opportunity to lose their transformative powers and to become normal adolescents, with all the complications that entails.

Subsequent to *Secret Life of a Mermaid*, a number of other aficionado productions featuring and largely made by pre-teen and teen girls, almost exclusively in the US, were produced and made available online, including:[217]

Mermaid Secrets (2011-2013)
Deep Sea Tails (2012-2013)
My Magical Mermaid Life (2012-2013)
Forever Scales (2012-2013)
Truly H₂O (2013)
Tennessee Tailz (2013-2015)
The Mermaid Mysteries (2014-2015)
The Tail of 2 Mermaids (2014-2015)
Mermaid Island (2015-)
Ocean Star (2015-)
Maui Mermaids (2015-)
My Splash Side (2015-)

In addition to the short duration of individual episodes (usually 5–10 minutes), the above productions share a number of commons aspects, including:

- Small groups (often duos or trios) of young girls, usually Caucasian in appearance, who share secret mermaid identities

- Transitions to mer-form occurring at awkward moments

- Attempts to keep mer-identities secret

- Underwater sequences of mermaids swimming in pools

- Use of pre-recorded music, often by female artists

While writer and director credits are not always provided, one or more of the performers who appear on screen often function as writers and/or editors (camera operators are largely not identified). The close similarity between series suggests that innovation in style and content is not a key dynamic for the producers and that formulaic, low-production standards and predictability is core to the genre. These aspects might also suggest that the series are made primarily for the enjoyment of the participants. But viewing figures available for material uploaded to platforms such as YouTube and comments posted by viewers indicate that the series have considerable audiences who are familiar and comfortable with the programs' aesthetic formulae. Indeed, viewing figures for mermaid aficionado productions can be massive. One of the highest viewing totals I have encountered to date for an individual production is for *The Mermaid Experience: Mermaids of Georgia* (2013), a short, amateur video produced as a promotion for the Mermaid Experience, a company based in Dunwoody, in the US state of Georgia, run by three teenage mermaid aficionados.[218] The production (acted and directed by the girls) features a simple narrative that commences by showing a teenage mermaid trapped on a beach when her tail is wedged

---

217   See: youtubemermaid-shows.wikia.com for details of and links to other series.

218   See the company's website http://themermaidexperience.webs.com/ – accessed December 11th 2015.

under a rock. She is then rescued by a teenage human girl and reunited with her mermaid friends in the bay. The grateful mermaids then swim back to shore and transform the girl's legs into a tail in gratitude, allowing her to swim with them. As of December 11th 2015, this modest production had secured 37,287,595 viewers on YouTube.[219]

With regard to the series discussed above, *Mermaid Miracles* (2014–2015) stands out by virtue of combining a pre/early-teen creator and cast with more experienced (adult) creative personnel. In many ways it can be seen to mark the development of aficionado video production into a more standard independent mode – aspects reflected in its production standards, originality of scripting and quality of acting. Indeed, the opening sequence of *Mermaid Miracles'* pilot episode more closely resembles a sequence from the mermaid-themed feature films discussed in Chapters 2 and 3 than the standard aficionado video series. The episode opens with a clear, well-lit image of a glamorous, adult mermaid swimming underwater accompanied by an extract from Ocean Lab's song 'Underneath the Sea' (subsequently used as the title theme for Series 1).[220] A voiceover introduction by a young girl then states, "Let me tell you a story about how my momma and poppa met." The meeting concerned is shown as occurring when the mermaid swims up to a male surfer floating on a board at night. After she introduces herself flirtatiously to him, the voiceover states, "and this is where my story begins". The adult mermaid is played by Inga Tritt, the mother of the series' creator, Maya, with the two replicating their mother-daughter roles in the narrative. Maya has stated her inspiration to create the series in the following terms:

> *Ever since I was 6 years old, I always loved mermaids and the ocean... A few years later when I was 10, I thought "why not actually make this?" I had the idea in my head for a long time and thought it could help influence kids to clean up the ocean and bring awareness to mermaids. I've always been really drawn to water – I'd build a coral seaweed home underwater if I could – because it feels really safe and makes me feel at home.* (Young 2015: online)

Maya features in the series as a young girl who lives on the mid-California coast and who unexpectedly gains the ability to become a mermaid when wet. She is joined in her adventures by a small group of other young girls with mer-powers, including her cousin, Ashley (Ashley Hannon). One key difference between *Mermaid Miracles* and the series discussed above is the former's utilisation of mermaid folk- and media-lore for narrative and thematic purposes in scripts developed by Tritt and co-writer/director Brett Mazurek for Series 1. This is most apparent in Episode 4, in which Inga provides an explanation to Maya and Ashley about their heritage and explains the 'Golden Rules' of being a mermaid (see Figure 24). This occurs in an extended sequence that provides a visually complex and well-researched interpretation of mermaid folk- and media-lore. Over a monochrome, silent film-style sequence that represents the events related by Inga in a voiceover, she informs the girls that their heritage began in the early 1800s on Sylt island, off the Atlantic coast of northern Germany, when their "great-great-great grandpa and grandma" found a mermaid in a nest on the beach, took her in, named her Ana and raised her as their child.

---

219   See: https://www.youtube.com/watch?v=HrOLiJ6pyII – accessed December 11th 2015.

220   The music featured in the series is markedly more adult in orientation than other aficionado series, including tracks by artists such as Sigur Rós and Abel Okugawa.

Figure 24 – Production still of sequence from *Mermaid Miracles* Series 1 Episode 4, where Inga (left) informs Maya (centre) and Ashley (right) about their family mermaid history.

After identifying that Ana subsequently discovered that she was from a "clan" of North Sea nereids, Inga informs the girls that one of Ana's nereid friends, named Marina, "fell in love with some Prince of Denmark and died tragically". When Ashley and Maya interrupt her to point out that this sounds like Andersen's 'The Little Mermaid' story, Inga brushes their comments aside by stating, "that story was told for years but he just published it". Responding to a question from Maya as to whether there are other mermaid clans, Inga states that there are many and identifies "Mami Watas from Africa, Iaras from the Amazon, there's the Lasirene from the Caribbean and the list goes on, my little mermaids, sea nymphs, water fairies, selkies and sirens", with the screen showing a montage of still images to illustrate this role call of types.

Having provided this introduction, Inga states the '3 Golden Rules' for mermaids:

- We love, respect and protect the ocean at all times, she has the power to help you or hurt you, so always stay true to mother ocean.[221]

- Material things and money come in and out of our lives like the tides. When the tide is high, you give and help others. When the tide is low, be open to receive from others.

- Be careful to whom you give your heart to. We mermaids have a lot of love to give to everyone but we only have one chance to fall in love. If the person you give your heart to doesn't give the same love back, well one can end up like Marina, a tragic love story.

As will be apparent, these rules are as much broad New Age ones as a specific mermaid code but nevertheless form moral compass points for the young mermaids to follow in subsequent adventures.

Along with its depiction of the girls achieving awareness of their status and responsibility as mermaids, the first series also entwines two other narrative strands. One involves the arrival of a pair of comically eager video-makers intent on making an episode of their independent show *Mermaid Hunters*. This representation parodies two Animal Planet

---

221 The environmental message of the first is prominent throughout the series (including sequences representing Surfrider Foundation activists).

network programs, namely the *Finding Bigfoot* show (2011–2014) and two hoax mermaid documentaries broadcast in 2012 and 2013 (discussed in detail in Chapter 7). Despite staking out the beach and following suspected transformative mermaids into town, the bumbling duo are easily outwitted by the girls who distract and divert them by staging a fake Bigfoot attack on their campsite. The arrival of a quartet of sirens in town is represented as a far more problematic event, with the series providing an innovation to mermaid media-lore by representing mermaids and sirens as antagonistic. The sirens arrive in Episode 8 in human form trying to find the tempest, a magic artefact that controls the power of the sea. The sirens, three alluring young women with hypnotic powers over men (later joined by a fourth), are represented as acting as agents of "the old man of the sea" (a vague off-screen presence), who wants to secure the tempest in order to attack humans in retaliation for their degradation of the marine environment. The sirens capture Inga and her husband and force them to give information as to where the tempest is. In parallel with this, Maya and Ashley also set out to seek the tempest, aided by a book of mermaid spells. The first series ends with them setting out on their quest with a young male friend.

The high production standards and originality of the first series delivered high viewing figures, with YouTube statistics indicating that individual episodes secured over a million views. These viewing figures attracted the attention of Maker Studios, a company that was founded in 2009 by a number of audiovisual producers who had gained a profile from independently produced material uploaded to YouTube. The company negotiated a deal to partner the production of *Mermaid Miracles* that involved a number of modifications and reorientations,[222] including the involvement of director Vincente Cordero and co-writer Travis Livingstone in Series 2. This resulted in a more conventional television youth drama orientation, longer episodes (around the 20-minute mark), the inclusion of a wider range of magical entities and a reduction in mermaid-tailed swimming sequences in favour of the key female characters appearing predominantly in human form. There was also an unlikely link back to the seminal *The Little Mermaid* film in that Maker Studios' success in developing new, low-budget material attracted the attention of Disney, who bought the company out for $500 million in 2014. Despite their financial injection into the operation, Disney's involvement with Maker Studios did not benefit *Mermaid Miracles'* profile. YouTube viewing figures for Series 2 and 3 showed a considerable decline on the first series, suggesting that the marked reduction of core mermaid aficionado elements substantially lost that audience sector and did not replace it with a broader one.

Conclusion

The films and television programs that have represented teenage girls transformed into mermaids (and vice versa) and the video dramas subsequently produced by teen and pre-teen mermaid aficionados share a number of aspects. Prime amongst these is sororal solidarity, a 'sisterhood of the finned' that allows small groups of girls to mature and

---

222 These included a new, original theme song, 'Open Your Eyes Under the Water', sung by Maya Tritt, which was retailed through iTunes and accompanied by a music video. Series 2 and 3 also replaced the varied pre-recorded music tracks that were a prominent element of Series 12 in favour of more homogenous original scoring by Lenny Bunn.

develop together as they explore the possibilities their transformative states can grant them. Unlike the standard Western girls that Pipher characterises as having their "assertive, energetic and 'tomboyish'" attributes stripped away in adolescence (1994: 19), the mermaid/girls featured in the productions discussed in this chapter retain theirs and, indeed, often enhance them through the magical (telekinetic and/or hypnotic) powers that their mer-forms give them. Their mer-identities also allow them access to a liquid realm in which they are particularly confident, empowered and powerful, one located outside of the strictures of social normality and the interference and domination of boys and men. Rather than any developmental Bermuda Triangle, in which they "crash and burn" (ibid), the watery spaces available to them enhance their self-confidence and self-belief. This situation is all the more poignant as they are only "mermaid-like a while". No audiovisual productions show the mermaid/girls either progressing to adulthood and/or developing the romantic and/or sexual relationships with human males, mermen or other mermaids or girls that traditionally mark transition to adulthood. The situations represented in the audiovisual productions are effectively "temporary autonomous zones", of the kind originally identified by Bey (1985) as constituted by corsairs roaming the seven seas beyond the reach of formal authoritarian mechanisms – ones whose dynamic intensity is premised on their brevity and their essentially improvised nature. The uncertainty of identity – mermaid or girl? girl or mermaid? – creates a liminal richness that provides points of intense identification for aficionados. The aficionado investment in producing audio-visual texts within parameters established by mainstream media productions emphasises the manner in which the former might be characterised as having tapped into the collective psyche of female adolescents. In this, the mermaid anima manifests itself as an appealingly mutable entity who is an "active protagonist in dreams and fantasies" (Relke 2007: online) such as those represented on screen.

Chapter Seven

At the Margins:
Mermen on the Screen

As previous chapters have elaborated, representations of mermaids proliferated during the 19th and 20th centuries. Mermen, by contrast, remained far more obscure.[223] The most obvious explanation for the merman's marginalisation from cultural representation, particularly in modern realist media such as cinema and television, concerns the awkwardness of his anatomy, in that the nature of his tail precludes anything resembling a human penis. The merman is thus symbolically un-manly. While the mermaid possesses (human) breasts that are frequently subject to representation in a conventionally erotic manner (in combination with her tresses, mirrors and/or combs), the merman has no such obvious gender markers. This serves to variously de-gender and/or feminise the 'male of the mermaid'.[224] There is also a sense of symbolic pointlessness to the merman's tail within the psychoanalytic frameworks advanced in the Introduction to this book. If the mermaid's tail can be considered as a phallic symbol that offsets her lack of a phallus (at the same time as it effaces the female genitalia that confirm that lack) the merman's tail is a more perplexing appendage. It could be considered as a phallic symbol that offsets his lack of an actual phallus but there is a circularity to this in that the lack of that phallus is clearly manifest through the presence of a tail that shows no visible male genitals. In this regard, the merman floats in an ambiguous place. While aspects of his upper body, face, voice and/or character may indicate his masculinity, his lower body destabilises those associations. The merman, in this sense, is a complex figure whose presence has to be negotiated in various ways by the occasional texts that feature

---

223 As discussed in Chapter 1, there is considerable ambiguity as to whether the Sea King in Andersen's 'Den lille Havfrue' was fish-tailed in form – an aspect that is also apparent in the two most famous poetic interpretations of the story, Alfred Lord Tennyson's 'The Merman' (1830) and Matthew Arnold's 'The Forsaken Merman' (1849). Fish-tailed mermen were, however, featured in Clara Guernsey's little-known fantasy novella 'The Merman and The Figurehead' (1871), which merits greater critical attention than it has received to date.

224 Indeed, as discussed in Chapter 2, films such as *Miranda* (Kenn Annakin, 1948) include dialogue that identifies the unappealing nature of mermen to mermaids (as opposed to the more virile masculinity that mermaids perceive in human males).

him. One such negotiation occurred in the mermaid-themed episode of the TV series *Voyage to the Bottom of the Sea* (Jerry Hooper, 1967), discussed in Chapter 2. Following the submarine captain's capture of a mermaid, a male from her undersea community comes on board to rescue her and wreaks havoc. In contrast to the mermaid (played alluringly in fish-tailed form by Dianne Webber) the male is an aquatic humanoid with legs, similar in bodily form to the titular protagonist of *Creature from the Black Lagoon* (Jack Arnold, 1954). Its masculinity is made clear through its muscularity and violent behaviour, which contrast to the mermaid's subtle wiles. The creature is not so much 'the male of the mermaid' as a counterpart in an aquatic 'beauty and the beast' duo. Actual fish-tailed mermen are conspicuous by their absence from the episode.

The principal exception to the above characterisation of absence, and to the symbolic disempowerment of the merman in 19th and 20th Century Western culture more generally, occurs in the form of a patriarchal figure derived from Triton, the son of the Greek sea gods Poseidon and Amphitrite. Unlike his parents, who had human physiques, classical renditions of Triton usually represent him with a fish-tailed lower body.[225] As Chapter 1 details, a Triton-like figure occurs in several 1930s' Disney short films (where he is referred to as King Neptune) and in Disney's *The Little Mermaid* and its spin-off films and television series (as King Triton). In these productions other aspects of his form and persona effectively bypass his anatomical deficiencies. The figure's grey-haired and bearded patriarchalism gives the character a particular set of associations. He has established his potency by siring a considerable number of offspring (by means unknown) but is represented as essentially post-sexual (in that he no longer has, nor appears to seek, a sexual partner). The visible absence of genitals on his tail is compensated by his regular accessory of a trident, with its triple phallic symbolism and its ability to function as either a blast weapon or as a magic wand. Indeed, in Disney's films and television series King Triton is represented as hyper-masculine, prone to issuing edicts and to losing his temper in a dramatic and often violent manner (often in response to the insubordination of females). The figure has been less frequently represented in live-action cinema, but a giant Triton makes a brief appearance in a sequence in Ray Harryhausen's *Jason and the Argonauts* (1963), when he helps the mariners through a narrow, rocky strait by holding back crumbling cliffs. He also appears, albeit as an off-screen presence, in *Aquamarine* (Elisabeth Allen, 2006), whipping up storms to indicate his displeasure at his daughter's inclination to explore the pleasures of romance onshore with young human males. These powerful figures also have a faint echo in the form of the lone merman who appears in the TV film *Mermaids* (Ian Barry, 2003) as the father of the film's female protagonists. He features as a far less commanding presence than his predecessors, appearing in most of the narrative as a corpse. Accidentally killed by fishermen using explosives, his body is kept on ice by them in anticipation of being able to profit from selling it as a scientific curiosity while his daughters, who have assumed human form, strive to locate and reclaim it.

Aside from versions of the Triton figure, and a brief appearance in the idiosyncratic 1965 feature film *Eve and the Merman*, the merman has principally featured in a disparate cluster

---

225 Although he is represented in human form in two episodes of *Hercules: The Legendary Journeys*: 'Love on the Rocks' (Rick Jacobson, 1999) and 'My Best Girl's Wedding' (Andrew Merrifeld, 1999).

of audiovisual texts produced subsequent to the representation of mermen in the promotional video for Madonna's 1991 single 'Cherish'.[226] These texts are discussed below with particular regard to their representations of what might be referred to as 'mer-masculinity'.

I. The Outlier Merman

The only feature film produced to date that includes the term merman in its title[227] is an obscure 1965 production directed by Chev Royton entitled *Eve and the Merman*. Royton's film was a niche product that straddled two particular strands of early 1960s' erotic cinema, the nudist film genre, pioneered by Doris Wiseman (in which the representation of activities at nudist camps provided an excuse for the representation of female nudes on screen) and the subsequent 'nudie cutie' genre, pioneered by Russ Meyer (which featured frequent, gratuitous screen nudity without the camps as a context). The former aspects are apparent in the film's opening sequences, which indicate that its production was supported by the American Nudist Association.[228] Despite the film's low budget, which seems to have precluded the inclusion of synch-sound dialogue, a somewhat surprising conceptual ambition is evident from the outset. The film commences with underwater footage of fish and cetaceans and a voiceover that anticipates Elaine Morgan's 'Aquatic Ape' thesis[229] by proposing a "tie" between humans and cetaceans and "possibly a link between the mysterious world of water and the home of man on dry land". The film emphasises the latter aspect with a cut from an image of a porpoise to that of a naked young woman swimming across a pool. A different voice then picks up the narrative thread over images of the woman diving underwater:

> *It's not strange for man to look for some link with the fish. There is a great pleasure to be found in the water. In the water is found a freedom to move without the restraint of gravity. Floating gracefully, it's a place for man to unleash the bonds that bind him to land.*

The narration then shifts to discuss present-day humans as "creatures of amazing skill and beauty" who enjoy the simple pleasures of being together. This comment accompanies images of nude people playing and watching sports in a hilltop camp. Buttressed by standard nudist rhetoric that describes the camp as a latter-day Garden of Eden, "a natural and complete free world to run and simply be joyful", a high proportion of the film's opening screen time provides representations of naked young women. Twelve minutes into the film a narrative thread emerges as the voiceover declares that, "our story is about the water and the mysteries of the deep" before introducing the film's three main protagonists: Brenda, "a lovely legal secretary" (Laura Kane); Suzette, a dance instructor (Marcia LeRoux); and Eve, a shy school teacher (Lori Dawson). The narration informs us that the cool climate of the mountain region in which the camp is located has prompted

226 Similarly, the merman reappeared in late 20th and early 21st Century literary fiction in the period after Madonna's video was produced. (See the 'Listopia' list of merman-themed fiction online at: http://www.goodreads.com/list/show/43227.Good_Merman_Mermen_Books – accessed December 28th 2015.)

227 Natasha Huk also directed a short film entitled *Merman* in 2007, concerning a man with a skin condition who seeks relief by submerging his body in water.

228 This organisation appears to be an obscure one, given the dearth of contemporary records confirming its existence; the acknowledgement may be an invented one aimed to give the film some notional legitimacy.

229 See the discussion of this in Chapter 8.

Figure 25 – Promotional poster for *Eve and the Merman*.

the girls to seek a warmer location to relax in. Unsure as to where to go, the girls seek advice from the camp supervisor who suggests a tropical island he has heard of. He shows them the island's position on a map but adds the somewhat alarming caution that many beautiful women have disappeared from there without trace and that "strange fish-like creatures" are reported to inhabit the vicinity. Undaunted by what they regard as mere superstition the trio set off for the remote Caribbean island in question.

The film's island sequences are fragmented but commence with Brenda and Suzette sunbathing and with Brenda falling asleep and dreaming about being an exotic dancer. Eve initially stays inside before resolving to go out and expose her body to the sun. After paddling along the water's edge she strips off and sunbathes. At this point, a young, blonde-haired male (Johnny Salvo) surfaces in the water, holding a small metal trident, and watches her intently. She sees him and reacts in alarm, only for him to smile, wave to her to join him in the water and talk to her. The absence of synch sound makes it unclear quite what he is saying but she doesn't appear convinced by his overtures, shakes her head and mouths 'Goodbye', resulting in him swimming off, revealing his fish tail. The merman disappears from the narrative after this. In terms of the Eden scenario suggested in the film's title and elaborated in the film's promotional poster (Figure 25), Eve rejects the temptation offered by the merman (unlike the Biblical Eve who fell for the serpent's blandishments). Although brief snippets of female voice-over subsequently refer to Eve having fallen in love with a merman, the film basically gives up on this narrative element entirely after Eve spurns his advances. Somewhat bewilderingly, it ends with a lengthy sequence of nude women posing for photo shoots overdubbed with voiceover from a new character, Linda, complaining about the tedium of nude modelling. As this description suggests, the film is fairly incoherent and the merman theme is, despite the film's title and promotional poster images, minimal. Indeed, it is puzzling as to why this element is threaded through the film's series of nude modelling scenes. Nevertheless, the feature offers an early representation of a merman on screen that has some similarities to the re-insertion of the figure into popular cultural discourse that occurred two decades later.

II. Transformative Teen Mermen

The first live-action representation of a teenage merman on screen occurred in an episode of the Australian young adult-orientated TV series *Round the Twist* entitled 'Nails' (Esben Storm, 1992). The episode provided an unusual inflection to many of the transition narratives discussed in previous chapters in that its central male protagonist transforms from a human to a merman. The episode charts a budding romance between two teenagers, Linda (Joelene Crnogorac) and Andrew (Eamon Kelly) that is interrupted when the boy suffers mysterious ailments and becomes reclusive. The cause of his discomfort is revealed in the final minutes of the episode when he slips out of his wheelchair and dives into the sea. His glamorous, blond-tressed mermaid mother (Cheryle Street) then appears (accompanied by high female vocal melodies on the soundtrack) to summon him back to the sea.

1999 saw the release of two television films that featured mermen as central characters: *Sabrina, Down Under*, a spin-off from the TV series *Sabrina, The Teenage Witch* (1996–2003); and *The Thirteenth Year*, produced for The Disney Channel.[230] As the production contexts of both films suggest, they were targeted at a teen/pre-teen audience and featured lead characters who were themselves teenagers.

Like the TV series from which it was derived, *Sabrina, Down Under* (directed by Daniel Berendsen) featured Sabrina (Melissa Joan Hart) in the title role, using her supernatural abilities to negotiate adversity and to resolve injustice. The film involved her visiting Hamilton Island (off the north-east coast of Australia) on holiday with a young English witch named Gwen (Tara Charendoff). Flying in by helicopter, Sabrina first gets a brief glimpse of a merman in the sea and then meets the individual concerned, a sick teenager named Barnaby (Scott Michaelson). Like the male character in *Eve and The Merman*, Barnaby has a muscular upper torso, an attractive face and a full-fish tail. Given their familiarity with the supernatural, the teenage witches are less surprised to find a merman than might otherwise be expected. In order to get him medical help without attracting undue attention, Sabrina uses a spell that painlessly transforms his tail into legs for 48 hours. Once in human form he's successfully treated and Sabrina also goes to the lagoon where his community resides and gives his sister an ointment for her similar sickness. Narrative tension is generated when a scientist and his colleagues become aware of the mer-colony and seek to capture specimens of the new species. The scientist discovers Barnaby's true identity when Sabrina's spell expires and captures him, together with his sister, when she attempts to rescue him. Sabrina then intercedes to secure their release and the merfolk are finally allowed to return to their lagoon.

For a substantial proportion of the film Barnaby appears onshore in human form and

---

230 A third production made in the same year, an episode of the TV series *Hercules: The Legendary Journey* entitled 'My Best Girl's Wedding' (Andrew Merrifeld, 1999) also featured a human to merman transition at its end that enabled a character named Iolanthus (Michael Hurst) to go off and live in the sea with his love interest, a mermaid named Nautica (Angela Dotchin).

155

explores the novelty of having human legs and engaging in human pursuits (much like Madison in Ron Howard's *Splash* [1984]). With a similar wholesomeness to the TV series, the male and female characters enjoy each other's company without venturing into sexual interactions with each other. This latter aspect makes one of the film's throwaway jokes all the more notable. Prior to Sabrina uttering a transformation spell over Barnaby as he reclines in her hotel bathtub the girls show an awareness of physiological issues (and, implicitly, the anatomy that Barnaby lacks in mer-form but is shortly to acquire) when Sabrina gives him a towel to drape over his nether regions. This action leads Gwen to comment "spoilsport". This brief joke aside, the film avoids representing sexual issues or otherwise speculating on mermale sexuality. The otherness of the merman (and his mer-community) is diluted by its inclusion in a magic-themed scenario that also features humans transformed into talking cats. In this manner, the young merman essentially gives Sabrina a pretext to act in an assertive and confident manner in order to protect him and his mer-community.

The Disney Channel's *The Thirteenth Year* (Duwayne Dunham, 1999) has a similar plot structure to the episode of *Round The Twist* discussed above. Set on the north-east United States (US) coast, the film relates the story of a boy who experiences strange sensations and enhanced aquatic abilities around his 13th birthday and comes to realise that he is turning into a merman. The film's title refers to an invented folkloric theme that mer-children can live in human form onshore until they enter their teens, when their lower bodies transform. The film derives substantial aspects from *Splash*, not the least its representation of Cody's (unnamed) slim, long-haired mermaid mother (Stephanie Chantel Durelli) swimming underwater in a manner akin to representations of Madison in the earlier film. Like *Splash*, *The Thirteenth Year* also features an initial flashback sequence. This shows Cody being left on a boat as a baby while his mother evades pursuit by a fishing trawler. When she returns the boat has departed. The family who found her baby subsequently adopt and raise him. The film then moves to the week of Cody's 13th birthday and to the humour and drama caused by his gradual transformation. After initial developments, such as developing scaly hands and growing small side fins on his forearms, his real identity is fully realised in the final quarter of the film when his legs are revealed to have sprouted webbed flippers. This image is one that forms a minor strand within art historical representations of mermaids and mermen (cf Eriksen's famous Copenhagen statue of Andersen's mermaid) and represents a semi-mer form that does not problematise other aspects of his anatomy. It nevertheless shocks his girlfriend, who subsequently avoids his company until they are reconciled in the final scene. Cody's semi-mer form is soon revealed to be a transitional phase. After being reunited with his mother he is shown leaping athletically out of the water, sporting a full mer-tail, before departing with her to visit the undersea realm for the first time. This brief sequence (which has echoes of the mermen in Madonna's 'Cherish' music video leaping and showing off their physiques) represents Cody as accepting and proud of his transformation – a 'coming out' as a merman but one that is emphasised as firmly heterosexual through his promise to avoid "mer-girls" during his marine sojourn and to return to his human sweetheart.

An unexpected human to merman transition also occurs in the teen-oriented television series *Mako Mermaids*[231] (2013–), whose title refers to a pod of mermaids who live in the

Figure 26 –
Screen still
from *Mako
Mermaids*
showing Zac
holding a trident
(left of image)
(2013),
(Courtesy of
Jonathan M.
Shiff
Productions).

waters around (the fictional) Mako island off the south-east coast of the Australian state of Queensland. As discussed in the previous chapter, one of the series' main narrative threads is initiated by a human male gaining the power to transform to mer-form after accidentally falling into a magic pool on a deserted island. The series represents mermen and mermaids as adversaries with very different natures. The first program opens with the central trio of mermaids relaxing in a safe, amniotic, womb-like space inside the mountainous interior of Mako island, which is open to the sky via a vertical passage-way through which moonlight shines. When Zac (Chai Romruen), a handsome, mid–late teenage boy, accidentally falls down into the pool amidst them, he disturbs their exclusively female existence and gains the power to transform to mer-form (see Figure 26). Identified as having a human girlfriend early in the narrative, and also represented as being attracted to one of the mermaids, Zac's sexual orientation is far from ambiguous. His previous human physique and ability to transfer between forms at will offsets any perception of physical-symbolic lack his mer-form may suggest.[232]

A substantial proportion of the first series comprises interactions between Zac and the three mermaids he disturbs, who follow him back to land and assume human form as they attempt to remove his powers. Like Cody in *The Thirteenth Year*, Zac recovers from his initial surprise at having a tail and comes to enjoy the aquatic abilities and power that it brings. The mermaid trio's unease at a male being able to assume mer-form derives in substantial part from their lack of familiarity with mermen, who have not been seen by mermaids (or at least by members of the Mako pod) for hundreds of years. Some background to their disappearance is provided by an adult mermaid living on land in

---

231 Broadcast in Australia under the title *Mako: Island of Secrets*.

232 While the overwhelming majority of pre-teen and teen mermaid aficionado dramas discussed in the previous chapter only feature the female of the species, one, *Tail of a Mermaid and Merman* (2013–), produced in Scotland, also features a merman. The series was written, directed and edited by 16-year-old Nicky Crawford, who also performs as the lead mermaid, Jewel, alongside 16-year-old actor Alexander Warren, playing her brother Rin. The back-story to the series involves Jewel and Rin as the princess and prince of an underwater race of merfolk who are stolen by an evil shapeshifter who took them to land, where they became human, forgetting their origins until their 16th birthdays when they acquire the ability to alternate form. The majority of the drama involves the siblings combating the shapeshifter. Rin is shown in mer-form on several occasions but this aspect is not prominently featured in the series' dramatic vignettes.

human form who tells the trio that "aeons ago" a pod of warlike mermen rose up from Mako in possession of a powerful trident capable of destroying the mermaids' home and were only defeated by the combined efforts of pods of mermaids. The trident was subsequently concealed in a secret marine chamber beneath Mako by a sympathetic merman and remained hidden until Zac's transition to mer-form alerted him to its existence. Increasingly lured by the trident's power on full moon nights, Zac returns to the island, gains the trident and learns to use it. Once in possession of the trident he assumes a belligerent, alpha male persona and uses it against the mermaids. After wielding the trident to near fatal effect on one of them, he resolves to return it to its chamber and to form an alliance with the mermaids. When a male human friend discovers the trident's whereabouts, obtains it and attempts to use it to destroy the mermaid's island base, Zac intervenes to disarm him and to destroy the trident.[233] In a similar manner to Dundes' and Dundes' discussion of the significance of Triton's trident as a phallic symbol in Disney's *The Little Mermaid* (2002: 69–71), the trident stands for and embodies patriarchal power in *Mako Mermaids* and the threat of its power hangs over the mermaids until it is rejected by Zac.

III. Queering the Merman

While mermaids have been a theme in concert and popular music for several centuries, mermen have rarely featured in contemporary song lyrics. Perhaps the best-known exception is Jimi Hendrix's song '1983 ... (A Merman I Should Turn to Be)'. In the version featured on his 1968 album *Electric Ladyland*, the song's verse sections form the basis for an extended slow-paced, psychedelic improvisation featuring heavily distorted guitar sounds. The lyrics describe the song's vocal protagonist as despairing of the violent, war-torn state of the planet and represent him on the verge of entering the sea and transforming into a merman. Produced before videos became a standard aspect of music promotion, the song was not subject to any visual representation that helped disseminate the merman in popular culture.[234] But while Hendrix's song, and subsequent compositions such as Tori Amos's 'Merman',[235] referred to mermen in their lyrics, it was Madonna's 'Cherish' (1989), a light, uptempo pop song that did *not* verbally reference them, that prompted a spectacular re-inscription of mermen in audiovisual media. This occurred in the music video made for the track by prominent fashion and celebrity photographer Herb Ritts. 'Cherish' marked his debut as video director and his inclusion of mermen followed on from a number of his photo sessions that involved models appearing as mermaids. The first of these featured Stephanie Seymour wearing an "iridescent, pearlized fabric" tail made by designer Sharon Simonaire after Ritts failed to get access to the tail used by Daryl

---

233 At the time of writing, the DVD for the second series of *Mako Mermaids* was due to be released but this did not occur in time for the series to be included in my analysis.

234 Although the track inspired the name of the San Francisco rock band The Mermen, formed in 1989 and who are still performing.

235 The song is a delicate, piano-accompanied ballad with subtle and allusive lyrics. One repeated phrase describes that the merman "doesn't need your voice" (the "your" in question seemingly referring to a female protagonist). In another line which refers to the merman the singer has invited to go to bed, being "a merman to the knee"; the latter phrase suggesting that he has a conventional middle-body anatomy. Amos has identified the figure of the merman as symbolising complex aspects of masculinity and the lyrics as having been addressed to her husband (see: http://www.hereinmyhead.com/lyrics/soundtracks/merman/ – accessed August 16th 2015).

Hannah in *Splash* (Churchward 2010: 201).[236] While Ritts initially requested similarly flimsy tails for the mermen represented in 'Cherish', Simonaire opted for stronger rubber ones that allowed the models to use them propulsively and to appear vigorous in the water (ibid).

The 'Cherish' video features five characters: Madonna (implicitly as herself), a young boy who initially appears in human form, running across the beach, and subsequently in mer-form; and three young mermen, who cavort in the ocean. In place of narrative, the video blends three main performance strands: Madonna lip-synching, vamping for the camera and/or playing at the edge of the sea; the mer-boy shot alone in frame or interacting with Madonna; and the frolicking mermen. Vernallis (1998) produced a detailed analysis of the interaction of music and visual elements of the video that emphasised the manner in which the video was shot and edited so as to make the musical elements appear to complement and support the visual track:

> the snare and tambourine, the voice, the multi-layered chorus accompanied by its glittery synthesized timbres, the sibilants 'ch' and 'sh' all have a white noise component that we might associate with foaming, rushing water and the prismatic light reflected off the ocean and the sand. Each character corresponds by association to one of the song's countermelodies, and these correspondences – built upon a familiar connection between physical size and registral placement – reflect gender and power stereotypes. The mermen are associated with a synthesized saxophone in its lower register, Madonna with a sassy synthesized trumpet in the middle register, and the merboy with a slightly comic synthesizer patch in the high register. (ibid: 163–164)[237]

Vernallis argues convincingly that these elements operate to produce a highly coherent audiovisual sequence that minimises any sense of disconnection of the visual track from the lyrics. Indeed, the manner in which the camera lovingly tracks the bodies of the mermen and Madonna's interactions with the mer-boy suggests that the repeated verbal refrain of "cherish" can be understood to denote the female vocal protagonist's feelings towards the males featured in the video.

One intriguing element of the video concerns the nature of the inter-relation between the various characters and the assumptions necessary for any interpretation of these. Madonna and the mer-boy are represented in a playful and affectionate relationship that could be taken to suggest her as his mother. If this is the case, and if Madonna is wholly human in the video scenario (rather than being a transformative mermaid), then (ignoring issues of anatomical lack) a merman, such as one of those swimming off the beach, might be the mer-boy's father. In an earlier essay on the 'Cherish' video (Hayward, 1991) I identified

---

236 The photo shot was published in Playboy magazine in March 1991 under the title of 'Stephanie: A Herb Ritts Portfolio'.

237 Vernallis also contends that: *Much of what we know about the disposition of the figures in 'Cherish' is defined through the harmony. For example, the child commonly appears at the same time as the subdominant in second inversion. This chord is pulled in two directions: it is often subsumed by the tonic, while it also resists the dominant. This harmonic pull might contribute to the way that the child is volleyed back and forth between the mermen and Madonna. The mermen tend to land on the relatively stable chords of I, IV and V, and the way they seem to float suspended in space, performing a slight acrobatic twist, suggests their freedom from the influence of the song's harmonic motion. Madonna's appearances, on the other hand, coincide with passing chords; these correspondences make her seem somewhat hemmed-in by the harmony. In each section of the video, she forges a winding path towards us, yet monumental harmonic forces towards the end of the section pull her back towards the water's edge ... Later in the video, Madonna breaks free of these constraints, affecting the video as a whole.* (1998: 165–166)

159

the representation of the legs of a male figure standing over Madonna in the video's penultimate image as representing the re-imposition of the (human) patriarchal order after sequences in which gender identities were represented in a fluid manner. This was an overly prescriptive characterisation of a sequence that is highly ambiguous; the masculine legs might also be considered to be those of the mer-boy in human form or of a merman transformed into human form. Whatever reading may be adopted, Madonna's charismatic star power, at its apex in the early 1990s, and the strength of her persona, embodying sexual confidence and assurance, provided the catalyst for the reassertion of the merman in popular culture.

Madonna revisited the music video's representations of mermen in her 1990 Blond Ambition world tour, which included 57 performances across Asia, Europe and North America. Her elaborate stage performance featured young male dancers whose routines included drag-style sequences and performances as mermen during renditions of 'Cherish'. On the tour, the song's instrumental introduction was accompanied by three mermen rising up at the front of the stage clustered around a large concert harp. After greeting them ("Hi boys, will you play with me?"), Madonna commenced singing the first verse while one of the mermen flexed his tail vertically and the other two swayed. On the chorus, opening "Cherish the love" she knelt, cuddled, caressed and nuzzled the mermen, singing directly to them, with their tails flexing appreciatively in response. During the second verse Madonna and the mermen performed similar gestures and body moves, before progressing into the second chorus where the mermen performed a set of synchronised moves on the floor. In the final section of the number Madonna's moves become more suggestive, including her grabbing the mermen's tails. Footage of her tour performances show a distinct blurring of gender roles, including several occasions when she lifted a merman's tail and thrust her hips into his rear in what appeared to be the mimicking of sexual penetration (as she intoned "I will always cherish you")[238]. Such representations of the male form are part of a pattern in Madonna's work in this period that critics such as Skeggs (1993) assert destabilise the fixed natures of gender and of normative heterosexuality. Already queer, in the traditional use of the term, the mermen are readily deconstructed and recontextualised in manners that enhanced Madonna's imperious shuffling of sexual signs and symbolism.[239]

238 See, for instance, the extract from her performance onstage at Cannes, online at: https://www.youtube.com/watch?v=e-WGSHtB8j0 – accessed September 3rd 2015.

239 In addition to Madonna's work with merman imagery it is also notable that several other prominent American female vocal performers assumed the role of mermaids in the 1980s and early 1990s. Bette Midler regularly performed in a mermaid costume in the early 1980s. For performances of 'I Will Survive' in her 'Dolores Delago' persona she initially wriggled across the stage in a mermaid tail before climbing onto a motorised wheelchair during performances of a novelty medley accompanied by three, similarly-clad back-up singers. (See the video of a 1983 performance of the song online at: https://www.youtube.com/watch?v=L_vdlhsvI1M – accessed September 14th 2015). It is also notable that Lady Gaga, often regarded as something of a successor to Madonna in terms of prominence and outrageousness, attracted criticism from Midler for plagiarism when she appeared as a mermaid in a wheelchair during stage performances of her song You And I in 2011 (drawing on imagery from the song's accompanying music video). (See Gagapedia [n.d.] for a discussion of Gaga's broader 'Yüyi the Mermaid' persona.) Cher also appear in mermaid fancy dress costume in sequences from the film comedy Mermaids (Richard Benjamin, 1990), providing images that were used prominently in the film's promotion. Cyndi Lauper, perceived as something of a rival to Madonna in the late 1980s and early 1990s, also appeared as Cyd, one of three performers who swim in mermaid costumes in a large nightclub tank in Edward Bianchi's crime heist comedy Off and Running (1991).

While causality cannot be easily established, Ritts's representations of mermen as desirable objects of the gaze prefigured the merman's renewed representation in a variety of audiovisual contexts,[240] a number of which further explored the merman's queering of masculine identity. Two notable examples occurred in films where mermen were used as comic details.[241] The best known of these was *Zoolander* (Ben Stiller, 2001), in which the director plays Derek Zoolander, a somewhat dimwitted male model who gets involved in a political conspiracy. With his career in decline he attempts to reconnect with his (working class) family and, as part of that process, goes into a local bar with his father. To his father's embarrassment, the television screens a commercial for a skin care product that features Derek as a merman. He is represented swimming underwater, accompanied by a wordless female vocal melody, before he theatrically declaims to camera, "water is the essence of wetness and wetness is the essence of beauty". In response to derisive laughter from the men in the bar, his father disowns him and, referring to Derek's deceased mother, states, "I just thank the Lord that she didn't live to see her son as a mermaid". Devastated, Derek's only response is to repeat, "mer-<u>man</u>" and exit the bar. The scene emphasises the effeminate nature of the merman (at least, as portrayed by Derek in the ad), an aspect that is, if anything, reinforced by Derek's assertion of a masculine identity for a figure that so obviously lacks male genitalia in the full-frontal images shown on screen.

In 2007 an actual television advert used the figure of the merman to less comic effect. As part of a re-launch campaign for Levi's 501 jeans, male 'supermodel' Patrick Ribbsaeter starred as a merman in a 40-second TV ad for the product.[242] Made with high production values, the ad featured Ribbsaeter (in merman form) swimming up from the depths to interact with two beautiful mermaids before farewelling them and swimming off powerfully underwater. Breaking the surface again, he emerges onshore in fully-human form, his tail having transformed itself into legs clad in tight blue Levis, walking in a manner that suggests that he is having trouble re-adjusting to having legs instead of a tail. Implicitly referring to the merman's transformation, the advert then screens the slogan "501: The original re-born".[243] The dialogue-free sequence is strongly reliant on musical score for dramatic colouration and emphasis, utilising elements such as opening choral textures, shifting melodic harmonies and indecipherable word-like sounds (all of which derive from the sonic traditions of representing mermaids discussed in Chapter 3). Ribbsaeter's facial and bodily beauty is the central element of the video in a more clearly erotic manner than Stiller's more effete, comic performance in *Zoolander*, 'normalised' by his assumption of human form.

Aspects of Ribbsaeter's performance and visual appearance as a merman prefigured that of Eric Ducharme, a custom tail-maker who became absorbed in aquatic performance

---

240   Also see the 2000+ images of mermen collected at: http://photobucket.com/images/merman – accessed September 2nd 2015.

241   See, for instance *Cabin in the Woods* (Drew Goddard, 2012), in which one of the evil controllers twice bemoans the lack of mermen in the action sequences enacted in the film, only to be confronted by a monstrous merman at the film's conclusion who immediately kills him.

242   I have been unable to ascertain the director's identity.

243   The ad also had a significant predecessor in the form of Michele Condrey's 1997 Levis ad that featured three mermaids interacting with a sailor knocked overboard while just wearing his jeans.

culture at an early age (see Figure 27). An account published on his 'Mertailor' company website describes how:

> He grew up in the shadow of the Weeki Wachee Springs, Florida's legendary roadside mermaid attraction, and was enthralled from the first time his grand-parents took him to see the parks [sic] underwater theater, where a beautiful gold-tailed creature swam across the window, waving and blowing kisses to the audience. When Eric turned six, his father surprised him by having two glim-mering mermaids swim up to the dock at Weeki Wachee's waterpark, Buccaneer Bay, where Eric sat eating his birthday cake, so they could all chat and the mermaids could give the boy a birthday kiss and, with it, seal his fate... At age nine, Eric attended his first camp at Weeki and finally got to swim in the springs himself. This is where he met former mermaid Barbara Wynns, who gave him his first tail, got him scuba certified, and imparted to him all her secret mermaid knowledge. For years she picked him up every day after school and on the weekends and took him to swim at the park, and they remain best friends to this day. (themertailor.com n.d.: online)

Ducharme's profile as a performer and tail-maker was significantly boosted when he was featured in a segment of the TLC network's *My Crazy Obsession* series in 2013.[244] Entitled 'The Little Merman', the item acknowledged his identity as a gay male but represented the complex gender in-betweenness of mermen through reference to his fascination with mermaids as inspiring his costume, demeanour and appearance as a merman.

The item opens with a parody of the opening sequence of *Jaws* (Stephen Spielberg, 1975). As menacing music plays, a mysterious finned figure swims beneath and then breaks the surface of a waterway. The image then reveals the figure to be a merman, who rises up out of the water, states his name to the camera and introduces himself as being "obsessed with mermaids". Lingering shots of his bare, hairless upper torso and glittering tail are then intercut with his own comments about his interest in mermaids being a "lifestyle". Interview snippets with his mother, Candy, and his boyfriend, Matthew Quijano, attest to the depth of his obsession. Shown pulling a tight mer-tail over his legs, Ducharme explains, "when I put on a tail I feel transformed". The screen then shows images of Ducharme performing graceful balletic movements underwater in his tail, together with a voiceover that describes him as a merman. The segment then addresses gender issues and prejudices as Quijano relates how people find Ducharme's appearance problematic ("sometimes we get those people with their scolding looks, because they're just like 'why is there a guy in a tail? It's supposed to be a girl'"), accompanied by on-screen images of men looking at the water where Ducharme is swimming. This is followed by a supporting statement from Ducharme that states, "I'm sure I get 'mean fire' from this, I mean that's just how the world is, unfortunately" as the image shows another (large and muscular) man staring into the waterway in a distinctly unfriendly manner.

The segment goes on to discuss the obscurity of mermen. After his mother comments, "you don't hear about mermen, I really don't understand why", Quijano comments (in a manner that recalls the sequence from *Zoolander* discussed above), "when people see Ducharme in a tail sometimes they call him a mermaid, and usually I just turn around

---

244 The segment was included in Season 2 Episode 2 'Star Chaser and the Little Merman', originally broadcast in the US on April 3rd 2013.

Figure 27 – Eric Ducharme in merman tail (2013 – courtesy of Chiara Salomoni, Project Mermaids).

and say 'mer-man'". This discussion sets up the final part of the item, which shows Ducharme auditioning to be a performer at the Florida Aquarium, which features mermaid performers in several of its display tanks. Despite attempting to persuade Aquarium staff to employ him on the grounds that having a male performer would encourage young boys to emulate him, they reject his overtures. As Aquarium mermaid performer Erin Gallagher then relates to camera, "unfortunately at this time the Aquarium just doesn't have the demand for mermen to join our team of mermaids". After shots of Ducharme, shown as tired and disappointed, Gallagher then adds, "seeing Eric in a tail, seeing a man in a tail, was totally different, was a bit of a surprise at first. We do get very used to seeing just girls in the mermaid tails, it sort of lends itself a little more to a delicate feminine move".

The comments provided by Gallagher in response to Ducharme's audition echo those made by female staff at Weeki Wachee Springs in response to an audition given to another aspirant merman, comedian Tom Kelly, featured in his online video series *The Merman* (2006). The series tracks Kelly's impulse to quit stand-up comedy in New York and to become what he refers to at one stage as a professional "mermaid guy" at the Springs. After driving down to Florida he manages to talk his way into an audition. The majority of female staff at Weeki Wachee interviewed in the series express a distinct unease about men donning a mer-tail, regarding it as transgressing traditional gender roles. In Episode 3, for instance, "mermaid manager" Vici comments that "a man that wants to dress up like a girl … would be like drag a little bit … would make you question their masculinity"; while the Springs' general manager, Robyn Anderson, expresses her disinclination to incorporate mermen in the show as deriving from her concern to "protect the integrity of

163

Weeki Wachee". This comment identifies the troubling nature of mermen to a society with rigid gender roles and to a commercial operation that has always traded heavily on images of female beauty.

Media coverage of the *My Crazy Obsession* segment on Ducharme in both mainstream media (e.g. Golgowski 2013) and gay websites (e.g. Towle 2013) elevated Ducharme's profile as a champion of merman identity. Ducharme's representation as an actual gay mermale performer complemented and realised an aspect that was previously exploited for comic effect in *Another Gay Sequel: Gays Gone Wild!* (Todd Stephens, 2006).[245] The film featured a group of young gay men on Spring break in Fort Lauderdale participating in an informal contest to see who could have the most sex during their vacation. Lead character Nico (Jonah Blechman) encounters an attractive young blond merman, named Stan (played by gay porn star Brent Corrigan) and is charmed by his good looks and tail-flexing. After meeting Nico by the pool one evening, Stan climbs onto the pool edge and reveals an unusual configuration to his tail, which scoops at the rear to reveal human buttocks. Despite this inviting point of access for penetrative sex, the merman represents an unattainable fantasy for Nico, his enigma remaining a key part of his appeal.

The comments section to Towle's aforementioned article on Ducharme's appearance in *My Crazy Obsession* gave respondents the opportunity to discuss both the specific TV item and the nature of the merman within gay culture. One significant response came from Gregoire, who contrasted Ducharme's image to the more common male impersonation of mermaids in gay culture, stating, "I'm fine with this. At least he's not some creepy Drag mermaid" (ibid). The latter reference points to the manner in which incongruous impersonations of Ariel (and mermaids in general) had become a feature of parades, fancy dress events and drag shows in the decades since the release of Disney's *The Little Mermaid*. As Ng has identified, "camp" performances of animation characters can be challenging for essentialist perspectives of the human body and gender and sexual identity:

> Due to their artificiality, or lack of human biology, animated characters are not an accurate representation; nor are they produced through a single axis of gendered norms. Rather, the animated body retains its ambiguity because it is derived from a network of desires and anxieties that are comprised of different values and practices. (2011: 586)

In these regards, Gregoire regards even the problematic identity of a male obsessed with mermaids who performs as a merman as less problematic than a male impersonating an animated figure of a mermaid (ibid). Despite this, the "creepy Drag" tradition of camp, gay, male mermaid performance referred to above was crystallised in a music video in which the lead character combined drag traditions of representing Ariel with a more novel re-interpretation of King Triton. It also concluded with him choosing to transform, like Ariel, for similar reasons.

The music video in question, made for Big Dipper's 2015 track 'Vibin', provides a very different image of gay mermanity to that offered by Ducharme. The Big Dipper is a hirsute, New York-based singer who identifies as a gay 'bear' man[246] and performs hip hop songs

---

245 A follow-up to the director's first romantic comedy feature, *Another Gay Movie* (2008).

246 'Bear' is gay slang term referring to a large and hairy male.

Figure 28 – Big Dipper –
publicity still for 'Vibin' (2015).

from that perspective. The music video for 'Vibin' (directed by Tobin Del Cuore) is introduced as set on "Merbear Island" off the coast of the "Furry Mountains" of "Skankland". An animated map shows a sailing ship being wrecked off adjacent rocks and the image sequence then cuts to Big Dipper, bare-chested with long red hair, a beard and a turquoise tail, clasping a large golden trident, blending the representation of Ariel and King Triton from Disney's *The Little Mermaid*.[247] After Big Dipper-as-King Triton caresses his tail and hair during the song's chorus and touches the prongs of his trident, four sailors wade ashore from the wreck and move in on him suggestively, one caressing his beard with a fork (again in echo of the Disney film). After a further chorus a fifth male emerges from the sea, while the other four perform a dance routine on the sand. After caressing the new arrival during the next verse, Big Dipper kisses him and, following the line "take me home sweet boy, let's seal the deal", he is shown transformed by a video effect into fully-human form, ready and equipped to deal with human males on their own terms. Wearing turquoise swimming trunks, he leads the seamen's dance routine. The remainder of the video alternates images of Big Dipper dancing and images of him in mer-form (see Figure 28). The production combines the humour of incongruity with an effective statement of claim for 'bear' men to be able to assume and perform a variety of cultural figures and, more broadly, shows mer-identity as one potential path for gay performers wishing to destabilise and refigure gendered cultural stereotypes.[248]

247 In the 'Making of' video Big Dipper describes that he is about to "become a mermaid", online at: https://www.youtube.com/watch?v=o6-jXMbjjCM – accessed September 26th 2015.

248 The video's playful exploration of mermale identity is also explored in the low-budget video accompanying the track's 'Mighty Mark remix' (Meg Skaff, 2015), which shows Big Dipper hosting a backyard summer party where he splashes around in a small paddling pool before being pulled out and having his tail stripped off him by three men.

Outside of gay-themed popular culture, a notable representation of the merman was provided in the music video for Vancouver rock trio The Poles' 2013 song 'Merman', shot by Gavin Kennedy. The song's lyrics concern powerlessness and alienation and are declaimed in a harsh, distorted style by guitarist and lead singer Scott Budgie. Budgie is represented as a merman in the video, dressed in a fluorescent green mermaid tail with a bare chest and shell pendant, perching on a rock, lying in a hollowed tree trunk, wriggling at the edge of the sea and, more coherently within the logic of the song, miming playing its solo lead guitar break. Budgie has identified the video as deliberately representing a vulnerable and physically imperfect image of masculinity, which offers "a different take on the typical fantasy merman", as represented by King Triton and similar "noble and strong creatures"; one that reflects the song, "which is written from the perspective of someone frightened and desperate, and unable to cope with life's hardships" (p.c. August 23rd 2015). Appropriately in these regards, the merman in The Poles' song is a bizarre, isolated individual, reinforcing the central awkwardness of the merman for the patriarchal cultural order.

Conclusion

The limited number and generic diversity of the productions discussed above do not facilitate any straightforward characterisation of the function and affective power of mermen in contemporary audiovisual media. The merman in Royton's 1965 film *Eve and the Merman* features so briefly that we are unsure as to what his powers or attributes may be. Similarly, the mermen in Madonna's 'Cherish' video also appear so briefly that we are unsure whether they have transformative (or other) abilities. The mermen featured in the pre-teen/teen-oriented productions discussed in Section II all either have transformative abilities or else are subject to transformation by external forces. Few of the productions feature mermen in any kind of romantic interaction with human women (or mermaids) (although 'Cherish' might be read to suggest this). The exceptions are *The Thirteenth Year* and *Mako Mermaids*, where the mermen's romances with their human girlfriends are initiated before their transitions to mer-form. It is significant that many of the mermen discussed above have access to human genitalia (and related phallic power) for part of their screen time. It is only the briefly rendered comic figure from *Zoolander* or the more forlorn character from The Poles' music video that exhibit phallic lack as their defining condition. But the latter factor also frees the merman up for more complex symbolism, most notably as playthings of Madonna's highly flexible sexuality in the performances of 'Cherish' on her 1992 world tour and as a fantasy figure in *Gays Go Wild!* One aspect lacking in the screen fictions discussed above is that (aside from Zac in *Mako Mermaids*, who is a human who has acquired mer-form) the only mermen who are represented as active masculine agents within the aquatic realm are aged patriarchs. In this regard, the two hoax documentary productions discussed in the following chapter are both surprising and innovative, providing identities for mermen that give them a dignity and agency they lack in many of the disparate audiovisual texts discussed in this chapter.

Chapter Eight

Crypto-Science and Hoax TV: The Animal Planet's Mermaid Documentaries

D espite the variety of audiovisual representations of mermaids and mermen discussed in previous chapters, they were not subject to representation in film or television as a coherent, living species until the early 21st Century, in the form of the Animal Planet hoax documentaries discussed in detail in this chapter. Their representation in the two programs was significant for enhancing their status as popular cultural figures and for indicating the porous boundary between factual and fictional programming in contemporary audiovisual media.

A binary division between factual and fictional forms of audio-visual media has been identified and asserted since the earliest days of cinema (when it appeared most clearly manifest in the schism between the Lumière Brothers' supposedly objectivist footage of actual events and Georges Méliès' various trick films, including *La Sirène* [1904]).[249] Definitions of and debates about documentary-making and its aesthetics occurred at an

---

249 See the special issue of *The Historical Journal of Film, Radio and Television* (v22 n3 2002) for discussion of early forms of non-fiction cinema.

early stage in film criticism[250] and have persisted to the present. But wherever the line has been drawn between documentary and fiction forms, critical and industrial consensus for most of the 20th Century was that there *was* one. However in recent decades this sense of separation has been increasingly blurred as a result of various media tendencies. Two of particular note are a type that Rhodes and Singer (2006) term *docufiction* (including the so-called 'mockumentary' – a parodic form of documentary exemplified by *This is Spinal Tap* [Rob Reiner, 1984]) and the cycle of hand-held camera/found footage films popularised by *The Blair Witch Project* (Daniel Myrick and Eduardo Sánchez, 1999). The blurring has involved both the textual styles of productions and their promotion.[251] Particularly in the case of hand-held camera/found footage films, much of the genre's frisson has arisen from ambiguity as to whether the events depicted are true and/or have been recorded truthfully. Indeed publicity campaigns have regularly sought to encourage perceptions of the films' veracity. This approach has also been pursued in televisual production[252] and, particularly since the proliferation of low-cost digital cameras and desktop post-production software, through the widespread uploading of video material to platforms such as YouTube. More problematically, in many ways, there has been a blurring of lines between documentaries that involve CGI visualisation and/or dramatic enactment as part of their conventional documentary function and programs that have sought to use CGI and/or enactments to represent scenarios that are so significantly removed from evidential bases that they are quasi-fictional. As Jordan (2013) identifies, for instance, pseudo-archaeology has become particularly prominent on the (supposedly) factually-oriented History Channel in recent years. As he argues, such content is all the more problematic when it appears as part of standard scheduling rather than as 'specials' (whose promotion suggests them as distinct from standard programming).

As a result of such tendencies, there is a blurred intersection between forms of film and television that adopt pseudo-documentary techniques and two congruent media forms: hoax documentaries and quasi-documentary expositions of crypto-science. Over the last sixty years there has been a number of film, television and, more latterly, Internet-circulated hoax science documentaries whose material has been science fiction in all but its characterisation.[253] As distinct from these pseudo-documentary presentations of fictional material, another burgeoning genre is that of documentary-style expositions of crypto-science. In this context, the 'crypto' prefix indicates that the existence of the subject being addressed by the 'science' has been overlooked and/or concealed for various (and often implicitly nefarious) reasons. Common themes within this field are alien visitations,

250   As exemplified by responses to the work of pioneering documentary film-makers Robert Flaherty and Walter Ruttmann in the 1920s and 1930s and a number of idiosyncratic directors in the 1930s and 1940s, such as Humphrey Jennings and Alberto Cavalcanti (see Aufderheide 2007 for an overview).

251   See Rhodes (ed) (2006).

252   See Hight (2010) for a discussion of examples of television mockumentary and their contexts.

253   One of the earliest examples of this type was *Unidentified Flying Objects: The True Story of Flying Saucers* (Winston Jones, 1956), a film that attracted media attention in the US and United Kingdom (UK) at its time of release with regard to its possible veracity. One of the best-known televisual hoaxes of this kind was *Alternative 3* (Christopher Miles, 1977). Broadcast by Britain's Anglia TV in 1977 in their weekly 'Science Report' slot, *Alternative 3* purported to document a secret project to establish a manned colony on Mars in order for humanity to survive an impending terrestrial collapse. The only clue within the program as to its entirely fictional nature was an end-credit caption that declared it "Copyright April 1st 1977"

supposedly lost secrets of Nazi technologies and/or legendary animals.[254] The latter topic belongs to the enduringly popular field of crypto-zoology, the quest for and pseudo-scientific study of a cast of fantastic creatures including the yeti and Bigfoot. These creatures differ from (but partially overlap with) folkloric and mythological ones. The key distinction is whether there has been a tradition of their having been observed by humans in the modern era (in this schema, for instance, sphinxes are absent whereas the Loch Ness Monster is included). Mermaids, and their more reclusive partners, mermen, straddle mythological, folkloric and crypto-zoological realms and thereby provide rich material for representation.

The most substantial discussion of the mermaid within a crypto-zoological context was provided in a hoax concocted by eminent oceanographer Karl Banse in the journal *Limnology and Oceanography* in 1990 (a publication not otherwise prone to publishing such material but complicit on this occasion). In order to provide some credible pretext for a scientific study of what had hitherto been perceived as a purely folkloric entity, Banse's paper begins with a statement that, on account of limited data, his research note[255] is "situated between science as it normally should, and archaeology or historical work as it often must, be conducted" (1990: 148). Banse contends that his paper was "critical but also daring, setting out from an anatomical observation about mermaids that Linnaeus (1758) cited but was afraid to pursue" (ibid: 148–149). The latter reference is to the work of seminal biological taxonomist Carl Linnaeus, who included the mermaid in the 2nd edition of his 'System Naturae' as one of fourteen *animalia paradoxa* (contradictory animals) that had some presence in 18th Century European folklore. The section on *animalia paradoxica* was dropped from the 6th edition and is now regarded as a whimsical side note to early editions of the scientist's major taxonomic work,[256] but the siren was subsequently re-inserted in the 10th edition (1758) in a note on the *Trichechus* (manatee), which refers to a specimen of a mermaid supposedly kept in a museum in Leyden. As Bondeson (2014: 42) identifies, Linnaeus had a particular interest in mermaids and sought to secure access to a specimen supposedly caught off Nyköping in Denmark before ascertaining that it was a fake (ibid).

Based on his readings of a number of sources, apparently taken at face value, Banse contends that:

> *The hindbody lacked external limbs, and the end usually was drawn with rays as in fishes, but actually it was a homocercal fluke ... As with the fishy tail, the common depicting of scales covering the entire hindbody was caused, of course, by the artists never having seen specimens; truly, the "scales" were more or less distinct horny skinfolds similar to those in some of the Xenarthra [placental mammals]. (1990: 149)*

---

254 It is notable in this regard that several short videos purportedly discussing the work of a marine scientist named Professor Mandelhoff have been uploaded to YouTube. These include two that refer to mermaids, one of which discusses the Nazi's alleged recruitment of mermaids during World War Two to search for the lost city of Atlantis (see the latter online at: https://www.youtube.com/watch?v=TxOD9ReApzo – accessed December 12th 2015).

255 A research note is a short paper that sets out aspects of a research agenda and/or case study without the detailed substantiation and/or analysis expected of a full journal article.

256 It first appeared in the 1740 edition and was first omitted in 1748.

This characterisation neatly avoids the most obvious factor preventing any credibility for the mermaid as an actual creature, namely the absurdity of a biological system that could accommodate a piscine lower half and mammalian upper one. Linnaeus and Banse concur in classifying the mermaid as a mammal, and Banse elaborates on Linnaeus by identifying three species within a new sub-order entitled *Nixi:* the Mediterranean-Lusitanian *siren sirena*, the western Atlantic *siren indica* and the *siren erythraea* of the Red and Arabian Seas and Indonesian archipelago (ibid).[257] The latter part of Banse's research note goes on to speculate about the life patterns and social organisation of mermaids (a term he uses to refer to both females and males), characterising them as having an aquapelagic lifestyle. He speculates, for instance, whether:

> *the young were held in nurseries and protected by some structure built from driftwood, coral blocks, and the like (cf. the shallow-water data on "baby-sitting" by similarly large-brained dolphins ...) Nothing of these edifices, of course, remains since preservation in the physically highly energetic inshore environment is almost impossible. Moreover, marine transgression since the end of the ice age has submerged everything.* (ibid: 150-151)

Banse goes on to characterise mermaid territories as: "areas or provinces with rather dense populations and appreciable political organization, separated by rocky or very exposed sandy stretches that were frequented only during food-gathering or hunting expeditions, if at all" (ibid). The research note ends with discussion of what he regards as the recent extinction of the mermaid, which he dates "as late as after World War 2" (ibid: 152) and his speculation that this was caused by or related to "human technology intruding the marine arena since the later decades of the last century" (ibid: 152).[258] As this chapter goes on to discuss, the makers of the hoax documentaries *Mermaids: The Body Found* (henceforth referred to as *Mermaids: TBF*) and *Mermaids: The New Evidence* (*Mermaids: TNE*) attempted to establish a similar legitimacy to Banse's journal paper by representing their subject as one explored and documented by scientists associated with government agencies and universities.

I. Production Context

Mermaids: TBF and *Mermaids: TNE* were produced for the Animal Planet network. The network was established in 1996 as a joint venture between the United States (US)-based Discovery Channel and the British Broadcasting Corporation (BBC) to transmit material on various aspects of wildlife and on nature in general. The Animal Planet's initial programming (in 1996–2007) was strongly influenced by the BBC tradition exemplified by broadcaster David Attenborough's various carefully-scripted and scientifically-informed programs (such as *Life on Earth* [1979] and *The Living Planet* [1984]). Despite early

257 Curiously, eastern Atlantic and Baltic mermaids are left out of this framework, unless considered as included within the Mediterranean-Lusitanian type.

258 Banse also included the speculation that "the resulting removal of planktivorous visual predators (principally finfishes) shifted the ecological balance of open waters toward invertebrate predators, including jellyfish ... Because mermaids had thin skin and no access to clothing, they were helpless, especially at night, against the stings of jellyfish" (1990: 152).

170

success with audiences, by the mid-2000s the network's educational, family-oriented approach was increasingly at odds with newer forms of reality TV programming that favoured 'rawer', less apparently mediated representations of environments and of human and animal behaviour. Following a decline in the network's overall viewing figures in 2005–2006, Animal Planet Media's president, Marjorie Kaplan, announced a re-launch that aimed to provide "more aggressive" programming "tapping into the instinctual nature of compelling animal content" (Becker 2008: online).

There are interesting parallels here between Animal Planet's shift away from an ethos acquired from a state-subsidised broadcasting operation (i.e. the BBC) and the BBC's own move into higher-profile, audience-grabbing programming from the late 1990s on. As Wheatley (2004) discusses, the approach the corporation adopted was one that prioritised big-budget specials in order to attract audiences to a wider range of BBC material. One such production was *Walking with Dinosaurs* (1999), a six-part series that attempted to marry scientifically-informed scenarios and narrative interpretation with eye-catching CGI sequences that aimed to present the natural history of a range of species only known from the fossil record. Animal Planet's revamp represented a somewhat different strategy, one that substantially shifted from established notions of educational media into a more sensationalist style of programming.

Animal Planet's revamped format was successful in securing an increased viewing share and also signalled the network's readiness to seek novel ways of refreshing and innovating its content. This included a venture into crypto-zoology in the form of *Finding Bigfoot*, a series that followed the activities of the amateur enthusiasts who constitute the Bigfoot Field Researchers Organization.[259] The series initially documented the group's attempts to find the eponymous creature (a hairy hominid reputed to inhabit remote areas of the Pacific Northwest) before branching further afield to (unsuccessfully) seek similar creatures in other continents. In January 2012 the network announced that its annual schedule would include a special 'Monster Week'. The network's publicity release referred to this week as a "programming stunt" and went on to describe its climax as:

> *a stunning, two-hour feature that claims the existence of the lost, mythical sirens of the sea in MERMAIDS: THE BODY FOUND. Throughout history, people from nearly every culture have spotted or spoken about this half-man, half-fish anomaly. Amped by stunning CGI and animation, MERMAIDS: THE BODY FOUND details the first-hand accounts of a team of government scientists who testify they've found the remains of a never-before-identified sea creature with ties to human origins. In a story about evolutionary possibility grounded in scientific theory, experts reveal the natural history of mermaids and show us what they looked like, how they lived and how they could have evolved but remained hidden ... until now.* (Animal Planet 2012)

The juxtaposition of two statements, one identifying a "programming stunt" as about to occur and the other referring to the testimony of government scientists, reflects the

---

259 Which was parodied in the series *Mermaid Magic*, as discussed in Chapter 7.

generally ambiguous approach the network took to its theme week, in which actual documentaries were mixed with the climactic program in question.[260]

While Animal Planet may have been venturing into unknown territory as a natural science-oriented broadcaster tackling the theme of mermaids in a non-folkloric context, the topic was familiar to the viewing public due to prior exposure to the series of fictional films and TV series on the topic discussed in previous chapters.[261] But in terms of the history of media representations discussed above, *Mermaids: TBF* (directed by Sid Bennett) had significantly novel elements. Rather than the bizarrely sutured physicality of fish and human that we have learned to suspend our disbelief in, *Mermaids: TBF* presented viewers with an anatomically more functional and credible species. In this regard, the creatures presented in *Mermaids: TBF* more closely resemble a hybrid of the classic mermaid and the representations of aquatic humanoids in Jack Arnold's 1954 film *Creature from the Black Lagoon* and its 1955 and 1956 sequels[262] (or the similar creature featured in Reinhardt Peschke's *Aquanoids* [2003]), in that their physique was integrated into a coherent humanoid form. As a result of this, the virgular aspect of mermaids and mermen central to their character as media-loric figures and to their manifestation of psychoanalytic tropes was largely effaced in favour of a revised perception and representation of them as an actual, credible species (similar to that described by Banse in his hoax scientific paper). While the issue of their possession of genitalia is not resolved in the program's visual representation, their identification as a species of mammal implies the types of organs and reproductive patterns typical of mammals. The mermen featured in the program are therefore not characterised in terms of physical/symbolic lack and appear to be able to sire offspring with mermaids without any difficulty.

Mermaids: TBF proved a decided hit with TV audiences, being watched by 3.4 million viewers when first broadcast in May 2012,[263] and prompted extensive discussions on Twitter and social media sites. This publicity also resulted in a reported 1.5 million online

260 Although the network did not acknowledge it, their mermaid special had a notable predecessor in the form of a feature-length fictional program produced by Darlow Smith Productions in 2004 for Channel 4 (UK) entitled *The Last Dragon*. This program featured CGI sequences similar to those used in the BBC's speculative documentary series *Walking with Dinosaurs*. Like *Mermaids: TBF*, *The Last Dragon* combined CGI visualisations of its subjects in historical contexts (commencing with a sequence labelled "Montana 65 million years ago") with the discoveries of a contemporary scientist (a palaeontologist, in this case), who uncovers evidence that the fabled flying creatures actually existed and, indeed, survived until the Middle Ages (when human expansion rendered them extinct). In contrast to *Mermaids: TBF*, the fictional nature of the 2004 production was made explicit in its initial voice-over, which describes the program as "a scientific exploration of a remarkable species ... the natural history of the most extraordinary creature that *never existed*" (my emphases).

261 The program's most obvious predecessor in terms of representing merfolk as a coherent species encountered by undersea explorers was in an episode of the TV fantasy/science fiction series *Sanctuary* entitled 'Requiem' (Martin Wood, 2008). The series includes a mermaid as one of the non-humans housed in its titular sanctuary facility (introduced in its opening episode 'Sanctuary for All' [Martin Wood, 2008]). Referred to as Sally, since her mer-name is unpronounceable to humans, she senses trauma in her marine community, located in the so-called Bermuda Triangle of the Atlantic. This prompts the series' lead characters Dr Helen Magnus and Dr Will Zimmerman to go into the area in a submarine and investigate. They find that the merfolk have been infected by a parasite and appear to have turned on each other and massacred each other. While this element principally provides the pretext for a drama on board the submarine when Magnus also gets infected, the program provides a relatively unusual representation of merfolk as a coherent species that does not require interaction with humans.

262 *Revenge of the Creature* (Jack Arnold, 1955) and *The Creature Walks Among Us* (John Sherwood, 1956).

263 Source: www.thefutoncritic.com – accessed October 10th 2015.

streams of footage from the program (Quigley 2013: online) and subsequent DVD sales. The following sections provide detailed analyses of the scenarios and hypotheses presented in *Mermaids: TBF* and its follow-up, *Mermaids: TNE*, the nature of the representations of the aquatic humanoids featured and the manner in which sound design and musical scoring combined with CGI sequences and narrative to render the program's merfolk as humane.

NB: Despite the programs' titles, the creatures depicted in *Mermaids: TBF* and *Mermaids: TNE* are both male and female (i.e. mer-*men* and -*maids*). The program's use of the female variant for its title principally emphasises the low profile of the 'male of the species'. In order to avoid confusion, throughout this chapter I refer to groups of mixed mermaids and mermen as 'merfolk', following a contemporary tendency to use that term.[264]

II. Introducing The Bloop

The objective was to take the viewers on the ride, from a far-fetched, instantly dismissible, premise and drag them in to the point where they no longer knew what was real and if possible, create such a strong, unwavering case, that they might even believe. (Sound designer Damien Trotta, p.c. March 3rd 2014)

A 2-minute, 25-second pre-title credit sequence to *Mermaids: TBF* sets up the narrative that follows and also establishes sound as both a key element in the 'evidence' provided by the program and as a key dramatic device within it. Sound is initially used as a disturbing, unsettling element. Swishing helicopter rotors, sirens, and recurring short crescendos of indefinable environmental sounds are used to accompany blurry, hand-held camera images of people in protective full-body suits carrying something on a stretcher. The impression that someone is making an un-authorised film of this activity is confirmed as a hand moves towards the camera to block the lens. An electronic beep signals a sudden cessation of the introductory scenes. Sound elements are also used to reinforce the authenticity of the subsequent interview scene, with (supposed) pre-interview chatter between the recording team and the interview subject (a scientist later identified as Paul Robertson, played by actor Sean Michael) intentionally left in the broadcast program. The program then succinctly addresses an issue central to audience engagement with its narrative (i.e. its credibility) and introduces (what is presented as) a key evidential underpinning of that credibility. After having announced that "as a scientist" he never previously believed in conspiracy theories (such as the one he is about to be principal narrator of) Robertson states that he is well aware of the need to provide conclusive proof of his claims. Moving straight to this aspect, Robertson relates that:

In 1997, scientists from NOAA recorded a sound in the deep Pacific. It's thought to be organic in nature and it has never been identified. It's called 'the Bloop'.

Complementing the statement, a sequence using high-pitched notes with glissandos, suggestive of whale songs, plays on the soundtrack and a computer monitor shows a sound wave form (implicitly that of the Bloop in question). The screen image then cuts to archival footage of whales washed up on a beach as Robertson continues:

---

264 ftnalt See for instance the eponymous Wikipedia site dedicated to them: http://en.wikipedia.org/wiki/Merfolk – accessed February 12th 2015.

> *In the early 2000s it was proved that the Navy beached whales while testing sonar weapons. For years the Navy denied that they were responsible for these beachings. These are facts. And in some of the incidents there were reports of something else washing up with the whales.*

Retaining the association of the 1997 Bloop sound from the previous sequence, the voice-over and beach sequences are accompanied by sounds with similar timbres before the visual scene cuts to footage that shows a blurry body on a beach. Higher, treble tones suggest an urgency and tension, as Robertson relates that:

> *In 2004 two boys were the first to arrive on a mass whale beaching in Washington State. They captured it on a cell-phone. The boys claim that they saw something that day. They claim they saw a body.*

The last words of the voice-over are accompanied by the image of a webbed humanoid hand and, as the boy turns to face his friend in surprise, a sound like a distorted human roar startles the viewer and the image cuts to black. The screen then shows a caption that states: "The footage that you are about to see has not been broadcast until now." After this dramatic interjection the program cuts to shots of an aquarium tank as Robertson's narration continues: "that official record was later changed and the Navy took the remains of what the boys found". As the image cuts to a close-up of a porthole in an aquarium tank and slowly zooms into it, Robertson declares: "I know this because I was part of the team investigating that beaching and what the Navy did that day and I believe that I know what it is that they took." In synch with the last words of the statement a webbed hand is shown reaching from inside the tank and blocking out the porthole, accompanied by a distorted slamming sound, as the image fades to black once more.

The scientific references presented in the pre-credit sequence provide an apparently credible underpinning of its topic. The NOAA is an actual organisation – the National Oceanic and Atmospheric Administration – and the Bloop was an actual sound recorded by them in 1997 that has attracted much discussion. One notable deviation from these solid referents is that the predominant scientific view is not that the sound was "organic" in nature (as stated in the earlier quote). Despite this, recordings of the (actual) Bloop (which are readily available online[265]) do have a rhythmic groaning quality that might be taken as suggestive of animal utterances. This has led a number of writers (and subsequent Internet posters) to promulgate accounts of the Bloop as being generated by undersea animals. One of the most influential of these was provided by David Wolman, writing in the prestigious *New Scientist* magazine in 2002, who reported comments made about the Bloop by NOAA scientist Christopher Fox:

> *Fox's hunch is that the sound nicknamed Bloop is the most likely to come from some sort of animal, because its signature is a rapid variation in frequency similar to that of sounds known to be made by marine beasts. There's one crucial difference, however: in 1997 Bloop was detected by sensors up to 4800 kilometres apart. That means it must be far louder than any whale noise, or any other animal noise for that matter. Is it even remotely possible that some creature*

---

265 See for instance http://www.wired.co.uk/news/archive/2012-11/29/bloop-mystery-not-solved-sort-of - – accessed November 28th 2014.

bigger than any whale is lurking in the ocean depths? Or, perhaps more likely, something that is much more efficient at making sound?Ɔ (2002: online)

Wolman's speculations amplified Fox's "hunch" and – through use of the word "likely" – opened the door for subsequent speculation as to what such an "efficient" noise-making entity might be. Over the last decade consensus has, in fact, supported the argument that the noise is produced by ice fracturing processes (see Steadman 2012). This has not deterred enthusiasts from providing more colourful explanations and *Mermaids: TBF* plays off this strand of pseudo-scientific folklore.

After the introductory sequence discussed above the program proceeds to discuss the connections between mass beachings and Navy sonar experiments and suggests that testing of ultrasound weapons was the cause. In response to this, the scientists reveal that NOAA had underwater audio recorder arrays in an area of beachings on the Pacific Northwest in 2004. Robertson relates that these recorders had captured a sequence that comprised whale sounds, a sound that they later understood to be the priming of the sonar weapon, the explosive detonation of the weapon and, finally, a cluster of sounds reminiscent of the 1997 Bloop recording discussed above. Robertson describes the last section of these sounds as:

the most complex, intricate animal call I had ever heard and we had no idea what had made the sound ... all we knew was that a creature that had only been heard once in human history had just resurfaced.

Note the condensation and elision of evidence and opinion here. An ambiguous sound of uncertain origin is briskly characterised as sonic evidence of a unique, barely-known creature capable of "intricate" sonic communication.

Despite the program's explicit linkage, the particular sound Robertson refers to (and which is played to illustrate Robertson's discussion) is significantly different from actual recordings of the original (i.e. 1997) Bloop, particularly in terms of its complexity. The new sound passage comprises multiple high-frequency tones, many of which slide off in pitch and volume, together with sustained high-frequency white-noise elements. The underscore also subtly introduces a low rhythmic pulse and some low-frequency sustained notes, enhancing the dramatic tension and blending with the Bloop featured on the soundtrack.

Robertson's narration then describes continual Navy denials about the sonic-induced beachings and the scientists' lack of proof of their occurrence, stating:

We continued to build profiles of these events and we went over the one thing that we did have, which was the recording ... we listened to and analysed this recording I don't know how many times and we made comparisons with whales and dolphins but this thing to our ears sounded much more intricate, much more advanced and we thought we had a reasonable chance to crack the code but it was still beyond us, we needed help.

Rather like the previous narrative step's contention that the original Bloop was "organic" and produced by a mysterious "creature", the narration both posits and accepts that the fourth section of the (fictional) 2004 Bloop recording includes sonic "code" that, by definition, is open to de-coding.

At this point the program introduces us to a new scientist (identified as an expert on cetacean communications) who comments that he can recognise "literally hundreds of signifiers" in the final section of the sound recording and can "arrange these into recognisable patterns". The reference to "signifiers" here moves the program's contentions into acceptance of there being a language expressed in the 2004 Bloop recording (requiring the "creature" that made them to have a sufficient level of intelligence to articulate such a language). This is reinforced by the expert's subsequent comments, referring to pitch changes visible on a screen visualisation of the sound pattern found in frequencies above the human hearing range. Slowing the recording down by a third and playing it back, the program's soundtrack presents us with multiple discernible sonic elements, which the expert describes in the following terms: "multiple individuals ... literally thousands of different [sonic] signifiers ... at least half a dozen individual voice prints – so what you see here is language ... they're talking to one another". The sample played takes the form of a thick cluster of overlapping sounds (with predominant upper frequencies) and that combines sustained sounds that rise and/or fall within a variety of frequency ranges. The sample ends with a crescendoed cacophony of high-pitched sounds. The sequence then cuts back to Robertson asking, "what other animal could have a language so complex, so sophisticated?"

With regard to representations of the conventional siren/mermaid, it is notable that the seductive vocalisations associated with the female of the species in both folklore and mainstream cinema are delivered *above* the surface of the water, as she perches on rocky outcrops, reclines on the shore or else sings with her head above the waves. Her voice floats across the water and is heard in the air, emphasising her ability to exist in both aquatic and terrestrial environments. By contrast, the radical aspect of the merfolk about to be revealed in the program's narrative is their complete aquaticism. Through repeated sequences of Bloop recordings on the soundtrack, graphic representations of Bloop elements as wave forms (as if the latter somehow confirm the veracity of the former) and frequent statements emphasising their significance, *Mermaids: TBF* transmutes different abstract sound sequences into crucial evidence that brings the narration, narrative and, implicitly, the audience to the cusp of a radical contention. As Robertson reveals in the statement that sets the program on a new tangent, "our theory was that this was a new species of dolphin but there was another theory we should have considered sooner, the aquatic ape theory".

III. Aquatic Apes and their Evolution into Merfolk

Cued by Robertson's reference, the program shifts into a discussion of the aquatic ape theory. Aspects of the theory were initially propounded in the 1920s, when German anatomist Max Westenhöfer contended that various elements of human physique suggested an aquatic phase early in human evolution (see de Sarre 2003). Alister Hardy, a British zoologist and researcher into comparative religions, propounded a similar idea with regard to a significantly later stage in evolution, most notably in an article in *The New Scientist* magazine entitled 'Was Man More Aquatic in the Past?' (1960).[266] Important as Hardy's work was, the individual who succeeded in raising more major and sustained

---

266 Hardy gave a number of talks subsequent to his 1960 article but never wrote the book on the topic that he foreshadowed in various fora

discussion of the concept was British writer Elaine Morgan. The theory rose to prominence in the 1970s following the publication of her book 'The Descent of Woman' in 1972 and was extended in two further books by the author (1982, 1990) and a BBC documentary on her work (*The Aquatic Ape*, Richard Chambers, 1998). Informed by Hardy's ideas, Morgan reacted to what she and other feminist theorists saw as the male bias of the so-called 'Savannah Theory' of human evolution. This proposed that male hunters venturing from the jungle into the savannahs of Africa led the development of contemporary humans. Her work sought to problematise the theory and to pose an alternative version. There were two pivots to her account. The first was that it was women's activities that spurred the surge in human development that led to our contemporary form. The second was that these activities took place in an area of East Africa that was substantially inundated by the sea around 5 million years ago and, in particular, around one elevated fragment (the present-day Danikil Alps region) that was 'islanded' by the flooding of adjacent lowlands. She contended that humans adapted to become essentially aquapelagic in this period and that changes in their foraging patterns led them to evolve so as to lose body hair. She also argued that their diet, high in Omega-3 fatty acids, facilitated their rapid mental development and their evolution into modern humans.

Illustrating its account of Morgan's ideas with images such as those of young (human) infants instinctively swimming underwater, *Mermaids: TBF* sets up two parallel strands that the remainder of the program cuts between. One is the gradual unfolding of Robertson and his colleagues' investigation of what the mysterious beached creature and Bloop sounds might be. The second is a series of historical re-enactments, initially performed by actors in ape costumes and subsequently by CGI sequences (reminiscent of those in James Cameron's film *Avatar* [2009]). The re-enactments show the possible outcome of a group of humans becoming increasing integrated with aquatic environments and evolving into a separate species, with elongated manatee-like tails, webbed hands and particular cranial characteristics that enable them to sense and communicate in undersea environments. These sequences are presented in a series of vignettes, introduced by screen captions, such as "Africa 7 Million Years Ago", "Madagascar Coast 4.5 Million Years Ago" and "Indian Ocean 10,000 years ago". The African sequences echo Morgan's account of human origins in inundated areas of East Africa and the later one, set in warm oceanic waters, also recalls statements by researchers who have acknowledged that human inhabitation of such locales has elements that accord with aspects of Morgan's aforementioned theories. In the course of an article on marine shellfish gathering in Oceania, for instance (an area which offers various paradigmatic aquapelagic assemblages), ecologist Thomas Malm contends that:

> Some of the speculation made by proponents of the so-called "aquatic ape hypothesis" could benefit from observations of what is still being done in Oceania's coastal waters ... it could be argued that certain aspects of Oceanian lifestyle provide us with a mirror of what a semi-aquatic lifestyle might have meant in the remote evolutionary past of our species. (2009: 10)

These quasi-historical sequences serve to move the program's account towards the present and to the program's final CGI images of merfolk swimming with whales off the Washington coast.

177

The two strands outlined above are presented significantly differently and sound provides a key role in both delineating and creating the different affective dimensions of each. The first strand relies heavily on narration to camera by various scientists and witnesses, together with laboratory sequences and reconstructions of aquatic humanoid physiology. These serve to propel the narrative along to reveal that what the scientists have uncovered is the existence of merfolk and of a US Navy plot to cover up their existence so as to prevent public opinion from mobilising against the testing of sonar weapons that are killing them. Sustained tones incorporating a variety of electronic timbres are favoured within the underscore to support the development of the mysterious narrative, with low-frequency rumbles the most prominent element. These sustained, soft-edged elements, together with frequent sonic swells and scatterings of high-pitched sounds, also integrate well with the blurry graphic visual representations of the Bloop that are used regularly as corroborative visual proof of the sound's veracity and significance. By contrast, the highly speculative re-enactments of moments in merfolk evolution are accompanied by musical sequences. These aim to communicate emotions such as wonder, pathos, affection and admiration congruent with the scenes represented on screen and with the growing expressivity, intelligence and emotional complexity represented in the faces and actions of the CGI-generated merfolk.

The sequence entitled 'Madagascar Coast 4.5 million years ago' shows humanoid creatures swimming with confidence underwater as the narration relates that the creatures have become closely associated with dolphins, to the extent that they hunt collaboratively with them. The soundtrack includes individual melodic 'voices' at this point, analogous to those aggregated in the program's Bloop sound. The emotional uplift and inter-species bonding represented in the sequence is reinforced by an extract from American techno artist Moby's 2009 track 'A Seated Night', in which a sample of Haitian choral music is foregrounded. During the CGI sequence entitled "The Marianas Trench 3.1 Million Years Ago", the underscore makes prominent use of a gentle, evocative passage from the Kronos Quartet's arrangement of 'Flugufrelsarinn' by Sigur Rós. (It is also notable that the lyrics of the original Sigur Rós song include melancholic references to marine environments[267] and that, in turn, the excerpts from the Quartet's arrangement tend to be used to accompany melancholic and/or ominous scenes within the CGI sequences.)

The most dramatic and, arguably, most emotionally engaging CGI sequence, entitled "North America 1.6 million years ago", is accompanied by a complex and accomplished use of soundtrack elements. The sequence begins with watery sounds as a merman is seen in the ocean. When attention moves to the foreboding, snow-covered shore the underscore delivers a low rumble of synth notes and growling sound effects. These rumbling notes and sounds are replaced by a gentler and more uplifting underscore (featuring an A minor chord made up of pure-sounding 'sine' notes) as the visuals show a lone scout swimming gracefully in the ocean depths, with the CGI image showing a more intelligent, evolved humanoid face than that of the creatures featured in the 4.5 million-year-old Madagascar sequence. When the merman's attention moves to underwater feeding grounds, the

---

267 Such as "I can't breathe and I'm getting heavier with every wave, I need a miracle because I'm drowning" – translation from http://pdhinson.blogspot.com.au/2009/11/translation – flugufrelsarinn.html – accessed January 3rd 2015

inclusion of some mildly dissonant notes re-introduces some aural tension. These presage the representation of a gigantic megalodon shark attacking a whale. The attack is accompanied by a sudden percussive 'hit', followed by a cluster of dissonant notes mixed with sound effects that can be interpreted as the whale's agonised cries. The A minor chord re-emerges as a pod of merfolk is shown, with mermaids clutching the hands of their young to pull them along or else swimming with infants clinging around their necks. The sequence then features sounds that suggest that members of the pod are calling out in alarm to each other. Ominous-sounding, synthesised drumbeats introduce another layer of aural tension; a scout calls out to members of the pod, who pause and turn to look at him. His voice takes the form of a loud, complex, high-frequency screeching sound, and the pod responds with multiple, cleaner, high-frequency sounds. An individual mermaid and infant (implicitly his partner and child) are then shown looking back at him. The lone merman, who has chosen to sacrifice himself to save the pod, hangs in the water as the huge shark appears below him, and the ominous rhythmic pulses continue as he swims up towards the surface, attracting the shark's attention. Watery sounds move into the aural foreground as he calls to lure the shark away from the pod and the rhythmic pulses are then removed, creating a sparse aural texture that heightens the anticipation of the imminent attack. A recap of the gentle, evocative passages from the Kronos Quartet's arrangement of 'Flugufrelsarinn' conveys a further sense of the tragedy about to unfold, and the pod turns away to avoid witnessing the final horror. In a clever piece of understated sound design the underscore continues with a gentle melodic texture as the shark approaches and swallows the scout (rather than utilising dramatic percussive accents). The music used here plays a prominent role in establishing the complex emotional sensibilities of the merfolk and invites the audience to perceive them as intelligent and compassionate aquatic humanoids.

Following the drama of the sequence discussed above, with its representation of individual sacrifice for social good and poignant familial interaction, the next CGI sequence provides further emotional manipulation. The sequence commences with the caption title 'The South Pacific 150 Years ago' and is accompanied by narration that describes that the species so richly and sympathetically represented in previous CGI sequences is "in decline" but "still clings on" despite increasing human intrusion into its environment. The sequence again incorporates an expanded use of material from 'Flugufrelsarinn'. After initially presenting more of the evocative Dorian chord progression and melody, the underscore shifts to an emphatically joyous-sounding section of the arrangement, featuring major tonality, accented string chords, and violin lines that soar into the upper range of the instrument as the visuals focus attention on a newborn mer-baby, inviting audience empathy and suggesting that the species has a future.

IV. The Cover-Up Intensifies

In parallel with the CGI sequences representing the evolutionary path from aquatic humans to fully-marine merfolk discussed above, *Mermaids: TBF* also has a second strand that relates the US Government's attempts to thwart Robertson and his fellow researchers (in a manner that recalls the recurrent theme of *The X-Files* TV series [1993–2002][268]). In addition to evidence of the 2004 Bloop data discussed in Section I, the scientists' growing certainty about the existence of merfolk is consolidated through their visit to South Africa. Here two important strands of proof come together. The first involves analysis of a South African scientific recording of another Bloop event. This is similar to the 2004 example but has an additionally significant element. The South African recording appears to have captured an inter-species communication between dolphins and an unknown creature. The second strand follows from the extrication of fragments of an unknown animal from a shark's stomach. Careful examination of the remains and deductive reconstruction by a forensic anthropologist reveal the body parts to be those of an aquatic humanoid with an elongated manatee-like tail, webbed hands and a ridged cranium. As the narration specifies, with regard to the latter, "the parts which in humans correspond to sound interpretation were greatly enlarged". Drawing on this, the scientists also conclude that a hole in the creature's cranium is related to a sound organ that can sense space and movement and can be used for communication. This evidence of highly evolved communication faculties leads the scientists to conclude that the specimen they have reconstructed is the creature that was recorded participating in cross-species communication with dolphins in their recording. Having reached the sensational conclusion that merfolk exist and that they represent a highly intelligent, digressive wing of human evolutionary history, the narrative then robs the scientists of the opportunity to publicise their discovery, as security operatives seize the mer-skeleton and the majority of the scientists' other evidence, leaving them shattered and disillusioned. However, one more piece of evidence comes their way, the complete phone camera footage of the merman found on the Pacific Northwest beach in 2004 by two boys that is shown in extract earlier in the program. Tracking down one of the boys' families, Robertson and his colleagues finally see the complete recording, showing a severely damaged and traumatised merman, providing the scientists with their first, deeply saddening representation of a live mer-person.

The concluding CGI sequence, entitled "Washington Coast", provides the most orthodox natural history-style representation of the merfolk within the overall program. Having proved its case that merfolk exist, the narration conveys the scientists' realisation that merfolk migrate seasonally with whales (explaining their presence with whales in areas where sonic weapons have caused carnage). Rich, blue-dominated images show a stream of whales travelling along the coast accompanied by merfolk, set to the sounds of mer-voices and whale sounds. Having set up the audience with this wondrous New Age vision of whales and aquatic humanoids co-existing, the calm, authoritative voice-over informs the audience that the merfolk are no longer safe in the deep ocean due to the threats posed by US Navy weapons testing. The program then reveals that the scene we are watching is a representation of the moment before the sonar weapon blast recorded on the NOAA equipment played at the start of the program. While the impact of the sonic weapon's detonation on the merfolk and whales is not represented on screen, the idyllic migration scene is in stark contrast to the footage of beached whales and the distraught,

---

268   An episode of the *X-Files*, entitled 'Humbug', broadcast in season 2 of the series in 1995, briefly features a mermaid theme. It initially identifies the Feejee Mermaid as a potential suspect in the murder of a 'freak-show' performer but this suspicion is soon dismissed.

damaged merman included earlier in the program. The scenario depicted here represents a complete reversal of the sonic associations of the traditional siren/mermaid myth. Whereas the sirens of antiquity lured mariners to their death with irresistible songs and whereas the mermaids of folklore charmed and seduced mortal males away from everyday terrestrial concerns, *Mermaids: TBF* offers no such scenarios. Instead the situation is reversed and radically intensified. US Navy technologies do not so much distract merfolk as annihilate them via a form of indiscriminate sonic terrorism that the species is powerless to combat.

Adding further poignancy to the above, members of the scientific team subsequently seek contact with the merfolk that they have proved to exist. Having established that the merfolk migrate with whales on a seasonal basis, they try to contact them off the Washington coast. As the scientists' boat floats in the water, the underscore uses another lengthy, evocative quotation from 'Flugufrelsarinn'. High mer-voice sounds then become audible on the scientists' headphones, blending with the score's strings to suggest the merfolk's presence in the waters below the boat. The music then soars into a joyous, high-range violin section as the scientists believe they may be about to encounter the elusive creatures. But this moment of anticipation is abruptly shattered by the intrusion of the Navy, which intervenes to confiscate the scientists' equipment, with the joyful string sounds abruptly tapering off. The program ends on an emotional downbeat. Outmanoeuvred by government forces, with only the Bloops and odd snippets of visual evidence remaining, Robertson concludes that merfolk are safest hidden away in the deepest and most remote recesses of the ocean where humans may not be able to reach and eradicate them.

V. The New Evidence

Although *Mermaids: TBF* deviated from representations of mermaids in traditional form, its highly elaborate crafting as a documentary heavily dependent on sonic evidence and CGI visualisations led it to be widely accepted as providing actual documentary material by a significant proportion of its audience. As Robertson (2013) discusses, mermaids are the subject of considerable interest to a dispersed community of (in her nomenclature) "mermaiders", to whom they offer a sense of "re-enchantment" that involves senses of (human) "selfhood" being invested in an idealised semi-human 'other' that inhabits an aquatic realm. For such aficionados, the program's representation of merfolk as highly integrated with the natural world, swimming harmoniously with those most iconic examples of charismatic oceanic fauna, dolphins and whales, is highly potent. The merfolk depicted in *Mermaids: TBF* offer a vision of an alternative, Green and collectivist (quasi-) humanity that is the opposite of modern terrestrial communities that are out of synch with their spiritual side and complicit in damaging the planetary environment.

For a portion of its audience, the program's merfolk were not just potent figures that inspired identification and fascination but also ones that were credible as living crypto-zoological entities. This constituency was one that was particularly captivated by the Animal Planet program and social media postings representing their acceptance of the veracity of the program were widespread.[269] In many cases posters also condemned the US Navy for callous indifference to the damage it was doing to merfolk. The program was supported by a website (believeinmermaids.com) that 'mysteriously' had access to its content blocked shortly after the program's broadcast, further fanning perceptions of US Government censorship. As the main organisation identified as involved in the cover-up, NOAA found itself the target of inquiries and complaints, resulting in it issuing a press release in July 2012 entitled 'No evidence of aquatic humanoids has ever been found' (NOAA 2012). While the release did not deign to specifically debunk the Animal Planet hoax documentary, it clearly distanced itself from any aspect of the program's fiction. As might be expected, the NOAA press release received considerable publicity in its own right that explicitly linked it to the popularity of *Mermaids: TBF* and resulted in conspiracy theorists' further perceptions of a cover-up.

The Animal Planet network's success with *Mermaids TBF* prompted it to produce a follow-up in the following year's Monster Week, *Mermaids: The New Evidence*, which achieved similarly high viewing figures to its predecessor. Unlike the first program, and reflecting its lower budget, *Mermaids: TNE* eschewed CGI visualisations of merfolk evolution in favour of a studio catch-up with Robertson one year on and discussion of various strands of "new evidence" that supported the previous program's thesis. To that end, the program's format was basically that of its anchor (actual journalist Jon Frankel, 'playing himself') presenting Robertson with new material and seeking his comments on its veracity and the degree to which it was congruent with the research presented in the first program.

The "new evidence" presented in the program comes in various forms, one of which is historical. *Mermaids: TNE* introduces its audience to the historical case of the famous 'Feejee Mermaid', a fake dead mermaid (actually comprising the shrivelled upper torso of an orangutan and the lower half of a salmon). This concoction was acquired by sea captain Samuel Barrett Eades around 1820 and was initially exhibited in the United Kingdom. In 1842 the showman P.T. Barnum acquired it, gave it an identity as the 'Feejee Mermaid' (supposedly found in the South Seas) and publicised it with a woodcut illustration of a glamorous creature more in keeping with the mermaid's idealised form in fiction and folklore. His exhibition of it in New York created a brief but high profile sensation. The 'Feejee Mermaid' was subsequently exhibited elsewhere and then put into storage before apparently being destroyed in a fire in 1865 (see Bondeson 1999: 36–63). In terms of impact, Barnum's initial New York exhibition of his mermaid offers the most obvious historical precursor to Animal Planet's early 21st Century hoax broadcasts and it is fitting, in this regard, that the former is woven into the latter. This connection is forged through the narrative device of *Mermaids: TNE* purporting to have uncovered a second preserved mermaid corpse that was about to be exhibited by Barnum prior to the aforementioned fire at his premises. As the program reveals to an excited Robertson, the figure shown in handbills produced for the intended exhibition closely resembled the merfolk that Robertson discovered (and that were represented in the first program's CGI sequences).

Together with the Barnum evidence, *Mermaids: TNE* also used more contemporary

---

269   Members of the Kardashian family, for instance, were highly enthusiastic about the program, ensuring wide awareness among their Twitter followers - Kim Kardashian reportedly having 14 million Twitter followers alone (source: http://www.dailymail.co.uk/tvshowbiz/article-2115737/Kim-Kardashian-eclipses-Obama-Twitter-gains-14-million-fans.html accessed February 10th 2014).

footage that had allegedly come to light in the interim between the broadcast of *Mermaids: TBF* and its follow-up. In keeping with the first program, this is international in scope. One sequence showed supposedly amateur video footage of a mermaid filmed on rocks off the shore of an Israeli town named Kirat Yam and discussed the related story of the town council's offer of $1 million for a confirmed sighting of mermaids. The latter element, in particular, went viral, with various online news services reporting the reward and with posters on TripAdvisor's online travel forum reporting mermaid watching in the area as a planned activity.[270] The second sequence was of a creature allegedly caught on film during a British rescue boat exercise in the North Sea, accompanied by an earnest denial of the story from an official spokesman. These sequences were, however, principally the lead-in to the program's most effective (and most highly designed) sequence.

The climax of *Mermaids: TNE*, and of the major "new evidence" announced in its title, was a sequence that purported to show footage shot off the Jan Meyan Ridge in the North Atlantic by two Danish scientists surveying the ocean floor. The program features an actor playing the part of Torsten Schmidt, one of the fictional geologists, relating his experiences and commenting on footage taken from his submarine. Cued by the anchor's introduction ("You've not only seen some remarkable things down there you've heard some amazing things"), Schmidt relates how it was one of the team's jobs to undertake a 60-minute listening exercise to check that there were no marine animals in the vicinity before using sonar mapping that might disturb such creatures (a markedly different approach to the US Navy practices represented in *Mermaids: TBF*). Introduced by the host as a "terrifying" incident, the program then shows footage of the two geologists inside the submarine in 2010 listening, somewhat puzzled, to noises similar to the Bloop sounds from *Mermaids: TBF* that seem to surround their vessel and then reacting in alarm as the submarine is bumped by an unseen object. Schmidt relates that the survey administration attempted to explain the incident as an encounter with pilot whales and that it wasn't until he became aware of the research presented in *Mermaids: TBF*, and especially its analysis of recorded Bloops, that he began to conceive that he may have encountered aquatic humanoids. Schmidt then relates that he approached government agencies about an environmental study of the region where the incident happened, only to be thwarted by senior officials who reminded his team of confidentiality clauses in their contracts and instructed them not to play their audio-visual recordings to any outside party. As the program reveals, the team decided to seek further proof of the merfolk's existence in the region, which they duly obtained in 2013. Over a seven-month period they played a recording of the Bloop noises into the ocean during their survey missions while running two cameras to capture anything that the sounds may have attracted. As the program then reveals in its *coup de théâtre*, they were finally rewarded when they recorded fleeting images of a merperson on camera swimming to their porthole and (similar to an image early in *Mermaids: TBF*) pushing a webbed hand against the portal – as if rebuffing the playback of recordings of merfolk sounds into the water.

The sounds designed for these submarine sequences were as carefully crafted as those in

---

270   See, for instance, Barbie (2013: online).

the program's predecessor. As Trotta has identified, sound design was a crucial aspect of inviting audience credulity about and engagement with the new evidential footage:

> *The follow-up was ... "more of the same please" in the broad sense of hyper reality ... But again we weren't going to create "a mermaid" that you would need to buy into, we were bringing them to life by creating "realities" they would exist within. In the sightings, you heard the realities from which they were observed, a slap on the window of the submersible or the surf below with the mermaid in the distance. And if you did hear a vocalization, you didn't see them so you didn't have to connect the sound and visual which is important, your mind makes the connection, which keeps it vague and in some ways more real.* (p.c. 2014)

The program proved effective in engaging its audience and again Twitter and social media sites were abuzz with discussion as to the veracity of the footage. As Trotta has emphasised, the degree of affective engagement caused by clever deployment of sound was, again, a key element of the program's impact (ibid 2014). The "new evidence" arising from the submarine mission was both sonic and visual and the lure for the merfolk was their auditory signature, the 'Bloop' central to the programs' quasi-documentary conceits.

Conclusion

As stated in the Introduction to this chapter, *Mermaids: TBF* followed on from the Animal Planet's first successful foray into crypto-zoological programming in the form of *Finding Bigfoot*. In making *Mermaids: TBF* and its sequel, Animal Planet both exploited the popularity of crypto-zoology and, effectively, 'had their cake and ate it' by making the program as a hoax at the same time as actively seeking to reinforce perceptions of its veracity. The network's persistence in mixing hoax material with actual documentaries and, in particular, its perpetuation of the mermaid myth, severely aggravated elements of the scientific community. Bodies such as Deep Sea News went so far as to demand an apology from the network "for selling fiction based on fiction off as anything but fiction on a channel that should be celebrating the diversity of actual life" (deepseanews.com 2012). Unlike the Mercury Theatre of the Air's famous hoax broadcast adaptation of H.G. Wells' novel 'War of the Worlds' in 1938 – which caused public disturbance and actual physical harm to some of those who reacted in panic to it – *Mermaids: TBF* and its follow-up had less material impact but did serve to further blur the distinction between fiction and factual media production. While *Mermaids: TBF's* CGI sequences and their rich affective scoring may have proved particularly captivating to those open to believing in the evolution of merfolk, it was the program's careful exploitation of auditory material to provide a more sober evidential underpinning of its thesis that provided the pseudo-scientific aspect crucial to its fiction. Yet, despite this characterisation, the nature of the various Bloop sequences and their similarity to whale and other cetacean sounds allowed them to operate as both sonic evidence within the narrative/diegesis and as affective elements that functioned as score. The latter characterisation reflects perceptions of their musicality. Whale songs have come to be regarded as inherently musical, at least within New Age and/or Green discourse (hence the use of the term *songs* to characterise their sonic utterances), have been released on CDs[271] and have also been combined with (human-

---

271   See, for example, Paul Knapp Junior's *Rapture of the Deep: Humpback Whale Singing* (Compass Recordings, 2001) and Mark Franklin's *Songlines: Songs of the East Australian Humpback Whales* (Oceania, 2009)

originated) music in a number of recordings.[272] As such, cetacean sounds have been represented and understood to convey the creatures' intelligence and creativity – an aspect that makes the continuing slaughter of cetaceans by humans all the more tragic. Indeed it is the sound's ability to be heard and understood as musical (within the human concept of such a practice) that fosters cross-species identification and empathy.

The *Mermaids'* programs' use of Bloops similarly operates on a dual level, providing evidence and affect in dense sonic bundles that are complemented and gradually enhanced by the scored CGI sequences. In this manner, the programs' soundtracks provided highly effective support for the programs' narratives and visualisations and, thereby, the programs' success with viewing audiences and their broader *succès de scandale* in the public arena. The representations of merfolk that the programs provided were innovative in two ways. Firstly, they represented merfolk as physically credible creatures with an evolutionary back-story to account for their distinct form. This innovation shifts the nature of the program's representations from whimsical fantasy to a more docufictional account that invited audience empathy and delivered pathos. The second manner in which the programs were distinct concerned their depiction of male and female merfolk and their offspring in social circumstances. As Chapter 7 detailed, prior to *Mermaids: TBF* and *Mermaids: TNE*, the "male of the mermaid" was rarely represented in audio-visual culture. The Animal Planet network's programs were thereby a significant deviation from uni-sexual representations of mer-humanoids. While the programs did not cast any light on the precise location and operation of mermen's genitalia, the presence of merbabies and the hetero-normative behaviours evident amongst the pod also served to identify them as decidedly masculine in a less ambiguous manner than the figures represented in previous film, television and video texts. In this manner, the programs served to offset a major element of mermaid media-lore with regard to its central pairing of mermaids and human males – rendering merfolk as a distinct species rather than as primordial archetypes of humans' collective unconscious.

Author note: My thanks to Jon Fitzgerald for his assistance with analyses of the musical and sonic material discussed in Sections III and IV of this chapter.

---

272   Such as Kamal's *Reiki Whale Song* (New Earth, 2001) and David Rothenberg's *Whale Music* (Terra Nova, 2008).

Conclusion

I n the course of an extended reflection on Andersen's (1837) 'Den lille Havfrue', Easterlin contends that, "the mermaid and her kinfolk evoke a shifting constellation of concerns, not a fixed set of meanings" (2001: 256). She also asserts that it is "the complex relationship between individual adaptations, the total array of adaptations, subjective cognitive processes, and environmental circumstances" that gives cultural texts their particular significance (ibid: 252). My approach in this volume concurs with these characterisations and considers the "array" of audiovisual representations of mermaids and mermen made between 1904 (the date of Méliès' *La Sirène*) and 2015 from two main perspectives. The first focuses on the manner in which audiovisual representations have drawn on established aspects of folklore and/or on literary and dramatic inscriptions of these (see particularly Chapters 1 and 5). The second complements this by analysing a series of films, television programs and videos that have created distinctly modern forms of the folkloric figures.

The research presented in this volume has identified a number of thematic clusters that constitute contemporary mermaid media-lore. One common element concerns the mermaid's appearance. As per tradition – and almost without exception[273] – mermaids are depicted as slim, youthful, long-haired and conventionally beautiful. Similarly, they are overwhelming represented as Caucasian. In something of a deviation from folkloric accounts and representations of mermaids in pre-20th Century visual arts and design (which usually show mermaids' upper bodies unclothed) around two thirds of the mermaids represented in the 20th and 21st Century audiovisual media texts discussed in this volume are represented as wearing bikini-style tops or pasties. Given that many of the audiovisual productions they appear in are targeted at youth and/or family audiences, prevailing standards of modesty serve as a likely explanation for this visual design factor.

---

273 It is notable that the only representation of an older, unattractive mermaid developed for a live-action media text was cut from the film it was shot for after test screenings. The representation occurred in a sequence shot for *Splash* that involved Madison visiting a sunken ship to consult an aged mermaid about her plans to seek out Allen in New York. This sequence is discussed in Mayo (1984a: 97) together with an accompanying image of actress Marilyn Moe-Stader in role as the aged mermaid (referred to as a "mer-hag" by the production team [ibid]). Mayo describes that while "considerable time and expense was expended on the sequence" it was deleted after preview audiences found it too "foreboding and low key" (ibid). In contrast to Madison's sumptuously colourful tail, the "mer-hag's" tail was given a "folded, wrinkled appearance, and adorned with sculpted barnacles, dead sea specimens and other assorted scraps" (ibid).

187

In a similar deviation from folkloric traditions, while fixed-formed mermaids predominated in synch-sound cinema and television prior to the mid-1980s, the success of *Splash* (Ron Howard, 1984) and Disney's *The Little Mermaid* (1989) led to a continuing vogue for and consequent prominence of the figure of the transformational mermaid. Many television series and aficionado video dramas have also enshrined an element of *Splash* as a central motif, in that mermaids who transform to human form revert when their bodies and, in particular, their legs come into contact with water.

The figure of the transformative mermaid is central to contemporary mermaid media-lore and reflects the manner in which mer-form is, in many cases, one potential identity for mermaids who can also appear and perform as human. The analyses presented in this volume demonstrate that the polyvalence of the mermaid (and, to a lesser extent, the merman) has been key to their proliferation. The term 'polyvalence' is derived from chemistry,[274] but in cultural usage refers to the potential for multiple associations and combinations of elements and/or motifs to accrue and/or be ascribed to aspects of a text and/or cultural entity. Postcolonial discourse (including postcolonial feminist theory) has also used the term to refer to the multiple identities and identity affiliations available to human subjects.[275] The polyvalence I attribute to mermaids and mermen includes aspects of these associations. It is premised on their peculiar combination of physical elements from different genera and consequent lack of fit with a symbolic order premised on and reflective of male and female (human) bodies as the physical indexes of gender difference and as the loci of hetero-, homo- and inter-sexual desire.

The studies advanced in this volume identify the manner in which the scrambled symbolism of human upper-halves and fish-tailed lower bodies allows for markedly different deployments of mermaids and mermen. As Chapter 1 identified, while Disney represented Ariel as an attractive and alluring adolescent mermaid it only offered her the opportunity to pursue romantic/sexual interactions after transforming into human form. Complementing this, Chapter 2 addressed the central enigmatic 'tease' of the (fixed-form) mermaid for human suitors, namely the presence of her tail and the absence of genitalia. As earlier discussions elaborated, in such contexts the tail functions as a fetish object that substitutes for the absent female organ and, at the same time, suggests the phallus. Chapter 4 approaches this from a different angle by looking at processes of 'de-tailing' with regard to the figure of the transformative mermaid. This variety has similarities to the protagonist of Andersen's and Disney's stories, in that such mermaids are commonly represented as being able to assume human form, but as the chapter establishes this commonly occurs without the trauma experienced by the little mermaid and with more success in that the mermaids concerned can achieve emotional contact and/or copulation with terrestrial males. As Chapter 4 describes, *The Mermaid: The Siren of Seduction* (director unknown, 2011) also provides a unique alternative to the transformation of the mermaid into woman by representing its protagonist as becoming a highly phallic 'shemale'[276]. Chapter 3 also explores another aspect of transformative mermaids with regard to those whose beguiling

---

274 Where it refers to atoms that have the capacity to combine with two or more other atoms.

275 See, for instance, Grunkemeier (2012).

276 A term used within the Western sex industry to describe a pre-operative male–female transsexual presenting as a female in all but genital appearance and functionality.

appearance masks a more monstrous aquatic humanoid identity (as in the case of *She Creature* [Sebastian Guttierez, 2001]); Chapter 1 also discusses a mermaid who chose to exchange her fish-tailed lower body for a tentacled one (in the ABC series *Once Upon A Time* [2014]). In common with folkloric traditions, a majority of mermaids represented in conventional audiovisual media are motivated to engage with humans in order to establish romantic and/or sexual relations with men, either in fish-tailed form or in human guise. While it is unsurprising that (aside from versions of Andersen's heroine) a significant number of mermaids who transform to human form are successful in their quest, it is notable that a number are also successful in fish-tailed form.

Complementing these representations of mermaids as living, breathing creatures, Chapters 4, 5 and 6 analyse productions in which female characters assume aspects of mermaid identity in order to provide either spiritual and/or psychological motivation (as in the case of *The Mermaid Chair* [Steven Schacter, 2006], discussed in Chapter 5) or else in various types of role play. Chapter 6 details the development of mermaid-themed aficionado video dramas and the identifications involved, while Chapter 4 provides a discussion of *Mermaids and Unicorns* (Madison Young, 2013), in which women enact mermaid-themed sexual fantasies.

As these summaries suggest, mermaids take a multiplicity of forms and are used in significantly different scenarios. As a result, the media-lore that has developed around them is rich and complex, reflecting a variety of psycho-sexual motifs and tendencies. In these regards, we might identify the mermaid as a figure that can swim through the symbolic order, exploiting her duality to tease, provoke and problematise established gender relations and representations. By contrast, the merman is a more awkward figure, one not so appealing to the male, heterosexual hegemony of the established media industries, leaving him as a marginal other, a 'tailnote' to the mermaid's successful colonisation of 20th and 21st Century screens. But as Chapter 7 makes apparent, there are, nevertheless, significant aspects to his representation, most notably the various problematisations of social norms of masculine identity suggested by gay male merman performers or representations of mermen in various overtly gay productions.

Given that mermaids are frequently represented as closely associated with human males, it is unsurprising that mermaids and mermen are rarely shown as interacting with each other (aside from screen adaptations of Andersen's 'Den lille Havfrue'). Indeed, characterisations of mermen as non-existent/extinct (as in *Talk Dirty to Me Parts III* and *IV* [Ned Morehead, 1986 and 1986]), or else as so unappealing as to move mermaids to cross-genus miscegenation (as in *Miranda* [Ken Annakin, 1948]), are common. The principal exceptions to this are the two hoax documentaries produced by the Animal Planet network in 2012 and 2013 (*Mermaids: The Body Found* and *Mermaids: The New Evidence*), which are discussed in detail in Chapter 8. These essentially operate outside the parameters established in the Introduction and in Chapters 1–7 by representing 'mer-folk' as an anatomically coherent species with conventional male and female anatomies.

While singing abilities are a key element of many mythological and folkloric accounts of mermaids these form a relatively minor element of contemporary media-lore with regard to the representation of singing mermaids within narratives. This aspect is, however, more broadly inscribed within the musical scores of a number of film and television productions, diffusing the folkloric element into extra-diegetic aspects of texts. In addition to the focused discussion of music provided in Chapter 3, aspects of sonic representation are also offered in Chapters 1 and 5 and form a major element of Chapter 8. As these discussions elaborate, mermaids' songs are represented as exercising a powerful effect on human listeners (usually men). This effect can be seductive, in a sexual/romantic sense (as in *Miranda*), can be more akin to a mother's comforting lullaby (as in *Mr Peabody and the Mermaid* [Irving Pichel, 1948]) or else can lure mariners to their doom (as in *Pirates of the Caribbean: On Stranger Tides* [Rob Marshall, 2011]). As writers such as Murch (1994) and Naroditskaya and Austern (2006) suggest, the affective power of such voices evokes the amniotic environment of the womb (and the position of its foetal subjects between unbeing and being, between safety and danger, and between stability and instability).

As the Introduction to this volume identified, my research on mermaids and mermen was inspired by the development of the concept of the *aquapelago* within Island Studies. This concept identifies the manner in which groups of humans that inhabit particular island and/or coastal locales can become closely implicated with marine spaces through their livelihood activities. As I have contended elsewhere (Hayward 2012b), in some instances this leads to the development of aquapelagic cultures that reflect communities' engagements with marine environments in various ways. Fittingly, for this perspective, a significant number of the productions discussed in the volume point to the manner in which, while mermaids and mermen may be amphibious and able to slip between terrestrial and aquatic realms, humans are severely restricted in their abilities to enjoy reciprocal comfort in marine spaces. Indeed many of the films emphasise the impossibility of a fully-aquapelagic lifestyle for humans by variously representing the perils of sustained immersion (as in *Heart's Atlantis* [Andrew Macdonald, 2008]) or else offer magical ways of transcending biological limitation through the intervention of mermaids (as in the seemingly open-ended amphibianism offered to the male protagonist of *Splash*). In this context it is unsurprising that islands and their surrounding waters are often the centre of mermaids' territories and, consequently, key contact zones for contact with humans. These locations range from individual mermaid's bases (as in the case of Cay Oro islet, in *Mr Peabody and the Mermaid*), to mermaid pod bases (as in the titular location of the series *Mako Mermaids* [2013-]) or as ancient and mysterious ancestral homes (as in the case of the mid-Atlantic islands represented in *She Creature*). The liminality of these locations provides the context and opportunity for contact and for the subsequent elaboration of narratives that explore the interaction of human and mer-form subjects.

★ ★ ★ ★ ★ ★ ★

At the time of writing (February 2016), a number of new mermaid- and merman-themed audiovisual works are in various stages of production and/or are slated for release. This indicates the extent to which mermaids and mermen are actively in play in contemporary culture. Like the texts discussed in this volume, the new productions will, in all likelihood, draw on mythic, folkloric and/or previous popular cultural representations in both derivative and innovative manners, solidifying and elaborating some aspects of 20th and 21st Century mermaid and merman media-lore while innovating others. In this regard, this volume captures the first 110 years of a field of production and offers models against which subsequent developments can be considered.

In parallel with research for this book I have established a website that also links to an associated exhibition at Sydney's Macquarie University Art Gallery. The website will be maintained and updated with essays on new mermaid audio-visual productions as they emerge. My current intention is to update this volume to accommodate the new material likely to emerge over the next decade. Correspondence on these and related matters is welcome (see details on the website).

Mermedia Research site: http://www.mermedia.com.au

Bibliography

AFI (American Film Institute) (2015) 'Underwater!', Catalogue of Feature Films, online at: http://www.afi.com/members/catalog/DetailView.aspx?s=&Movie=51711 – accessed December 18th 2015

Amon, Maria Patrice (2014) 'Performances of innocence and deviance in Disney cosplaying' *Transformative Works and Cultures* v17: http://journal.transformativeworks.org/index.php/twc/article/view/565/452 – accessed November 5th 2015

Andersen, Hans Christian (1829) *Fodreise fra Holmens Canal til Østpynten af Amager i Aarene 1828 og 1829*, Copenhagen: self published

——- (1833) 'Agnete og Havmanden', Copenhagen: self published

Andersen, H.C. (1837) 'Den lille Havfrue', Copenhagen: C.A. Reitzel, archived online by Det Kongelige Bibliothek: http://wayback-01.kb.dk/wayback/20101108104437/ http://www2.kb.dk/elib/lit/dan/andersen/eventyr.dsl/hcaev008.htm – accessed March 5th 2015; (unattributed) English translation (as 'The Little Mermaid') archived online by Project Gutenberg: http://www.gutenberg.org/files/27200/27200-h/27200-h.htm#li_mermaid – accessed December 3rd 2014

Andersen, Jens and Nunnally, Tina (2005) *Hans Christian Andersen*, New York: Overlook Books

Animal Planet (2012) 'We've Created a Monster!', January 13th, online at: http://press.discovery.com/us/apl/press-releases/2012/weve-created-monster-animal-plane t-proclaims—1754/ – accessed February 4th 2014

Arne, Anti and Thompson, Stith (1955–1958) *Motif-index of Folk-literature: a classification of narrative elements in folktales, ballads, myths, fables, medieval romances, exempla, fabliaux, jest-books, and local legends*, Bloomington: University of Indiana Press, archived online at: http://www.ruthenia.ru/folklore/thompson/ – accessed April 2nd 2015

Arnold, Matthew (1849) 'The Forsaken Merman', online at: http://www.poetryfoundation.org/poem/172845 – accessed November 1st 2015

Aufderheide, Partricia (2007) *Documentary Film: A Very Short Introduction*, Oxford: Oxford University Press

Austern, Linda Phyllis (2006) '"Teach Me to Heare Mermaides Singing": Embodiments of (Acoustic) Pleasure and Danger in the Modern West', in Austern, Linda Phyllis and Naroditskaya, Inna (eds) *Music of the Sirens*, Bloomington: University of Indiana Press: 52–104

Austern, Linda Phyllis and Naroditskaya, Inna (eds) (2006) *Music of the Sirens*, Bloomington: University of Indiana Press

Baker Brown, Isaac (1866) *On the Curability of Certain Forms of Insanity, Epilepsy, Catalepsy and Hysteria in Femmales*, London: Hardwicke

Banse, Karl (1990) 'Mermaids – their biology, culture and demise', *Limnology and Oceanography* v35 n1: 148–153

Barbie, P (2013) 'Haifa then Kirat Yam for Mermaid Spotting', posting on TripAdvisor, December 3rd, online at: http://www.tripadvisor.com.au/ShowTopic-g293982-i4592-k7022553-Haifa_then_Kirat_Yam_for_sunset_mermaid_spotting-Haifa_Haifa_District.html – accessed February 15th 2014

Barnes, Mo (2015) 'TS Madison rises from prostitution to porn mogul, part 2', *Rollingout* February 4th, online at: http://rollingout.com/2015/02/04/ms-madison-rises-prostitution-porn-mogul-pt-2/ – accessed December 19th 2015

Barrie, J.M. (1904) *Peter Pan or the Boy Who Would Not Grow Up*, online at: http://gutenberg.net.au/ebooks03/0300081h.html – accessed March 20th 2015

———- (1911) *Peter and Wendy*, London: Hodder and Stoughton

Barthes, Roland (1975) *The Pleasure of the Text* (translated by Richard Miller), New York: Hill and Wang

Becker, Anne (2008) 'Animal Planet Changes Its Stripes', *Broadcasting and Cable* January 14th, online at: http://archive.is/AdT2D – accessed February 4th 2014

Begg, Ean (1989) *Cult of the Black Virgin*, London: Arkana

Bendix, Regina (1993) 'Seashell Bra and Happy Ending: Disney's Transformations of *The Little Mermaid*', *Fabula* n34: 280–290

Berger, Pamela (1985) *The Goddess Obscured: Transformation of the Grain Protectress from Goddess to Saint*, Boston: Beacon Press

Betcher, G. J. (1996) 'A Tempting Theory: What Early Cornish Mermaid Images Reveal about the First Doctor's Analogy in "Passio Domini"', *Early Drama, Art, and Music Review* v18 n2: 65–76

Bey, Hakim (1985) *The Temporary Autonomous Zone: Ontological Anarchy, Poetic Terrorism*, online at: http://hermetic.com/bey/taz_cont.html – accessed October 10th 2015

Bilde, Per (1990) 'Atargatis/Dea Syria: Hellenization of Her Cult in the Hellenistic-Roman Period?' in his *Religion and Religious Practice in the Seleucid Kingdom*, Aarhus: Aarhus University Press: 151–187

Bondeson, Jan (1999) *The Feejee Mermaid and Other Essays in Natural and Unnatural History*, Ithaca: Cornell University Press

Bottrell, William (1873) *Traditions and Hearthside Stories of West Cornwall, Second Series*, Penzance: Beare and Son

Boyle, Karen (2010) 'Porn Consumers' public faces: mainstream media, address and representation', in Boyle, Karen (ed) *Everyday Pornography*, New York: Routledge: 134–146

Brown, Ras Michael (2012) *African-Atlantic Cultures and the South Carolina Lowcountry*, Cambridge: Cambridge University Press

Bunker, Henry (1934) 'Voice as female phallus', *Psychoanalytical Quarterly* n3: 391–420

Chion, Michel (1990) *Audio-Vision: Sound On Screen* (translated by Claudia Gorbman), New York: Columbia University Press

———- (1999) 'The Siren's Song' (translated by Claudia Gorbman), in Chion, Michel *The Voice in Cinema*, New York: Columbia University Press: 109–122

Chung, Shu-Hua (2008) 'The Electra complex in Sylvia Plath and Anne Sexton's Poems', *Journal of National Taiwan Normal University: Humanities and Social Sciences* v53 n2: 87–97

Churchward, Charles (2010) *Herb Ritts: The Golden Hour*, New York: Rizzoli

Clay, Andreana (2013) 'Serving Fish: This One's a Snapper', *QueerBlackFeminist* Blog, online at: http://queerblackfeminist.blogspot.com.au/2013/02/serving-fish-this-ones-snapper.html – accessed October 20th 2015

Collins, Wilkie (1866) *Armadale*, London: Smith, Elder and Co./Cornhill

Connelly, Brendon (2011) 'Disney's Glen Keane on Tangled, Reboot Ralph and Bringing Old-School Technique to Animation', *Bleeding Cool,* online at: http://www.bleedingcool.com/2011/01/28/disneys-glen-keane-on-tangled-reboot-ralph-a nd-bringing-old-school-technique-to-cg-animation/ – accessed April 1st 2015

Coyle, Rebecca and Fitzgerald, Jon (2010) 'Disney does Broadway', in Coyle, Rebecca (ed) *Drawn to Sound: Animation Film Music and Sonicity*, London: Equinox: 223–248

Coyle, Rebecca (2012) 'North of Hollywood North: Bowen Island and screen production networks', *Shima: The International Journal of Research into Island Cultures* v6 n1: 67–82.

Craigie, William (1896) *Scandinavian Folk-Lore: Illustrations of Traditional Beliefs of the Northern Peoples*, London: Alexander Gardner

Cruz, Lenika (2014) 'The Feminist Legacy of The Little Mermaid's Divisive 'Sexy' Ariel, *The Atlantic* November 13th, online at: http://www.theatlantic.com/entertainment/archive/2014/11/the-little-mermaid-at-25-and-the-evolving-definition-of-strong-female/382581/ – accessed June 2nd 2015

Cuti, Nicola and Mas, Felix (1972) 'Cilia', *Vampirella* n16 April: 60–66

Dahlerup, Pia (1990) *'The Little Mermaid* Deconstructed', *Scandinavian Studies* n62: 154–163

Davis, Christine (nd) 'How it all started', online at: http://www.secretlifeofamermaid.moonfruit.com/#/about-me/4546248033 – accessed September 26th 2015

Deep Sea News (2012) 'RIP: Science on TV', online at: http://www.deepseanews.com/2012/05/rip-science-on-tv/ – accessed April 8th 2015

Deleuze, Gilles and Guattari, Felix (1972) *Capitalisme et schizophrénie - L'Anti-Oedipe,* Paris: Minuit

di Leonardo, Micaela (1998) *Exotics at Home: Anthropologies, Otherness, American Modernity,* Chicago: University of Chicago Press

——- (2006) 'Mixed and Rigorous Cultural Studies Methodology – an Oxymoron', in White, Mimi (ed), *Questions of Method in Cultural Studies*, Oxford: Blackwell: 205–220

Dick, Tom (2015) 'Chorographing the Vanuatu Aquapelago: Engaging with performatively constituted specificities of place', *Shima: The International Journal of Research into Island Cultures* v9 n2: 1–22

Dinnerstein, Dorothy (1999) *The Mermaid and the Minotaur*, New York: Other Press

Drewal, Henry John (ed) (2008) *Sacred Waters: Arts for Mami Wata and Other Divinities in Africa and the Diaspora*, Bloomington: University of Indiana Press

Driscoll, Catherine (2002) *Girls: Feminine Adolescence in Popular Culture and Cultural Theory*, New York: Columbia University Press

Dundes, Alan (2002) 'The Vampire as Bloodthirsty Revenant; A Psychoanalytic Post Mortem', in Dundes, Alan *Bloody Mary in the Mirror: Essays in Psychoanalytic Folkloristics*, Jackson: University Press of Mississippi: 16–32

Dundes, Alan with Dundes, Laura (2002) 'The Trident and the Fork: Disney's "The Little Mermaid" as a Male Construction of an Electral fantasy', in Dundes, Alan *Bloody Mary in the Mirror: Essays in Psychoanalytic Folkloristics*, Jackson: University Press of Mississippi: 55–75

Dunmore, Helen (2005) *Ingo*, London: Harper Collins

Easterlin, Nancy (2001) 'Hans Christian Andersen's Fish out of Water', *Philosophy and Literature* v25 n2: 251–277

Eliot, T.S. (1915) 'The Love Song of J. Alfred Prufrock', online at: http://www.poetryfoundation.org/poetrymagazine/poem/173476 – accessed June 2nd 2015

'Elsa' (1941) '"The Little Mermaid" – Preliminary Story Discussion', (unpublished) Disney production document (Disney Archives)

Fielding, Henry (1741) *Shamela*, London: A. Dodd

Finnell, Karin (2006) *Goodbye to the Mermaids: A Childhood Lost in Hitler's Berlin*, Columbia: University of Missouri Press

195

Freud, Sigmund (1963) *Sexuality and the Psychology of Love*, New York: Simon and Schuster

------- (1971) *The Wolf Man*, London: Basic Books

------- (2001a) 'Some psychical consequences of the anatomical distinction between the sexes', in Strachey, James (ed) *The Complete Psychological Works of Sigmund Freud, Volume 19*, London: Vintage: 248–260

------- (2001b) 'Female Sexuality, in Strachey, James (ed) *The Complete Psychological Works of Sigmund Freud, Volume 21*, London: Vintage: 225–245

------- (2001c) 'Femininity', in Strachey, James (ed) *The Complete Psychological Works of Sigmund Freud, Volume 22*, London: Vintage: 112–135

Gagapedia (nd) 'Yüyi the Mermaid', online at: http://ladygaga.wikia.com/wiki/Y%C3%BCyi_the_Mermaid – accessed September 14th 2015

Gitter, Elisabeth (1984) 'The Power of Women's Hair in the Victorian Imagination', *PMLA* v99 n5 October: 936–954

Glenza, Jessica (2015) 'Rise of the Mermaids: Weeki Wachee's biggest attraction makes quite a splash', *The Guardian* June 14th, online at: http://www.theguardian.com/us-news/2015/jun/14/rise-of-the-mermaids-weeki-wachee-florida – accessed July 1st 2015

Gn, Joel (2011) 'Queer simulation: The practice, performance and pleasure of cosplay', *Continuum: Journal of Media & Cultural Studies* v25 n4: 583–593

Gokcem, Seth (2012) 'Transperance Me I Want To Be Visible: Gay Gaze in Tom Ford's film A Single Man', *Cinema Journal* v1 n2, online at: http://cinej.pitt.edu/ojs/index.php/cinej/article/view/46/141 – accessed May 3rd 2015

Golgowski, Nina (2013) 'Meet Eric, 22, who lives as a MERMAN swimming underwater in Florida's springs wearing a latex tail – despite wide-eyed stares from local fishermen', *Daily Mail* April 3rd, online at: http://www.dailymail.co.uk/news/article-2303161/Eric-Ducharme-Meet-man-lives-life-merman-Floridas-natural-springs.html – accessed September 14th 2015

Grazer, Brian and Fishman, Charles (2015) *A Curious Mind: the Secret to a Bigger Life*, New York: Simon and Schuster

Grunkemeier, Ellen (2010) 'Writing a Zulu Woman back into History', in Gohrisch, Jana and Grunkemeier, Ellen (eds) *Cross/Cultures* n170 ('Postcolonial Studies Across the Disciplines'): 109–130

Grydehøj, Adam (2006) 'The Dead Began to Speak: Past and Present Belief in Fairies, Ghosts, and the Supernatural' (unpublished) Bachelor of Arts thesis, Evergreen State College, online at: www.islanddynamics.org/island-studies-research.html – accessed July 19th 2015

Guernsey, Clara (1871) *The Merman and the Figure-Head*, Philadelphia: Lippincott

Guinness, Katherine Hunt (2013) 'Rosemarie Trockell: the Problem of Becoming' (unpublished) PhD Thesis, University of Manchester School of Arts, Languages and Cultures, online at: https://www.escholar.manchester.ac.uk/api/datastream?publicationPid=uk-ac-man-scw:196225&datastreamId=FULL-TEXT.PDF – accessed November 4th 2015

Hale, Lindsay (2009) *Hearing the Mermaid's Song: The Umbanda Religion in Rio de Janeiro*, Albuquerque: University of New Mexico Press

Hampton, Howard (2007) *Born in Flames: Termite Dreams, Dialectical Fairy Tales, and Pop Apocalypses*, Cambridge: Harvard University Press

Hanson, Bruce (2010) *Peter Pan on Stage and Screen, 1904–2010*, Jefferson: McFarland

Hardy, Alister (1960) 'Was man more aquatic in the past?', *The New Scientist* n7: 642–645

Hayward, Philip (1989) 'Rhapsodies of Difference: The Mermaid Myth and its radical re-interpretation in Ulrike Zimmerman's *Touristinnen* and the Tom Tom Club's *Suboceania*', *Mediamatic* v4 n1–2: 13–20

------- (1991) 'Desire Caught By Its Tail: The Unlikely Return of the Merman in Madonna's *Cherish*', *Cultural Studies* v5 n1. 98–106

——- (2011) 'Salmon Aquaculture, Cuisine and Cultural Disruption in Chiloé', *Locale: The Australasian-Pacific Journal of Regional Food Studies* n1: 87–110

——- (2012a) 'Aquapelagos and Aquapelagic Assemblages', *Shima: The International Journal of Research into Island Cultures* v6 n1: 1–10

——- (2012b) 'The Constitution of Assemblages and the Aquapelagality of Haida Gwaii', *Shima: The International Journal of Research into Island Cultures* v6 n2: 1–8

—— (2013) 'Englamoured: Mermaid Iconography as a Contemporary Heritage Asset for Catalina Island', *Contemporary Legend: The Journal of the International Society for Contemporary Legend Research* v3: 39–62

——- (2015a) 'Sounding the Aquapelago: The cultural-environmental context of ni-Vanuatu women's liquid percussion performance', *Perfect Beat: The Pacific Journal of Research into Contemporary Music and Popular Culture* v15 n2: 111–128

——- (2015b) '*The Mermaid Chair*: Transplanting Cornish Folklore to an American Island', *Cornish Studies* Series 3 n1: 62–83

Hight, Craig (2010) *Television Mockumentary: Reflexivity, Satire and a Call to Play*, Manchester: Manchester University Press

Hoffman, Alice (1995) *Practical Magic*, New York: Putnams

——- (2001) *Aquamarine*, New York: Scholastic Press

Holford-Strevens, Leofranc (2006) 'Sirens in Antiquity and the Middle Ages', in Austern, Linda and Naroditskaya, Inna (eds) *Music of the Sirens*, Bloomington: Indiana University Press: 16–51

Hughes, Caroline (2010) 'Cahoon's mermaids focus of new exhibit', *Cape Cod Times* August 7th, online at: http://www.capecodtimes.com/article/20100807/LIFE/8070303 – accessed July 29th 2015

Hunt, Robert (1865) *Popular Romances of the West of England – or – Traditions and Superstitions of Old Cornwall*; section on 'Romances of the Mermaids: Morva or Morveth (sea-daughters)', archived online at: http://alternatewars.com/Mythology/PopRom_WEngl_Excerpt.htm

Ingemann, Bernhard (1812) 'Havfruen', online at: http://www.poemhunter.com/poem/havfruen/ – accessed April 12th 2015

Irigaray, Luce (1996) 'Divine Women', in Garry, Ann and Pearsall, Marilyn (eds) *Women, Knowledge, and Reality: Explorations in Feminist Philosophy*, New York: Routledge: 471–484

Jacques, Elliott (1965) 'Death and the mid-life crisis', *International Journal of Psychoanalysis* v46 n4: 502–14

James, Ronald M. (2015) 'Curses, Vengeance, and Fishtails: The Cornish Mermaid in Perspective', *Cornish Studies*, Series 3 n1, Exeter: University of Exeter

Jones, Guy and Jones, Constance (1946) *Peabody's Mermaid*, New York: Random House

Jordan, Alexis (2013) 'Dealing with electric pandas: Why it's worth trying to explain the difference between archaeology & pseudoarchaeology', *Field Notes* v5 n1: 66–75

Jung, Carl (1913) 'The Theory of Psychoanalysis', *Psychoanalytic Review* n1: 1–40

——- (1968) 'Archetypes of the Collective Unconscious', in *Collected Works of C.G Jung* v9 n1: *The Archetypes and the Collective Unconscious*, Princeton: Princeton University Press Bollingen Series: 3–42

Kaplan, E. Anne (ed) (1978) *Women in Film Noir*, London: British Film Institute

Karpowitz, Christopher and Mendelberg, Tali (2014) *The Silent Sex; Gender, Deliberation and Institutions*, Princeton: Princeton University Press

Kazickdas, Jurate (1972) 'Is the Missing Link a Mermaid?', *The Stars and Stripes* July 6th: 14–15

Kennedy, Michael P.J. (1997) 'The Sea Goddess Sedna: An Enduring Pan-Arctic Legend from Traditional Orature to New Narratives of the Late Twentieth Century', in Moss, John (ed) *Echoing Silence: Essays on Arctic Narrative*, Ottawa: University of Ottawa Press: 211–224

Kidd, Sue Monk (1996) *The Dance of The Dissident Daughter*, New York: Harper One

------ (2002) *The Secret Life of Bees*, New York: Penguin

------ (2005a) *The Mermaid Chair*, New York: Penguin

------ (2005b) 'The Mermaid Chair', Sue Monk Kidd 'Reflections' website: http://www.suemonkkidd.com/Reflections.aspx?t=m&i=27 – accessed May 2nd 2014

------ (2006) 'The Mermaid Chair: A Visit to the Movie Set', Sue Monk Kidd 'Reflections' website: http://www.suemonkkidd.com/Reflections.aspx?t=m&i=7 – accessed January 12th 2015

Kinemathek (2008) 'Lost Films', online at: http://www.lost-films.eu/index/whylf – accessed July 22nd 2015

Klara, Robert (2014) 'How a Topless Mermaid Made the Starbucks Cup an Icon (She's a little more modest today than in the '70s)', *AdWeek* September 29th, online at: http://www.adweek.com/news/advertising-branding/how-topless-mermaid-made-starbuck ks-cup-icon-160396 – accessed December 1st 2015

Kokai, Jennifer (2011) 'Weeki Wachee Girls and Buccaneer Boys: The Evolution of Mermaids, Gender, and "Man versus Nature" Tourism', *Theatre History Studies* v31: 67–89

Kramer, Nat (2013) '"Ud maate jeg": Andersen's Fodreise as Transgressive Space', *Scandinavian Studies* v85 n1: 39–66

Kramer, Lawrence (2006) '"Longindyingcall": Of Music, Modernity, and the Sirens' in Austern, Linda Phyllis and Naroditskaya, Inna (eds) *Music of the Sirens*, Bloomington: Indiana University Press: 194–215

La May, Thomasin and Armstrong, Robin (2006) 'The Navel, the Corporate, the Contradictory: Pop Sirens at the Twenty-first Century', in Austern, L.P. and Naroditskaya, I. (eds) *Music of the Sirens*, Bloomington: University of Indiana Press: 317–348

Lacan, Jacques (1977) 'The Mirror-Stage as Formative of the I as Revealed in Psychoanalytic Experience', in Lacan, Jacques *Écrits: A Selection*, London: Tavistock: 1–6

Lauritsen, Pernille (2001) 'Rabat pa misbrug af havrfrue', *Politiken* March 10th: - accessed November 8th 2015

Liberator Magazine (2013) 'Nijla Mu'min's "Deluge"/Magical Realism, post-BP oil spill New Orleans and Black Mermaids', *Liberator Magazine*, online at: http://weblog.liberatormagazine.com/2012/05/nijla-mumins-deluge-magical-realism.html – accessed January 30th 2016

Malm, Thomas (2009*)* 'Searching for clues in the lagoon: Is marine gathering a reflection of our evolutionary past?', *SPC Women in Fisheries Information Bulletin* n20: 10–16

Martin, Manjula (2012) 'The Rumpus Interview with Madison Young', online at: http://therumpus.net/2012/05/the-rumpus-interview-with-madison-young/ – accessed July 19th 2015

Mattson, Kelcie (2014) 'TIFF Women Directors: Meet Shahad Ameen – "Eye and Mermaid"', *IndieWire* September 13th, online at: http://blogs.indiewire.com/womenandhollywood/ tiff-women-directors-meet-shahad-ameen-eye-mermaid-20140913 – accessed August 22nd 2015

Maxwell, Ian (2012) 'Seas as Places: Towards a Maritime Chorography', *Shima: the International Journal of Research into Island Cultures* v6 n1: 22–24

Mayo, Michael (1984a) 'Splash', *Cinefantastique* v14 n3: 15–17

------ (1984b) 'How to Make a Mermaid', *Cinefantastique* v14 n3: 92–99

McCarthy, Imogen (2012) 'Saint Senara's Prayer', online at: http://lighthousestudiosydney. tumblr.com/post/38152767695/saint-senaras-prayer-may-your-soul-always#.Vw9Tu6a2 D7A – accessed May 2nd 2015

------ (2013) 'Saint Senara and the Mermaid', online at: http://saintsenara.com/ the-mermaid-saint/ – accessed May 4th 2014

MissMerFaery (2012) 'The Legend of the Mermaid of Zennor', online at: http://missmerfaery.squidoo.com/the-mermaid-chair – accessed May 4th 2014

Miller, Julie (2015) 'Rob Reiner Says There's Too Much Sex In Today's Rom-Coms', *Vanity Fair Hollywood,* September 15th, online at: http://www.vanityfair.com/hollywood/2015/09/rob-reiner-romantic-comedies-sex – accessed December 12th 2015

Milliken, Roberta (2012) *Ambiguous Locks: An Iconology of Hair in Medieval Art and Literature,* Jefferson: McFarland

Mills-Kronborg Collection of Danish Church Wall Paintings (2015) *The Index of Christian Art*, Princeton University, online at: https://ica.princeton.edu/mills/– accessed November 8th 2014

Monaghan, Patricia (2004) *Encyclopedia of Celtic Mythology and Folklore*, New York: Infobase

Morgan, Elaine (1972) *The Descent of Woman*, London: Souvenir Press

——- (1982) *The Aquatic Ape*, New York: Stein and Day

——- (1990) *The Aquatic Ape Hypothesis*, London: Penguin

Moss, Leonard and Cappannari, Stephen (1982) 'In Quest of the Black Virgin: She is Black because She is Black', in Preston, James (ed) *Mother Worship: Theme and Variations*, Chapel Hill: University of North Carolina Press: 53–74

Mostert, Linda Ann (2011) 'Feminist Appropriations of Hans Christian Andersen's "The Little Mermaid" and the ways in which stereotypes of women are subverted or sustained in selected works', (unpublished) Master of Arts thesis, Nelson Mandela Metropolitan University

Movieline (1989) 'Daryl Hannah: Rich Little Rich Girl', *Movieline* November 1st, online at: http://movieline.com/1989/11/01/daryl-hannah-rich-little-girl/3/ – accessed December 31st 2015

Mulvey, Laura (1975) 'Visual Pleasure and Narrative Cinema', *Screen* v16 n3: 6–18

Murch, Walter (1994) 'Foreword' in Chion, Michel *Audio-Vision: Sound On Screen* (translated by Claudia Gorbman), New York: Columbia University Press: vii–xxiv

Naroditskaya, Inna and Austern, Linda (2006) 'Introduction: Singing Each to Each', in Austern, Linda and Naroditskaya, Inna (eds) *Music of the Sirens*, Bloomington: University of Indiana Press: 1–15

Narvaez, Peter (1991) 'Newfoundland Berry Pickers "In the Fairies": Maintaining Spatial, Temporal, and Moral Boundaries Through Legendry', in Narvaez, Peter (ed) *The Good People: New Fairylore Essays*, New York: Garland: 336–368

National Oceanic and Atmospheric Administration (NOAA) (2012) 'No evidence of aquatic humanoids has ever been found', online at: http://oceanservice.noaa.gov/facts/mermaids.html – accessed February 15th 2014

Nicholson, Steve (2011) *The Censorship of British Drama 1900–1968 Volume 3: The Fifties*, Exeter: University of Exeter Press

Nickell, Joe (2014) 'Song of a Siren: A Study in Fakelore', *Skeptical Inquirer* v24 n1, online at: http://www.csicop.org/sb/show/song_of_a_sirena_study_in_fakelore/ – accessed May 8th 2015

Nielsen, Kai (1941) 'The Little Mermaid', (unpublished) initial treatment for Disney (Disney Archives)

Nikunen, Kaarina, Paasonen, Susanna and Saarenmaa, Laura (eds) (2008) *Pornification: Sex and Sexuality in Media Culture,* New York: Berg

Ofek, Galia (2006) 'Sensational Hair: Gender, Genre, and Fetishism in the Sensational Decade', in Harrison, Kimberly and Fantina, Richard (eds) *Victorian Sensations: Essays on a Scandalous Genre*, Columbus: Ohio State University Press: 102–114

Payton, Philip (2005) *The Cornish Overseas: A History of Cornwall's 'Great Emigration'*, Fowey: Cornish Editions

Pedersen, Tara (2015) *Mermaids and the Production of Knowledge in Early Modern England*, Farnham: Ashgate

Peters, Caradoc (2015) 'The Mermaid of Zennor: A Mirror on Three Worlds', *Cornish Studies* Series 3 n1: 62–83

Peterson, Brenda (2013) 'Dolphins, Sharks, and Mermaids, Oh, My! Interview With Hannah Foster', *Huffington Post* February 8th, online at: http://www.huffingtonpost.com/brenda-peterson/dolphins-sharks-and-mermaids_b_3691691.html – accessed August 20th 2015

Pipher, Mary (1994) *Reviving Ophelia*, New York: Random House

Pisters, Patricia (2003) *The Matrix of Visual Culture: Working with Deleuze in Film Theory*, Stanford: Stanford University Press

Pratt, Mary (1991) 'Arts of the Contact Zone', *Profession 2006*: 33–40

Prick, A. et al (2001) 'Homosociality in the Classical American Stag Film: Off-Screen, On-Screen', *Sexualities* v4 n3: 275–291

Prior, Richard (1860) *Ancient Danish Ballads translated from the originals Volume III*, London: Williams and Northgate

Quigley, Rachel (2013) 'How HOAX Mermaid "mockumentary" gave Animal Planet its biggest audience EVER', *Daily Mail* May 30th, online at: http://www.dailymail.co.uk/news/article-2333515/Mermaid-hoax-How-mockumentary-gave-Animal-Planet-biggest-audience-EVER.html – accessed February 9th 2014

Rajs, Jessie (2015) 'Interview with Iconic Mermaid Maker Robert Short', *Cosplay Culture* September 5th, online at: http://www.cosplayculture.com/article/interview-iconic-mermaid-maker-robert-short – accessed September 9th 2015

Relke, Joan (2007) 'The Archetypal Female in Mythology and Religion; The Anima and the Mother', *Europe's Journal of Psychology* v3 n1, online at: http://ejop.psychopen.eu/article/view/389/html – accessed April 30th 2015

Reynard, E. (1934) *The Narrow Land*, New York: Riverside Press: 41–44, archived online at: http://www.humanity.org/voices/folklore/mermaids/squant/# – accessed August 1st 2015

Rhodes, Gary and Springer, John (eds) (2006) *Docufictions: Essays on the Intersection of Documentary and Fiction*, Jefferson: McFarland & Company

Richardson, Samuel (1740) *Pamela: or, Virtue Rewarded*, London: Rivington and Osborn

Rist, Peter (2005) 'A Brief Introduction to Brazilian Cinema', *Off Screen* v9 n6, online at: offscreen.com/view/intro_braziliancinema – accessed July 27th 2015

Robertson, Venetia (2013) 'Where Skin meets Fin: The Mermaid as Myth, Monster and Other-Than-Human Identity', *Journal for the Academic Study of Religion* v26 n3: 303–323

Russian Laboratory of Theoretical Folkloristics (2104) 'Conference "Mechanisms of Cultural Memory: From Folk-Lore to Media-Lore", RANEPA website: http://www.ranepa.ru/eng/activities/item/604-cultural-memory.html – accessed July 10th 2015

Schlumpf, Heidi (2003) 'All Abuzz about the Black Madonna: An Interview with Sue Monk Kidd', *U.S. Catholic* November, online at: http://www.thefreelibrary.com/All+abuzz+about+the+Black+Madonna%3A+an+interview+with+Sue+Monk+Kid d.-a0110266645 – accessed May 2nd 2014

Schneider, Daniel (1946) 'A Psychoanalytic Approach to the Painting of Marc Chagall', *College Art Journal* v6 n2: 115–124

Schnier, Jacques (1956) 'Mythology of a symbol: the octopus', *American Imago* n13: 3–31

Scott, Jill (2005) *Electra After Freud: Myth and Culture*, Ithaca: Cornell University Press

Scriptshadow (2013) 'Screenplay Review – the Mermaid', online at: http://scriptshadow.net/screenplay-review-the-mermaid/ – accessed July 16th 2015

Scull, Andrew and Favreau, Diane (1986) 'The Clitoridectomy Craze', *Social Research* v53 n2: 243–260

Secret, Mosi (2014) 'A Strip Club in Manhattan Proves that Vice Is Hard To Kill', *New York Times* May 30th, online at: http://www.nytimes.com/2014/06/01/nyregion/a-strip-club-in-manhattan-proves-that-vice-is-hard-to-kill. html?_r=0 – accessed August 1st 2015

Sells, Laura (1995) '"Where do the Mermaids Stand?": Voice and Body in *The Little Mermaid*', in Bell, Elizabeth, Haas, Lynda and Sells, Laura (eds) *From Mouse to Mermaid: The Politics of Film, Gender and Culture*, Bloomington: Indiana University Press: 175–191

Silber, Austin (1981) 'The Influence of the Medusa Myth on the Psychology of the Female', in Orgel, Shelley and Fine, Bernard (eds) *Clinical Psychoanalysis*, New York: Jason Aronson: 159–173

Silverman, Kaja (1988) *The Acoustic Mirror: The Female Voice in Psychoanalysis and Cinema*, Bloomington and Indianapolis: Indiana University Press

Skeggs, Beverley (1993), 'A Good Time For Women Only' in Fran Lloyd, *Deconstructing Madonna*, London: Batsford: 271–281

Slide, Anthony (2012) *The Encyclopedia of Vaudeville*, Oxford: University of Mississippi Press

Soracco, Sabrina (1990) 'A Psychoanalytic Approach', *Scandinavian Studies* n62: 145–149

Spencer, Leland (2014) 'Performing Transgender Identity in The Little Mermaid: from Andersen to Disney', *Communication Studies* v65 n1: 112–127

Spyer, Patricia (ed) (1998) *Border Fetishisms: Material Objects in Unstable Spaces*, New York: Routledge

Starcevic, Vladan (2007) 'Dysphoric About Dysphoria: Towards a Greater Conceptual Clarity of the Term', *Australasian Psychiatry* v15 n1: 9–13

Steadman, Ian (2012) 'The Bloop mystery has been solved: it never was a giant sea monster', *The Wire* November 29th, online at: http://www.wired.co.uk/news/archive/2012-11/29/bloop-mystery-not-solved-s ort-of – accessed February 7th 2014

Stryker, Susan (2006) 'Desubjugated Knowledges: An introduction to Transgender Studies' in Stryker, Susan and Whittle, Stephen (eds) *The Transgender Studies Reader*, New York: Routledge: 1–19

Stuart, Tessa (2013) 'When fanfic becomes porn', *Buzzfeed*, July 7th, online at: http://www.buzzfeed.com/tessastuart/when-fanfic-becomes-porn – accessed August 8th 2015

Suwa, Juni'chiro (2012) 'Shima and Aquapelagic Assemblages: A Commentary from Japan', *Shima: The International Journal of Research into Island Cultures* v6 n1: 12–16

The Shorter Oxford English Dictionary - On Historical Principals (Third Edition) (1973), Oxford; Clarendon Press

Tangherlini, Timothy (1994) *Interpreting Legend: Danish Storytellers and their repertoires*, Abingdon: Routledge

Taylor, Charles (2009) '*Talk Dirty to Me* (1980)' in Bernard, James (ed) *The X-List: the National Society of Film Critics' Guide to the Movies that Turn Us On*, Boston: Da Capo Press: 260–261

Tennyson, Alfred Lord (1830) 'The Merman', online at: http://www.litscape.com/author/Alfred_Lord_Tennyson/The_Merman.html – accessed November 6th 2015

The Futon Critic (2012) 'Ratings', online at: http://www.thefutoncritic.com/ratings/2012/05/30/animal-planet-slays-with-best-ever-ma y-in-network- history-143310/20120530animalplanet01/ – accessed February 5th 2014

Thompson, John O. (1978) 'Screen Acting and the Commutation Test', *Screen* v19 n2: 55–70

Thomson, David (2001) *People of the Sea*, Berkeley: Counterpoint

Towle, Andy (2013) 'Meet the Gay Man Living the Mermaid Lifestyle', *Towleroad* April 3rd, online at: http://www.towleroad.com/2013/04/meet-the-gay-man-living-the-mermaid-life style-video/ – accessed September 14th 2015

Trites, Roberta (1991) 'Disney's sub/version of Andersen's "The Little Mermaid"', *Journal of Popular Film and Television* v18 n4: 145–152

Turgeon, Carolyn (2011) 'Traci Hines, the Real-Life Ariel', *I am a mermaid Blog*, April 26th, online at: https://iamamermaid.com/2011/04/26/traci-hines-a-real-life-ariel/ – accessed November 5th 2015

Unattributed (nd) 'Mr. Peabody and the Mermaid – 1948', online at: http://anotheroldmovieblog.blogspot.com.au/2014/01/mr-peabody-and-mermaid-1948.html – accessed May 20th 2015

Unattributed (2004) 'The Dance of the Dissident Daughter – 10th Anniversary Interview', Sue Monk Kidd website: http://suemonkkidd.com/books/the-dance-of-the-dissident-daughter/10th-anniversary/ – accessed June 3rd 2015

Unattributed (2013) 'Halloween How-To: Get Mermaid Hair. MERMAID!' *Cosmopolitan* website October 7th, online at: http://www.cosmopolitan.com/style-beauty/beauty/how-to/a15897/sultry-mermaid-waves-halloween-tutorial/ – accessed May 12th 2015

Unattributed (2014) 'Permaid', *Issue*, online at: http://issuemagazine.com/permaidbrentwoodmanor/#/ – accessed August 31st 2015

Urban, Andrew (2007) 'Vision, Obsession and the School of Hard Knocks: Jonathan M. Shiff', *Lumina* n1: 1–12, online at: http://www.aftrs.edu.au/media/books/lumina/lumina1-ch6-3/index.html – accessed July 2nd 2015

Vernallis, Carol (1998) 'The Aesthetics of Music Video: An Analysis of Madonna's "Cherish"', *Popular Music* v17 n2: 153–185

Vickers, Lu and Dionne, Sara (2007) *Weeki Wachee: City of Mermaids*, Gainesville: University Press of Florida

Vickers, Lu and Georgiadis, Bonnie (2012) *Weeki Wachee Mermaids: Thirty Years of Underwater Photography*, Gainesville: University Press of Florida

Wheatley, Helen (2004) 'The Limits of Television? Natural History Programming and the Transformation of Public Service Broadcasting', *European Journal of Cultural Studies* n7: 325–339

Williams, Linda (1989) *Hard Core: Power, Pleasure and the "Frenzy of the Visible"*, Berkeley: University of California press

—— (2005) *The Erotic Thriller in Contemporary Cinema*, Bloomington: University of Indiana Press

Williams, Christy (2010) 'Mermaid Tales on Screen: *Splash*, *The Little Mermaid* and *Aquamarine*', in Frus, Phyllis and Williams, Christy (eds) *Beyond Adaptation: Essays on the Radical Transformations of Original Works*, Jefferson: McFarlane and Company: 194–205

Wilmington, Michael (1989) 'Movie Review: "Little Mermaid" Makes Big Splash', *Los Angeles Times* November 15th, online at: http://articles.latimes.com/1989-11-15/entertainment/ca-1802_1_big-leap – accessed February 15th 2015

Wolman, David (2002) 'Calls from the Deep', *New Scientist* June 15th, online at: http://www.science.org.au/nova/newscientist/102ns_001.htm – accessed February 3rd 2014

Woollacott, Angela (2011) *Race and the Modern Exotic: Three 'Australian' Women on Global Display*, Melbourne: Monash University Press

Wray, Tim (2003) 'The Queer Gaze', *Thesis* n4: 69–73

Young, Heather (2015) 'Popular YouTube series filmed and produced in North County', *Paso Robles Daily News* March 30th, online at: http://pasoroblesdailynews.com/popular-youtube-series-is-filmed-produced-in-north-county/33181/ – accessed September 28th 2015

Zipes, Jack (2006) *Fairy Tales and the Art of Subversion*, New York: Routledge

Žižek, Slavoj (1996) '"I Hear You with My Eyes" or The Invisible Master', in Žižek, Slavoj and Salect, Renata (eds) *Gaze and Voice as Love Objects*, Durham: Duke University Press: 91–126

Appendix

Chronology

Chronological catalogue of audiovisual productions featuring mermaids and mermen referenced in the volume

1904   *La Sirène* (Georges Méliès, France)
1910   *The Mermaid* (director unknown, USA)
1911   *Siren of the Sea* (director unknown, USA)
1911   *The Mermaid* (director unknown, USA)
1913   *Surf Maidens* (Leslie T. Peacock, USA)
1914   *Neptune's Daughter* (Herbert Brenon, USA)
1916   *A Daughter of the Gods* (Herbert Brenon, USA)
1916   *Undine* (Henry Otto, USA)
1918   *Queen of the Sea* (John Adolfi, USA)
1920   *Neptune's Bride* (Leslie T. Peacock, USA)
1924   *JM Barrie's Peter Pan* (Herbert Brenon, USA)
1924   *Venus of the South Seas* (James Sullivan, New Zealand)
1930   *Frolicking Fish* (Bert Gillett, USA)
1932   *King Neptune* (Bert Gillett, USA)
1935   *Mr and Mrs is the Name* (Fritz Freleng, USA)
1936   *Neptune Nonsense* (Bert Gillett, USA)
1938   *Merbabies* (Rudolf Isling and Vernon Stallings, USA)
1941   *Ikan Doejong* (Lie Tek Swie, Dutch East Indies)
1948   *Miranda* (Ken Annakin, UK)
1948   *Mr Peabody and the Mermaid* (Irving Pichel, USA)
1951   *Alle mine skibe* (Theodore Christensen, Denmark)
1953   *Dysebel* (Gerardo de Leon, Philippines)
1953   *Peter Pan* (Clyde Geronimi, Wilfred Jackson and Hamilton Luske, USA)
1954   *Mad About Men* (Ralph Thomas, UK)
1957   *Pekka Ja Pätkä Sammakkomiehinä* (Armand Lohirski, Finland)
1958   'Legend of the Mermaid' (episode of TV series *Sea Hunt*, Leon Benson, USA)
1961–62 *Diver Dan* (TV series, USA)
1961   *Night Tide* (Curtis Harrington, USA)
1961   *The Fisherman and his Soul* (Charles Guggenheim, USA/Brazil)

1961	'The Little Mermaid' (episode of TV series *The Shirley Temple Show*, Robert Kay, USA)
1962	*Mermaids of Tiburon* (John Lamb, USA)
1963	*Jason and the Argonauts* (Ray Harryhausen, USA)
1964	*Aqua Sex* (John Lamb, USA) – modified version of *Mermaids of Tiburon* (1962)
1964	*Anak ni Dysebel* (Gerardo de Leon, Philippines)
1965	*Beach Blanket Bingo* (William Asher, USA)
1965	*Eve and the Merman* (Chev Royton, USA)
1966	*The Glass Bottom Boat* (Frank Tashlin, USA)
1967	*Catalina Caper* (Lee Sholem, USA)
1967	'The Mermaid' (episode of TV series *Voyage to the Bottom of the Sea*, Jerry Hopper, USA)
1968	*Rusalochka* (Ivan Aksenchuk, USSR)
1969	'Catch of the Day' (episode of TV series *Rip Tide,* Michael Lange, USA)
1972	'Lindemann's Catch' (episode of TV series *Night Gallery*, Jeff Corey, USA)
1973	*Dysebel* (Emmanuel Borlaza, Philippines)
1973	*Undine* (Rolf Thiele, Austria) – also released as *Ondine '74*
1974	*The Little Mermaid* (Peter Sanders, USA)
1976	*Deep Jaws* (Perry Dell, USA)
1976	*Gums* (Robert J. Kaplan, USA)
1976	*Malá Morská Víla* (Karel Kachnya, Czechoslovakia)
1976	*Rusalochka* (Vladimir Bychkov, USSR)
1978	*Dysebel* (Anthony Taylor, Philippines)
1979	'The Mermaid' (episode of TV series *Fantasy Island*, Earl Bellamy, USA)
1980	'The Mermaid Returns' (episode of TV series *Fantasy Island*, Earl Bellamy, USA)
1984	*Splash!* (Ron Howard, USA)
1984	*Talk Dirty to Me Part III* (Ned Morehead, USA)
1984	'The Mermaid and the Matchmaker' (episode of TV series *Fantasy Island*, Philip Leacock, USA)
1985	*Mermaids of Tiburon* – modified version of *Mermaids of Tiburon* (1962)
1986	*Talk Dirty to Me Part IV* (Ned Morehead, USA)
1986	*Touristinnen: Über und unter Wasser* (Ulrike Zimmerman, West Germany)
1987	*The Little Mermaid* (episode of TV series *Faerie Tale Theater*, Robert Iscove, USA)
1988	'Better than Life' (episode of TV series *Red Dwarf*, Ed Bye, UK)
1988	*Manhoru no naka no ningyo* (Hidesho Hino, Japan)
1988	*Splash Too!* (Greg Antonaaci, USA)
1989	*Cherish* (Madonna music video, Herb Ritts, USA)
1989	*The Little Mermaid* (Ron Clements and John Musker, USA)
1990	*Dysebel* (Mel Chionglo, Philippines)
1990	*Little Mermaid Island* (Jim Henson, USA)
1990	*Mermaids* (Richard Benjamin, UK)
1991	*Hook* (Stephen Spielberg, USA)
1991	*Off and Running* (Edward Bianchi, USA)
1992	*Mermaid: A Flippant Tale* (Adele Smith and Charlie Simmonds, UK)
1992	'Nails' (episode of TV series *Going Round the Twist*, Esben Storm, Australia)
1992–95	*The Little Mermaid* (TV series, USA)
1992	*Undine* (Eckhart Schmidt, Germany)
1995	*Magic Island* (Sam Irwin, USA)
1995	'Submersible' (episode of TV series *Flipper*, Peter Fisk, USA)
1997	'Desert Island Dick' (episode of TV series *Captain Butler*, Iain McLean, UK)
1997	'Mermaid Island' (episode of TV series *Flipper*, Donald Crombie, USA)
1997	'Rendezvous' (episode of TV series *Baywatch*, Gus Trikonis, USA)
1999	'Love on the Rocks' (episode of TV series *Hercules: The Legendary Journeys*, Rick Jacobson, USA)
1999	'My Best Girl's Wedding' (episode of TV series *Hercules: The Legendary Journeys*, Andrew Merrifield, USA)

1999   *Sabrina Down Under* (Daniel Berendsen, USA)
1999   *The Thirteenth Year* (Duwayne Dunham, USA)
2000   'Married with Fishsticks' (episode of TV series *Xena: Warrior Princess*, Paul Grinder, USA)
2000   'Neptune's Daughter' (episode of TV series *Power Rangers Lightspeed Rescue*, Jonathan Tazachor, USA)
2000   'Ocean Blue' (episode of TV series *Power Rangers Lightspeed Rescue*, Jonathan Tazachor, USA)
2000   *The Little Mermaid II: Return to the Sea* (Jim Kammerud and Brian Smith, USA)
2001   *She Creature* (Sebastian Guttierez, Canada)
2001   *The Little Mermaid* porn parody video sequences (untitled, USA?)
2001   *Zoolander* (Ben Stiller, 2001)
2002   *A Ring of Endless Light* (Mike Schondek, USA)
2002   'A Witch's Tail' (double episode of TV series *Charmed,* James Conway, USA)
2002   *How Mermaids Breed* (Joan Ashworth, UK)
2003   *Hans Christian Andersen: My Life as a Fairy Tale* (Philip Saville, UK)
2003   *Mermaids* (Ian Barry, USA)
2003   *Peter Pan* (P.J. Hogan, USA)
2004   *Chudesa v Reshetov* (Mikhail Levin, Russia)
2004   *Demon of Temptation* (Luc Bernier and Laura Giglio?, USA)
2005   *Harry Potter and the Goblet of Fire* (Mike Newell, USA)
2005   'The Tale of the Knitted Map' (episode of TV series *My Parents are Aliens*, Tom Poole, UK)
2006   *Another Gay Sequel: Gays Gone Wild!* (Todd Stephens, USA)
2006   *Aquaman* (Greg Beeman, USA)
2006   *Aquamarine* (Elizabeth Arden, USA)
2006   *Barbie Mermaidia* (Walter Martishius and William Lau, USA)
2006–10 *H₂O: Just Add Water* (TV series, Australia)
2006   *The Mermaid Chair* (Steven Schachter, USA)
2006   *The Merman* (online video series, USA)
2007   'Dora Saves the Mermaids' (episode of TV series *Dora The Explorer*, director unknown, USA)
2007   *Fishtales* (Alki David, USA)
2007   Levi's 501s Merman ad (director unknown, USA)
2008   *Dyesebel* (TV series, Philippines)
2008   *Hearts Atlantis* (Andrew Macdonald, Australia)
2008   'Requiem' (episode of TV series *Sanctuary,* Martin Wood, USA)
2008   *Roxy Hunter and the Myth of the Mermaid* (Eleanor Lindo, USA)
2008   *The Little Mermaid: Ariel's Beginning* (Peggy Holmes, USA)
2008   *The Little Mermaid: Story Behind the Story* (director unknown, USA)
2008   'Underwater Menace' (episode of TV series *Primeval*, Jamie Payne, UK)
2009–14 *Secret Life of a Mermaid* (video drama series, USA)
2010   'A Mermaid's Tail' (episode of TV series *A Pair of Kings*, Andy Cadiff, USA)
2010   *Barbie in a Mermaid Tale* (Adam Wood, USA)
2010   *Mandelhoffs Mermaids: underwater research project Part 1* (Cyrax and Flyrax, UK?)
2011   *Arwah Kuntilanak Duyung* (Yoyo Dumpring, Indonesia)
2011–13 *Mermaid Secrets* (video drama series, USA)
2011-   *Once Upon A Time* (TV series, USA)
2011   *Pirates of the Caribbean: On Stranger Tides* (Rob Marshall, USA)
2011   *The Mermaid: The Siren of Seduction* (director unknown, USA)
2011   *You and I* (Lady Gaga music video, Laurieann Gibson, USA)
2012   *Barbie in a Mermaid Tale II* (William Lau, USA)
2012   *Cabin in the Woods* (Drew Goddard, USA)
2012–13 *Deep Sea Tails* (video drama series, USA, 2012–2013)
2012   'Dora's Rescue in Mermaid Kingdom' (episode of TV series *Dora The Explorer*, director unknown, USA)
2012–13 *Forever Scales* (video drama series, USA, 2012–2013)

2012   *Mermaids: The Body Found* (Sid Bennett, USA)

2102–13   *My Magical Mermaid Life* (video drama series, USA)

2012?   *Wild Little Mermaid* (director unknown, USA, 2012?)

2012   'Poseidon Adventure' (episode of TV series *The Glades*, Lee Rose, USA)

2013   *Brentwood Manor* (De Martino, USA)

2013   *Deluge* (Nijila Mu'min, USA)

2013   *Die kleine Meerjungfrau* (Irina Popow, Germany)

2013-   *Mako Mermaids* (TV series, Australia)

2013   *Mermaid Experience: Mermaids of Georgia* (Mermaid Experience, USA)

2013   *Mermaids and Unicorns* (Madison Young, USA)

2013   *Mermaids: The New Evidence* (Christina Bavetta, USA)

2013   Merman (*The Poles* music video, Gavin Kennedy, Canada)

2013   *SAGA: Curse of the Shadow* (John Lyde, USA)

2013–15   *Tennessee Tailz* (video drama series, USA)

2013-   *Tail of a Mermaid and Merman* (video drama series, Scotland)

2013   'The Little Merman' (episode of TV series *My Crazy Obsession*, USA)

2013   *The Little MerMILF* (director unknown, USA)

2013   *Truly H2O* (video drama series, USA)

2014   *Barbie: the Pearl Princess* (Ezekiel Norton, USA)

2014   *Destiny – The Vampire Mermaid: Crimson Currents* (Rusty Pietrzak and James Panetta, USA)

2014   *Destiny – The Vampire Mermaid: Death in the Dark* (Rusty Pietrzak and James Panetta, USA)

2014   *Dyesebel* (TV series, Philippines)

2014   *Eye and Mermaid* (Shahad Ameen, Saudi Arabia)

2014   *Ing-yeo gongju* (Baek Seung-ryong, South Korea)

2014   *Killer Mermaid* (Milan Todorovic, Croatia)

2014   *Lesbian Mermaids* (director unknown, USA)

2014   *Making of 'Part of Your World'* (Raiya Corsiglia, USA)

2014–15   *Mermaid Miracles* (video drama series, USA)

2014   *Part of Your World* (Traci Hines music video, Raiya Corsiglia, USA)

2014   *The Desert Fish* (Mohammad Ghorbankarimi, Iran/Canada)

2014   *The Little Spermaid* (Jordan Septo, USA)

2014–15   *The Mermaid Mysteries* (video drama series, USA)

2014–15   *The Tail of 2 Mermaids* (video drama series, USA)

2014   'Waves' (episode of TV series *Lost Girl*, Director X, USA)

2015   *Feeling My Fish* (TS Madison music video, Mitchell Hardage, USA)

2015-   *H2O: Mermaid Adventures* (TV series, Australia)

2015   *Fish Tale* (Steve Lewis, UK)

2015   *Maui Mermaids* (video drama series, USA)

2015   *Mermaid Island* (video drama series, USA)

2015   *Mermaids of New York* (Mica Scalin and Ilise Carter, USA)

2015   Merman (Ryan Bosworth, USA)

2015-   *My Splash Side* (video drama series, USA)

2015-   *Ocean Star* (video drama series, USA)

2015   *Pan* (Joe Wright, USA)

2015   *Pepper and the Salt Sea* (Don Downie, USA)

2015   *Vibin* (Big Dipper music video, Tobin del Cuore, USA)

2015   *Vibin (Mighty Mark remix)* (Big Dipper music video, director unknown (Meg Skaff, USA)

Index

Milton Keynes UK
Ingram Content Group UK Ltd.
UKHW052005220924
448637UK00008B/69